I0009980

# Machine Learning with Core ML

An iOS developer's guide to implementing machine learning in mobile apps

**Joshua Newnham**

**BIRMINGHAM - MUMBAI**

# Machine Learning with Core ML

Copyright © 2018 Packt Publishing

All rights reserved. No part of this book may be reproduced, stored in a retrieval system, or transmitted in any form or by any means, without the prior written permission of the publisher, except in the case of brief quotations embedded in critical articles or reviews.

Every effort has been made in the preparation of this book to ensure the accuracy of the information presented. However, the information contained in this book is sold without warranty, either express or implied. Neither the author, nor Packt Publishing or its dealers and distributors, will be held liable for any damages caused or alleged to have been caused directly or indirectly by this book.

Packt Publishing has endeavored to provide trademark information about all of the companies and products mentioned in this book by the appropriate use of capitals. However, Packt Publishing cannot guarantee the accuracy of this information.

**Commissioning Editor:** Amey Varangaonkar
**Acquisition Editor:** Tushar Gupta
**Content Development Editor:** Karan Thakkar
**Technical Editor:** Sagar Sawant
**Copy Editor:** Safis Editing
**Project Coordinator:** Nidhi Joshi
**Proofreader:** Safis Editing
**Indexer:** Tejal Daruwale Soni
**Graphics:** Tania Dutta
**Production Coordinator:** Arvindkumar Gupta

First published: June 2018

Production reference: 1260618

Published by Packt Publishing Ltd.
Livery Place
35 Livery Street
Birmingham
B3 2PB, UK.

ISBN 978-1-78883-829-0

www.packtpub.com

mapt.io

Mapt is an online digital library that gives you full access to over 5,000 books and videos, as well as industry leading tools to help you plan your personal development and advance your career. For more information, please visit our website.

# Why subscribe?

- Spend less time learning and more time coding with practical eBooks and Videos from over 4,000 industry professionals

- Improve your learning with Skill Plans built especially for you

- Get a free eBook or video every month

- Mapt is fully searchable

- Copy and paste, print, and bookmark content

# PacktPub.com

Did you know that Packt offers eBook versions of every book published, with PDF and ePub files available? You can upgrade to the eBook version at www.PacktPub.com and as a print book customer, you are entitled to a discount on the eBook copy. Get in touch with us at service@packtpub.com for more details.

At www.PacktPub.com, you can also read a collection of free technical articles, sign up for a range of free newsletters, and receive exclusive discounts and offers on Packt books and eBooks.

# Contributors

## About the author

**Joshua Newnham** is a technology lead at a global design firm, Method, focusing on the intersection of design and **artificial intelligence (AI)**, specifically in the areas of computational design and human computer interaction.

Prior to this, he was a technical director at Masters of Pie, a **virtual reality (VR)** and **augmented reality (AR)** studio focused on building collaborative tools for engineers and creatives.

*First and foremost, I would like give thanks to my incredible wife and son for their extraordinary support, encouragement, and inspiration throughout this book and life in general. Thank you both.*
*Writing a book is no small undertaking, and without the team at Packt continuously refining the work, you would likely be reading 400+ pages of late night ramblings. So, a big thanks to the team for helping me make this happen.*

# About the reviewer

**Shilpa Karkeraa** is a leading solution expert and the founder CEO of Myraa Technologies, an Artificial Intelligence Solutions Company. From being an independent entrepreneur to a hands-on developer, she has been an innovator with cutting edge technologies. Prior to Myraa, she spearheaded as a Team Lead—Data Engineering Group of a Bay Area start-up to a Top Corporates Financial Services Firm in India to being an architect at a Singaporean B2C company. She is an active global technology speaker. She hopes to commercialize research and innovation to touch human lives effectively!

> *Reviewing this book was indeed a page turner along with an excelling keyboard cruncher. Thanks Packt Publishing for an amazing experience with the book. Cheers to the author for his writing streak over the beauty of design and detail, to my dear friend Tanvi Bhatt and to my technologists at Myraa Technologies for the hands-on implementations.*

# Packt is searching for authors like you

If you're interested in becoming an author for Packt, please visit `authors.packtpub.com` and apply today. We have worked with thousands of developers and tech professionals, just like you, to help them share their insight with the global tech community. You can make a general application, apply for a specific hot topic that we are recruiting an author for, or submit your own idea.

# Table of Contents

# Preface

We are living on the verge of a new era of computing, an era where computers are becoming more of a companion than a tool. The devices we carry in our pockets will soon better understand our world and us a lot better, and this will have a profound impact on how we interact with and use them.

But right now, a lot of these exciting advancements are stuck in the labs of researchers and not in the hands of designers and developers, making them usable and accessible to users. This is not because the details are locked away; on the contrary, in most cases they are freely available.

This gap is somewhat due to our contentment with sticking to what we know, having the user do all the work, making them tap on the buttons. If nothing else, I hope this book makes you curious about what is out there and how it can be used to create new experiences, or improve existing ones.

Within the pages of this book, you will find a series of examples to help you build an understanding of how deep neural networks work and how they can be applied.

This book focuses on a set of models for a better understanding of images and photos, specifically looking at how they can be adapted and applied on the iOS platform. This narrow focus of image-based models and the iOS platform is intentional; I find that the visual nature of images makes the concepts easier to, well, visualize, and the iPhone provides the perfect candidate and environment for experimentation.

So, as you go through this book, I encourage you to start thinking about new ways of how these models can be used and what new experiences you could create. With that being said, let's get started!

# Who this book is for

This book will appeal to three broad groups of people. The first are intermediate iOS developers who are interested in learning and applying **machine learning** (**ML**); some exposure to ML concepts may be beneficial but are not essential as this book covers the intuition behind the concepts and models used throughout it.

The second group are those who have experience in ML but not in iOS development and are looking for a resource to help them to get the grips with Core ML; for this group, it is recommended to complement this book with a book that covers the fundamentals of iOS development.

The last group are experienced iOS developers and ML practitioners who are curious to see how various models have been applied in the context of the iOS platform.

# What this book covers

Chapter 1, *Introduction to Machine Learning*, provides a brief introduction to ML, including some explanation of the core concepts, the types of problems, algorithms, and general workflow of creating and using a ML models. The chapter concludes by exploring some examples where ML is being applied.

Chapter 2, *Introduction to Apple Core ML*, introduces Core ML, discussing what it is, what it is not, and the general workflow for using it.

Chapter 3, *Recognizing Objects in the World*, walks through building a Core ML application from start to finish. By the end of the chapter, we would have been through the whole process of obtaining a model, importing it into the project, and making use of it.

Chapter 4, *Emotion Detection with CNNs*, explores the possibilities of computers understanding us better, specifically our mood. We start by building our intuition of how ML can learn to infer your mood, and then put this to practice by building an application that does just that. We also use this as an opportunity to introduce the Vision framework and see how it complements Core ML.

Chapter 5, *Locating Objects in the World*, goes beyond recognizing a single object to being able to recognize and locate multiple objects within a single image through object detection. After building our understanding of how it works, we move on to applying it to a visual search application that filters not only by object but also by composition of objects. In this chapter, we'll also get an opportunity to extend Core ML by implementing customer layers.

Chapter 6, *Creating Art with Style Transfer*, uncovers the secrets behind the popular photo effects application, Prisma. We start by discussing how a model can be taught to differentiate between the style and content of an image, and then go on to build a version of Prisma that applies a style from one image to another. We wrap up this chapter by looking at ways to optimize the model.

Chapter 7, *Assisted Drawing with CNNs*, walks through building an application that can recognize a users sketch using the same concepts that have been introduced in previous chapters. Once what the user is trying to sketch has been recognized, we look at how we can find similar substitutes using the feature vectors from a CNN.

Chapter 8, *Assisted Drawing with RNNs*, builds on the previous chapter and explores replacing the the **convolution neural network (CNN)** with a **recurrent neural network (RNN)** for sketch classification, thus introducing RNNs and showing how they can be applied to images. Along with a discussion on learning sequences, we will also delve into the details of how to download and compile Core ML models remotely.

Chapter 9, *Object Segmentation Using CNNs*, walks through building an *ActionShot* photography application. And in doing so, we introduce another model and accompanying concepts, and get some hands-on experience of preparing and processing data.

Chapter 10, *An Introduction to Create ML*, is the last chapter. We introduce Create ML, a framework for creating and training Core ML models within Xcode using Swift. By the end of this chapter, you will know how to quickly create, train, and deploy a custom models.

# To get the most out of this book

To be able to follow through the examples in this book, you will need the following software:

- macOS 10.13 or higher
- Xcode 9.2 or higher
- iOS 11.0 or higher (device and simulator)

For the examples that are dependent on Core ML 2, you will need the following software:

- macOS 10.14
- Xcode 10.0 beta
- iOS 12 (device and simulator)

It's recommended that you use `https://notebooks.azure.com` (or some other Jupyter notebook service provider) to follow the examples using the Core ML Tools Python package, but those wanting to run locally or train their model will need the following software:

- Python 2.7
- Jupyter Notebooks 1.0
- TensorFlow 1.0.0 or higher
- NumPy 1.12.1 or higher
- Core ML Tools 0.9 (and 2.0 for Core ML 2 examples)

# Download the example code files

You can download the example code files for this book from your account at `www.packtpub.com`. If you purchased this book elsewhere, you can visit `www.packtpub.com/support` and register to have the files emailed directly to you.

You can download the code files by following these steps:

1. Log in or register at `www.packtpub.com`.
2. Select the **SUPPORT** tab.
3. Click on **Code Downloads & Errata**.
4. Enter the name of the book in the **Search** box and follow the onscreen instructions.

Once the file is downloaded, please make sure that you unzip or extract the folder using the latest version of:

- WinRAR/7-Zip for Windows
- Zipeg/iZip/UnRarX for Mac
- 7-Zip/PeaZip for Linux

The code bundle for the book is also hosted on GitHub at `https://github.com/PacktPublishing/Machine-Learning-with-Core-ML`. In case there's an update to the code, it will be updated on the existing GitHub repository.

We also have other code bundles from our rich catalog of books and videos available at `https://github.com/PacktPublishing/`. Check them out!

# Download the color images

We also provide a PDF file that has color images of the screenshots/diagrams used in this book. You can download it here: http://www.packtpub.com/sites/default/files/downloads/MachineLearningwithCoreML_ColorImages.pdf.

# Conventions used

There are a number of text conventions used throughout this book.

CodeInText: Indicates code words in text, database table names, folder names, filenames, file extensions, pathnames, dummy URLs, user input, and Twitter handles. Here is an example: "At the top of the class, we have the VideoCaptureDelegate protocol defined."

A block of code is set as follows:

```
public protocol VideoCaptureDelegate: class {
    func onFrameCaptured(
      videoCapture: VideoCapture,
      pixelBuffer:CVPixelBuffer?,
      timestamp:CMTime)
}
```

When we wish to draw your attention to a particular part of a code block, the relevant lines or items are set in bold:

```
@IBOutlet var previewView:CapturePreviewView!
@IBOutlet var classifiedLabel:UILabel!

let videoCapture : VideoCapture = VideoCapture()
```

**Bold**: Indicates a new term, an important word, or words that you see onscreen. For example, words in menus or dialog boxes appear in the text like this. Here is an example: "Select **System info** from the **Administration** panel."

 Warnings or important notes appear like this.

 Tips and tricks appear like this.

# Get in touch

Feedback from our readers is always welcome.

**General feedback**: Email `feedback@packtpub.com` and mention the book title in the subject of your message. If you have questions about any aspect of this book, please email us at `questions@packtpub.com`.

**Errata**: Although we have taken every care to ensure the accuracy of our content, mistakes do happen. If you have found a mistake in this book, we would be grateful if you would report this to us. Please visit `www.packtpub.com/submit-errata`, selecting your book, clicking on the Errata Submission Form link, and entering the details.

**Piracy**: If you come across any illegal copies of our works in any form on the Internet, we would be grateful if you would provide us with the location address or website name. Please contact us at `copyright@packtpub.com` with a link to the material.

**If you are interested in becoming an author**: If there is a topic that you have expertise in and you are interested in either writing or contributing to a book, please visit `authors.packtpub.com`.

# Reviews

Please leave a review. Once you have read and used this book, why not leave a review on the site that you purchased it from? Potential readers can then see and use your unbiased opinion to make purchase decisions, we at Packt can understand what you think about our products, and our authors can see your feedback on their book. Thank you!

For more information about Packt, please visit `packtpub.com`.

# 1
# Introduction to Machine Learning

Let's begin our journey by peering into the future and envision how we'll see ourselves interacting with computers. Unlike today's computers, where we are required to continuously type in our emails and passwords to access information, the computers of the future will easily be able to recognize us by our face, voice, or activity. Unlike today's computers, which require step-by-step instructions to perform an action, the computer of the future will anticipate our intent and provide a natural way for us to converse with it, similar to how we engage with other people, and then proceed to help us achieve our goal. Our computer will not only assist us but also be our friend, our doctor, and so on. It could deliver our groceries at the door and be our interface with an increasingly complex and information-rich physical world.

What is exciting about this vision is that it is no longer in the realm of science fiction but an emergent reality. One of the major drivers of this is the progress and adoption of **machine learning** (**ML**) techniques, a discipline that gives computers the perceptual power of humans, thus giving them the ability to see, hear, and make sense of the world—physical and digital.

But despite all the great progress over the last 3-4 years, most of the ideas and potential are locked away in research projects and papers rather than being in the hands of the user. So it's the aim of this book to help developers understand these concepts better. It will enable you to put them into practice so that we can arrive at this future—a future where computers augment us, rather than enslave us due to their inability to understand our world.

Because of the constraint of Core ML—it being only able to perform inference—this book differs vastly from other ML books, in the sense that the core focus is on the application of ML. Specifically we'll focus on computer vision applications rather than the details of ML. But in order to better enable you to take full advantage of ML, we will spend some time introducing the associated concepts with each example.

And before jumping into the hands-on examples, let's start from the beginning and build an appreciation for what ML is and how it can be applied. In this chapter we will:

- Start by introducing ML. We'll learn how it differs from classical programming and why you might choose it.
- Look at some examples of how ML is being used today, along with the type of data and ML algorithm being used.
- Finally, present the typical workflow for ML projects.

Let's kick off by first discussing what ML is and why everyone is talking about it.

# What is machine learning?

ML is a subfield of **Artificial Intelligence** (**AI**), a topic of computer science born in the 1950s with the goal of trying to get computers to think or provide a level of automated intelligence similar to that of us humans.

Early success in AI was achieved by using an extensive set of defined rules, known as **symbolic AI**, allowing expert decision making to be mimicked by computers. This approach worked well for many domains but had a big shortfall in that in order to create an expert, you needed one. Not only this, but also their expertise needed to be digitized somehow, which normally required explicit programming.

ML provides an alternative; instead of having to handcraft rules, it learns from examples and experience. It also differs from classical programming in that it is probabilistic as opposed to being discrete. That is, it is able to handle fuzziness or uncertainty much better than its counterpart, which will likely fail when given an ambiguous input that wasn't explicitly identified and handled.

I am going to borrow an example used by Google engineer Josh Godron in an introductory video to ML to better highlight the differences and value of ML.

Suppose you were given the task of classifying apples and oranges. Let's first approach this using what we will call classical programming:

Our input is an array of pixels for each image, and for each input, we will need to explicitly define some rules that will be able to distinguish an apple from an orange. Using the preceding examples, you can solve this by simply counting the number of orange and green pixels. Those with a higher ratio of green pixels would be classified as an apple, while those with a higher ratio of orange pixels would be classified as an orange. This works well with these examples but breaks if our input becomes more complex:

The introduction of new images means our simple color-counting function can no longer sufficiently differentiates our apples from our oranges, or even classify apples. We are required to reimplement the function to handle the new nuances introduced. As a result, our function grows in complexity and becomes more tightly coupled to the inputs and less likely able to generalize to other inputs. Our function might resemble something like the following:

```
func countColors(_ image:UIImage) -> [(color:UIColor, count:Int)]{
// lots of code
}

func detectEdges(_ image:UIImage) -> [(x1:Int, y1:Int, x2:Int, y2:Int)]
{
// lots of code
}

func analyseTexture(_ image:UIImage) -> [String]
{
// lots of code
}

func fitBoundingBox(_ image:UIImage) -> [(x:Int, y:Int, w:Int, h:Int)]
{
// lots of code
}
```

This function can be considered our model, which models the relationship of the inputs with respect to their labels (apple or orange), as illustrated in the following diagram:

The alternative, and the approach we're interested in, is getting this model created to automatically use examples; this, in essence, is what ML is all about. It provides us with an effective tool to model complex tasks that would otherwise be nearly impossible to define by rules.

The creation phase of the ML model is called **training** and is determined by the type of ML algorithm selected and data being fed. Once the model is trained, that is, once it has learned, we can use it to make inferences from the data, as illustrated in the following diagram:

The example we have presented here, classifying oranges and apples, is a specific type of ML algorithm called a **classifier**, or, more specifically, a multi-class classifier. The model was trained through **supervision**; that is, we fed in examples of input with their associated labels (or classes). It is useful to understand the types of ML algorithms that exist along with the types of training, which is the topic of the next section.

# A brief tour of ML algorithms

In this section, we will look at some examples of how ML is used, and with each example, we'll speculate about the type of data, learning style, and ML algorithm used. I hope that by the end of this section, you will be inspired by what is possible with ML and gain some appreciation for the types of data, algorithms, and learning styles that exist.

 In this section, we will be presenting some real-life examples in the context of introducing types of data, algorithms, and learning styles. It is **not** our intention to show accurate data representations or implementations for the example, but rather use the examples as a way of making the ideas more tangible.

# Netflix – making recommendations

No ML book is complete without mentioning recommendation engines—probably one of the most well known applications of ML. In part, this is thanks to the publicity gained when Netflix announced a $1 million competition for movie rating predictions, also known as **recommendations**. Add to this Amazon's commercial success in making use of it.

The goal of recommendation engines is to predict the likelihood of someone wanting a particular product or service. In the context of Netflix, this would mean recommending movies or TV shows to its users.

One intuitive way of making recommendations is to try and mimic the real world, where a person is likely to seek recommendations from like-minded people. What constitutes likeness is dependent on the domain. For example, you are most likely to have one group of friends that you would ask for restaurant recommendations and another group of friends for movie recommendations. What determines these groups is how similar their tastes are to your own taste for that particular domain. We can replicate this using the (user-based) **Collaborative Filtering** (**CF**) algorithm. This algorithm achieves this by finding the distance between each user and then using these distances as a similarity metric to infer predictions on movies for a particular user; that is, those that are more similar will contribute more to the prediction than those that have different preferences. Let's have a look at what form the data might take from Netflix:

| User | Movie | Rating |
|------|-------|--------|
| 0: Jo | A: Monsters Inc | 5 |
| | B: The Bourne Identity | 2 |
| | C: The Martian | 2 |
| | D: Blade Runner | 1 |
| 1: Sam | C: The Martian | 4 |
| | D: Blade Runner | 4 |
| | E: The Matrix | 4 |
| | F: Inception | 5 |
| 2: Chris | B: The Bourne Identity | 4 |
| | C: The Martian | 5 |
| | D: Blade Runner | 5 |
| | F: Inception | 4 |

For each example, we have a user, a movie, and an assigned rating. To find the similarity between each user, we can first calculate the Euclidean distance of the shared movies between each pair of users. The Euclidean distance gives us larger values for users who are most dissimilar; we invert this by dividing 1 by this distance to give us a result, where 1 represents perfect matches and 0 means the users are most dissimilar. The following is the formula for Euclidean distance and the function used to calculate similarities between two users:

Equation for Euclidian distance and similarity

```
func calcSimilarity(userRatingsA: [String:Float],
userRatingsB:[String:Float]) -> Float{
  var distance = userRatingsA.map( { (movieRating) -> Float in
    if userRatingsB[movieRating.key] == nil{
      return 0
    }
    let diff = movieRating.value - (userRatingsB[movieRating.key] ?? 0)
    return diff * diff
  }).reduce(0) { (prev, curr) -> Float in
    return prev + curr
  }.squareRoot()
  return 1 / (1 + distance)
}
```

To make this more concrete, let's walk through how we can find the most similar user for Sam, who has rated the following movies: `["The Martian" : 4, "Blade Runner" : 4, "The Matrix" : 4, "Inception" : 5]`. Let's now calculate the similarity between Sam and Jo and then between Sam and Chris.

**Sam and Jo**

Jo has rated the movies `["Monsters Inc." : 5, "The Bourne Identity" : 2, "The Martian" : 2, "Blade Runner" : 1]`; by calculating the similarity of intersection of the two sets of ratings for each user, we get a value of *0.22*.

**Sam and Chris**

Similar to the previous ones, but now, by calculating the similarity using the movie ratings from Chris (`["The Bourne Identity" : 4, "The Martian" : 5, "Blade Runner" : 5, "Inception" : 4]`), we get a value of *0.37*.

Through manual inspection, we can see that Chris is more similar to Sam than Jo is, and our similarity rating shows this by giving Chris a higher value than Jo.

To help illustrate why this works, let's project the ratings of each user onto a chart as shown in the following graph:

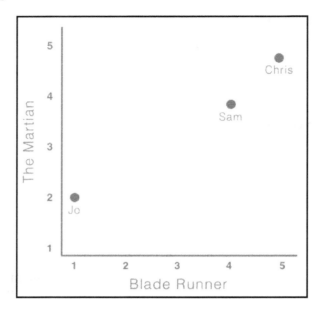

The preceding graph shows the users plotted in a preference space; the closer two users are in this preference space, the more similar their preferences are. Here, we are just showing two axes, but, as seen in the preceding table, this extends to multiple dimensions.

We can now use these similarities as weights that contribute to predicting the rating a particular user would give to a particular movie. Then, using these predictions, we can recommend some movies that a user is likely to want to watch.

The preceding approach is a type of **clustering** algorithm that falls under **unsupervised learning**, a learning style where examples have no associated label and the job of the ML algorithm is to find patterns within the data. Other common unsupervised learning algorithms include the Apriori algorithm (basket analysis) and K-means.

Recommendations are applicable anytime when there is an abundance of information that can benefit from being filtered and ranked before being presented to the user. Having recommendations performed on the device offers many benefits, such as being able to incorporate the context of the user when filtering and ranking the results.

# Shadow draw – real-time user guidance for freehand drawing

To highlight the synergies between man and machine, AI is sometimes referred to as **Augmented Intelligence (AI)**, putting the emphasis on the system to augment our abilities rather than replacing us altogether.

One area that is becoming increasingly popular—and of particular interest to myself—is assisted creation systems, an area that sits at the intersection of the fields of **human-computer interaction (HCI)** and ML. These are systems created to assist in some creative tasks such as drawing, writing, video, and music.

The example we will discuss in this section is shadow draw, a research project undertaken at Microsoft in 2011 by Y.J. Lee, L. Zitnick, and M. Cohen. Shadow draw is a system that assists the user in drawing by matching and aligning a reference image from an existing dataset of objects and then lightly rendering shadows in the background to be used as guidelines for the user. For example, if the user is predicted to be drawing a bicycle, then the system would render guidelines under the user's pen to assist them in drawing the object, as illustrated in this diagram:

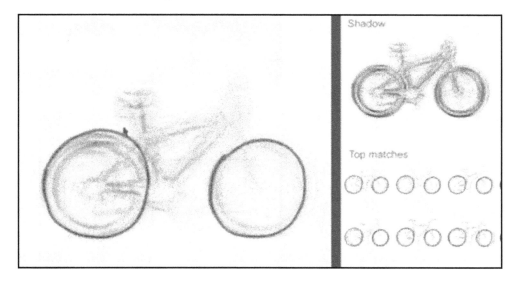

As we did before, let's walk through how we might approach this, focusing specifically on classifying the sketch; that is, we'll predict what object the user is drawing. This will give us the opportunity to see new types of data, algorithms, and applications of ML.

The dataset used in this project consisted of 30,000 natural images collected from the internet via 40 category queries such as face, car, and bicycle, with each category stored in its own directory; the following diagram shows some examples of these images:

After obtaining the raw data, the next step, and typical of any ML project, is to perform **data preprocessing** and **feature engineering**. The following diagram shows the preprocessing steps, which consist of:

- Rescaling each image
- Desaturating (turning black and white)
- Edge detection

Our next step is to abstract our data into something more meaningful and useful for our ML algorithm to work with; this is known as **feature engineering**, and is a critical step in a typical ML workflow.

One approach, and the approach we will describe, is creating something known as a **visual bag of words**. This is essentially a histogram of features (visual words) used to describe each image, and collectively to describe each category. What constitutes a feature is dependent on the data and ML algorithm; for example, we can extract and count the colors of each image, where the colors become our features and collectively describe our image, as shown in the following diagram:

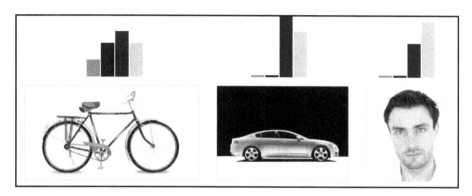

But because we are dealing with sketches, we want something fairly coarse—something that can capture the general strokes directions that will encapsulate the general structure of the image. For example, if we were to describe a square and a circle, the square would consist of horizontal and vertical strokes, while the circle would consist mostly of diagonal strokes. To extract these features, we can use a computer vision algorithm called **histogram of oriented gradients** (**HOG**); after processing an image you are returned a histogram of gradient orientations in localized portions of the image. Exactly what we want! To help illustrate the concept, this process is summarized for a single image here:

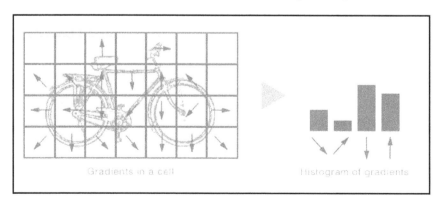

After processing all the images in our dataset, our next step is to find a histogram (or histograms) that can be used to identify each category; we can use an **unsupervised learning** clustering technique called **K-means**, where each category histogram is the centroid for that cluster. The following diagram describes this process; we first extract features for each image and then cluster these using K-means, where the distance is calculated using the histogram of gradients. Once our images have been clustered into their groups, we extract the center (mean) histogram of each of these groups to act as our category descriptor:

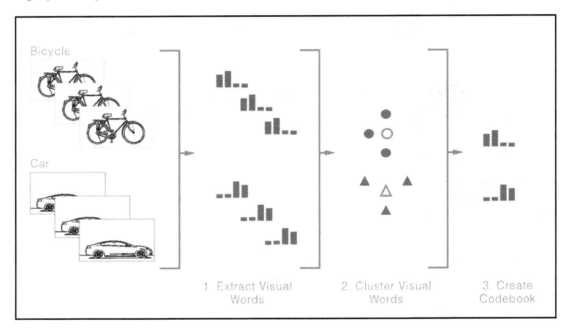

Once we have obtained a histogram for each category (codebook), we can train a **classifier** using each image's extracted features (visual words) and the associated category (label). One popular and effective classifier is **support vector machines** (**SVM**). What SVM tries to find is a hyperplane that best separates the categories; here, *best* refers to a plane that has the largest distance between each of the category members. The term *hyper* is used because it transforms the vectors into high-dimensional space such that the categories can be separated with a linear plane (plane because we are working within a space). The following diagram shows how this may look for two categories in a two-dimensional space:

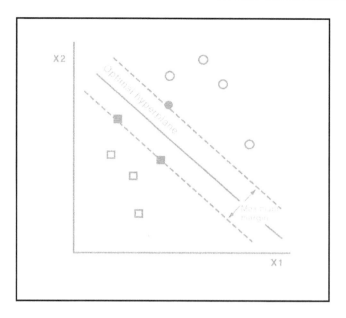

With our model now trained, we can perform real-time classification on the image as the user is drawing, thus allowing us to assist the user by providing them with guidelines for the object they are wanting to draw (or at least, mention the object we predicted them to be drawing). Perfectly suited for touch interfaces such as your iPhone or iPad! This assists not just in drawing applications, but anytime where an input is required by the user, such as image-based searching or note taking.

In this example, we showed how feature engineering and **unsupervised learning** are used to augment data, making it easier for our model to sufficiently perform **classification** using the **supervised learning** algorithm SVM. Prior to deep neural networks, feature engineering was a critical step in ML and sometimes a limiting factor for these reasons:

- It required special skills and sometimes domain expertise
- It was at the mercy of a human being able to find and extract meaningful features
- It required that the features extracted would generalize across the population, that is, be expressive enough to be applied to all examples

In the next example, we introduce a type of neural network called a **convolutional neural network** (**CNN** or **ConvNet**), which takes care of a lot of the feature engineering itself.

 The paper describing the actual project and approach can be found here: http://vision.cs.utexas.edu/projects/shadowdraw/shadowdraw.html.

# Shutterstock – image search based on composition

Over the past 10 years, we have seen an explosive growth in visual content created and consumed on the Web, but before the success of CNNs, images were found by performing simple keyword searches on the tags assigned manually. All this changed around 2012, when A. Krizhevsky, I. Sutskever, and G. E. Hinton published their paper *ImageNet Classification with Deep Convolutional Networks*. The paper described their architecture used to win the 2012 **ImageNet Large-Scale Visual Recognition Challenge** (**ILSVRC**). It's a competition like the Olympics of computer vision, where teams compete across a range of CV tasks such as classification, detection, and object localization. And that was the first year a CNN gained the top position with a test error rate of 15.4% (the next best entry achieved an test error rate of 26.2%). Ever since then, CNNs have become the de facto approach for computer vision tasks, including becoming the new approach for performing visual search. Most likely, it has been adopted by the likes of Google, Facebook, and Pinterest, making it easier than ever to find that right image.

Recently, (October 2017), Shutterstock announced one of the more novel uses of CNNs, where they introduced the ability for their users to search for not only multiple items in an image, but also the composition of those items. The following screenshot shows an example search for a kitten and a computer, with the kitten on the left of the computer:

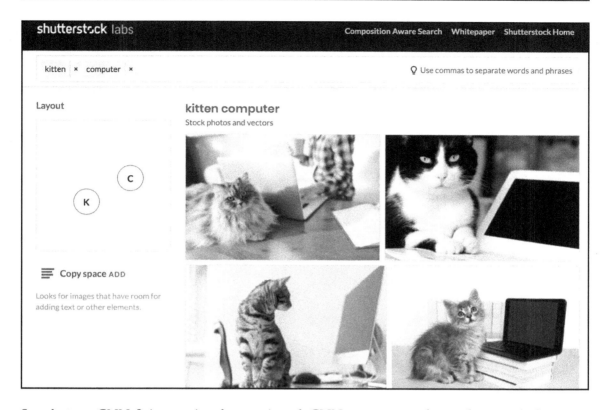

So what are CNNs? As previously mentioned, CNNs are a type of neural network that are well suited for visual content due to their ability to retain spatial information. They are somewhat similar to the previous example, where we explicitly define a filter to extract localized features from the image. A CNN performs a similar operation, but unlike our previous example, filters are not explicitly defined. They are learned through training, and they are not confined to a single layer but rather build with many layers. Each layer builds upon the previous one and each becomes increasingly more abstract (abstract here means a higher-order representation, that is, from pixels to shapes) in what it represents.

To help illustrate this, the following diagram visualizes how a network might build up its understanding of a cat. The first layer's filters extract simple features, such as edges and corners. The next layer builds on top of these with its own filters, resulting in higher-level concepts being extracted, such as shapes or parts of the cat. These high-level concepts are then combined for classification purposes:

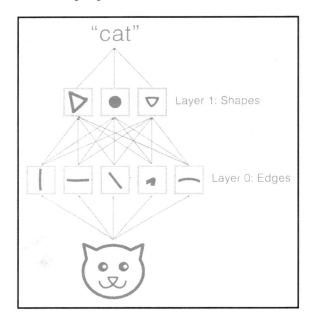

 This ability to get a deeper understanding of the data and reduce the dependency on manual feature engineering has made deep neural networks one of the most popular ML algorithms over the past few years.

To train the model, we feed the network examples using images as inputs and labels as the expected outputs. Given enough examples, the model will build an internal representation for each label, which can be sufficiently used for **classification**; this, of course, is a type of **supervised learning**.

Our last task is to find the location of the item or items; to achieve this, we can inspect the weights of the network to find out which pixels activated a particular class, and then create a bounding box around the inputs with the largest weights.

We have now identified the items and their locations within the image. With this information, we can preprocess our repository of images and cache it as metadata to make it accessible via search queries. We will revisit this idea later in the book when you will get a chance to implement a version of this to assist the user in finding images in their photo album.

In this section, we saw how ML can be used to improve user experience and briefly introduced the intuition behind CNNs, a neural network well suited for visual contexts, where retaining proximity of features and building higher levels of abstraction is important. In the next section, we will continue our exploration of ML applications by introducing another example that improves the user experience and a new type of neural network that is well suited for sequential data such as text.

# iOS keyboard prediction – next letter prediction

Quoting usability expert Jared Spool, *Good design, when done well, should be invisible.* This holds true for ML as well. The application of ML need not be apparent to the user and sometimes (more often than not) more subtle uses of ML can prove just as impactful.

A good example of this is an iOS feature called **dynamic target resizing**; it is working every time you type on an iOS keyboard, where it actively tries to predict what word you're trying to type:

Using this prediction, the iOS keyboard dynamically changes the touch area of a key (here illustrated by the red circles) that is the most likely character based on what has already been typed before it.

For example, in the preceding diagram, the user has entered `"Hell"`; now it would be reasonable to assume that the most likely next character the user wants to tap is `"o"`. This is intuitive given our knowledge of the English language, but how do we teach a machine to know this?

This is where **recurrent neural networks** (**RNNs**) come in; it's a type of neural network that persists state over time. You can think of this persisted state as a form of memory, making RNNs suitable for sequential data such as text (any data where the inputs and outputs are dependent on each other). This state is created by using a feedback loop from the output of the cell, as shown in the following diagram:

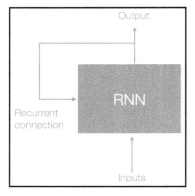

The preceding diagram shows a single RNN cell. If we unroll this over time, we would get something that looks like the following:

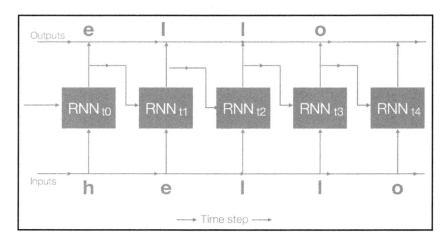

Using **hello** as our example, the preceding diagram shows an unrolled RNN over five time steps; at each time step, the RNN predicts the next likely character. This prediction is determined by its internal representation of the language (from training) and subsequent inputs. This internal representation is built by training it on samples of text where the output is using the inputs but at the next time step (as illustrated earlier). Once trained, the inference follows a similar path, except that we feed to the network the predicted character from the output, to get the next output (to generate the sequence, that is, words).

Neural networks and most ML algorithms require their inputs to be numbers, so we need to convert our characters to numbers, and back again. When dealing with text (characters and words), there are generally two approaches: **one-hot encoding** and **embeddings**. Let's quickly cover each of these to get some intuition of how to handle text.

Text (characters and words) is considered categorical, meaning that we cannot use a single number to represent text because there is no inherit relationship between the text and the value; that is, assigning **the** 10 and **cat** 20 implies that **cat** has a greater value than **the**. Instead, we need to encode them into something where no bias is introduced. One solution to this is encoding them using one-hot encoding, which uses an array of the size of your vocabulary (number of characters in our case), with the index of the specific character set to 1 and the rest set to 0. The following diagram illustrates the encoding process for the corpus **"hello"**:

| Corpus | Tokenize | Vocabulary | One-hot encoding |
|---|---|---|---|
| | | e | [ 1, 0, 0, 0 ] |
| | | h | [ 0, 1, 0, 0 ] |
| "hello" | ['h', 'e', 'l', 'l', 'o'] | l | [ 0, 0, 1, 0 ] |
| | | o | [ 0, 0, 0, 1 ] |

In the preceding diagram, we show some of the steps required when encoding characters; we start off by splitting the corpus into individual characters (called **tokens**, and the process is called **tokenization**). Then we create a set that acts as our vocabulary, and finally we encode this with each character being assigned a vector.

Here, we'll only present some of the steps required for preparing text before passing it to our ML algorithm.

Once our inputs are encoded, we can feed them into our network. Outputs will also be represented in this format, with the most likely character being the index with the greatest value. For example, if **'e'** is predicted, then the most likely the output may resemble something like [0.95, 0.2, 0.2, 0.1].

But there are two problems with one-hot encoding. The first is that for a large vocabulary, we end up with a very sparse data structure. This is not only an inefficient use of memory, but also requires additional calculations for training and inference. The second problem, which is more obvious when operating on words, is that we lose any contextual meaning after they have been encoded. For example, if we were to encode the words **dog** and **dogs**, we would lose any relationship between these words after encoding.

An alternative, and something that addresses these two problems, is using an embedding. These are generally weights from a trained network that use a dense vector representation for each token, one that preserves some contextual meaning. This book focuses on computer vision tasks, so we won't be going into the details here. Just remember that we need to encode our text (characters) into something our ML algorithm will accept.

We train the model using **weak supervision**, similar to supervised learning, but inferring the label without it having been explicitly labelled. Once trained, we can predict the next character using **multi-class classification**, as described earlier.

Over the past couple of years, we have seen the evolution of assistive writing; one example is Google's Smart Reply, which provides an end-to-end method for automatically generating short email responses. Exciting times!

This concludes our brief tour of introducing types of ML problems along with the associated data types, algorithms, and learning style. We have only scratched the surface of each, but as you make your way through this book, you will be introduced to more data types, algorithms, and learning styles.

In the next section, we will take a step back and review the overall workflow for training and inference before wrapping up this chapter.

# A typical ML workflow

If we analyze each of the examples presented so far, we see that each follows a similar pattern. First is the definition of the problem or desired functionality. Once we have established what we want to do, we then identify the available data and/or what data is required. With the data in hand, our next step is to create our ML model and prepare the data for training.

After training, something we hadn't discussed here, is validating our ML model, that is, testing that it satisfactorily achieves what we require of it. An example is being able to make an accurate prediction. Once we have trained a model, we can make use of it by feeding in real data, that is, data outside our training set. In the following diagram, we see these steps summarized for training and inference:

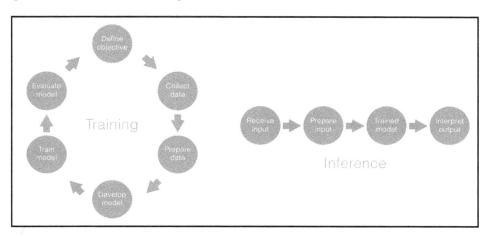

We will spend most of our time using trained models in this book, but understanding how we arrive at these models will prove helpful as you start creating your own intelligent apps. This will also help you identify opportunities to apply ML on existing data or inspire you to seek out new data sources. It's also worth noting that the preprocessing step on training data is equivalent to preprocessing on input data when performing inference—something we will spend a lot of time discussing and coding for throughout this book.

# Summary

In this chapter, we introduced ML and its value by contrasting it against classical programming. We then spent some time exploring different applications of ML, and for each we speculated about the type of data, algorithms, and learning style used. This approach was taken to help demystify how ML works and to encourage you to start thinking about how you can leverage data to improve user experience and/or offer new functionality. We'll continue this approach throughout this book with (obviously) more emphasis on making use of ML by way of example applications related to computer vision.

In the next chapter, we will introduce Core ML, iOS's specifically designed framework for making ML accessible to developers with little or no experience with ML.

# Introduction to Apple Core ML $2$

In this chapter, we are going to briefly introduce the framework that we will be using throughout this book - Core ML. But before doing so, we will elaborate on what training and inference are, specifically how they differ; and then we'll look at the motivation for performing **machine learning** (**ML**) on the edge, that is, your iOS device.

We will be covering the following topics in the chapter:

- Highlighting the difference between training a model and using the model for inference
- Motivation and opportunities for performing inference on the edge
- Introducing Core ML and the general workflow
- A brief introduction to some ML algorithms
- Some considerations to keep in mind when developing ML-enabled applications

## Difference between training and inference

The difference between training and inference is similar to that of a student being taught something like algebra at school and then applying it in the real world. In school, the student is given numerous exercises; for each exercise, the student attempts the question and hands his/her answer over to the teacher, who provides feedback indicating whether it is correct or not. Initially, this feedback is likely to be skewed toward the student being wrong more often than right, but after many attempts, as the student starts building his/her understanding of the concepts, the feedback shifts towards mostly being right. At this point, the student is considered to have sufficiently learned algebra and is able to apply it to unseen problems in the real world, where he/she can be confident of the answer based on his/her exposure to the exercises provided during the lessons at school.

ML models are no different; the initial phase of building the model is through the process of **training,** where the model is provided with many examples. For each example, a **loss function** is used in place of the teacher to provide feedback, which, in turn, is used to make adjustments to the model to reduce the loss (the degree to which the model's answer was incorrect). This process of training can take many iterations and is typically compute intensive, but it offers opportunities for being parallelized (especially for neural networks); that is, a lot of the calculations can run in parallel with one another. For this reason, it's common to perform training in the cloud or some dedicated machines with enough memory and compute power. This process of training is illustrated in the following diagram:

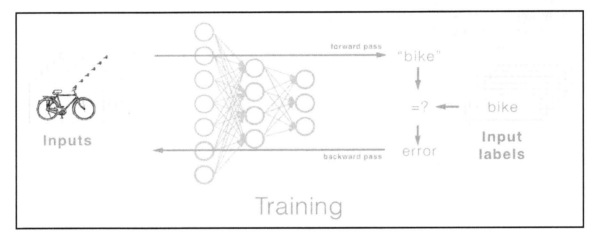

To better illustrate the compute power required, in the blog post *Cortana Intelligence and Machine Learning Blog,* Microsoft data scientist Miguel Fierro and others detail the infrastructure and time required for training on the ImageNet dataset (1,000 classes with over 1.2 million photos) using an 18-layer ResNet architecture. It took approximately three days to train over 30 epochs on an Azure N-series NC-24 virtual machine with 4 GPUs, 24 CPU cores, and 224 GB of memory. The full details are described here: https://blogs.technet.microsoft.com/machinelearning/2016/ 11/15/imagenet-deep-neural-network-training-using-microsoft-r- server-and-azure-gpu-vms/.

After the training is complete, the model is now ready for the real world; like our student, we can now deploy and use our model to solve unseen problems. This is known as **inference**. Unlike training, inference only requires a single pass through the model using its gained understanding from training, that is, weights and coefficients. Additionally, there are some sections in our model that are no longer needed, so there is a degree of pruning (the reduction of less important aspects that do not affect accuracy) that can be performed to further optimize the model:

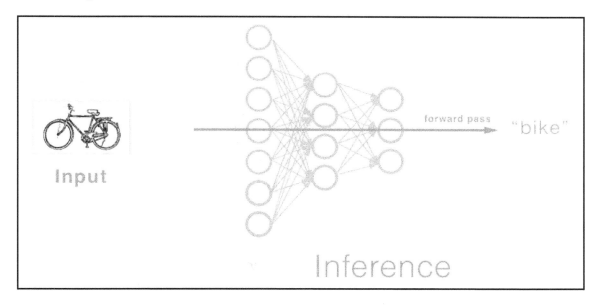

Because of these conditions, a single pass, and pruning, we can afford to perform inference on less performant machines, like our smartphone. But why would you want to do this? What are the advantages of performing inference on the edge? This is the topic of the next section.

# Inference on the edge

For those unfamiliar with the term **edge computing**, it simply refers to computation performed at the end, or edge, of a network as opposed to sending it to a central server for computation. Some examples of edge devices include cars, robots, **Internet of Things** (**IoT**), and, of course, smartphones.

The motivation for performing computation at the edge, where the data resides, is that sending data across the network is expensive and time-consuming; this incurred latency and cost restrict us with what experiences we can deliver to the user. Removing these barriers opens up new applications that would otherwise not be possible. Another benefit of performing inference at the edge is data privacy; removing the need of having to transmit personal data across the network reduces the opportunities that a malicious user has for obtaining it.

Luckily, technology advances at an astonishing rate and improvements in hardware and software have now made it feasible to perform inference at the edge.

As this book's focus is on applied ML on iOS; **detailed** model architectures and training have been intentionally omitted as training currently requires significant computational power that is still out of reach of most of today's edge devices - although this is likely to change in the near future as edge devices become increasingly powerful, with the most likely next advancement being around tuning and personalizing models using personal data that resides on the device.

Some common use cases for ML on the device include:

- **Speech recognition**: It's currently common to perform wake (or hot) word detection locally rather than continuously streaming data across the network. For example, **Hey Siri** is most likely performed locally on the device, and once detected, it streams the utterance to a server for further processing.
- **Image recognition**: It can be useful for the device to be able to understand what it is seeing in order to assist the user in taking a photo, such as applying the appropriate filters, adding captions to the photos to make them easier to find and grouping similar images together. These enhancements may not be significant enough to justify opening a connection to a remote server, but because these can be performed locally, we can use them without worrying about cost, latency, or privacy issues.
- **Object localization**: Sometimes, it is useful to know not only what is present in view, but also where it is in the view. An example of this can be seen in **augmented reality** (**AR**) apps, where information is overlaid onto the scene. Having these experiences responsive is critical for their success, and therefore there is a need for extremely low latency in performing inference.

- **Optical character recognition**: One of the first commercial applications of neural networks is still just as useful as it was when it was used in American post offices in 1989. Being able to read allows for applications such as digitizing a physical copy or performing computations on it; examples include language translation or solving a Sudoku puzzle.
- **Translation**: Translating from one language to another quickly and accurately, even if you don't have a network connection, is an important use case and complements many of the visual-based scenarios we have discussed so far, such as AR and optical character recognition.
- **Gesture recognition**: Gesture recognition provides us with a rich interaction mode, allowing quick shortcuts and intuitive user interactions that can improve and enhance user experience.
- **Text prediction**: Being able to predict the next word the user is going to type, or even predicting the user's response, has turned something fairly cumbersome and painful to use (the smartphone soft keyboard) into something that is just as quick or even quicker than its counterpart (the conventional keyboard). Being able to perform this prediction on the device increases your ability to protect the user's privacy and offer a responsive solution. This is not feasible if the request has to be routed to a remote server.
- **Text classification**: This covers everything from sentiment analysis to topic discovery and facilitates many useful applications, such as providing means to recommend relevant content to the user or eliminate duplicates.

These examples of use cases and applications hopefully show why we may want to perform inference on the edge; it means you can offer a higher level of interactivity than what could be possible with performing inference off the device. It allows you to deliver an experience even if the device has poor network connectivity or no network connectivity. And finally, it's scalable—an increase in demand doesn't directly correlate to the load on your server.

So far, we have introduced inference and the importance of being able to perform it on the edge. In the next section, we will introduce the framework that facilitates this on iOS devices: Core ML.

# A brief introduction to Core ML

With the release of iOS 11 and Core ML, performing inference is just a matter of a few lines of code. Prior to iOS 11, inference was possible, but it required some work to take a pre-trained model and port it across using an existing framework such as **Accelerate** or **metal performance shaders** (**MPSes**). **Accelerate** and MPSes are still used under the hood by Core ML, but Core ML takes care of deciding which underlying framework your model should use (**Accelerate** using the CPU for memory-heavy tasks and MPSes using the GPU for compute-heavy tasks). It also takes care of abstracting a lot of the details away; this layer of abstraction is shown in the following diagram:

| | | |
|---|---|---|
| | CoreML | |
| ML Performance Primitives | Accelerate | Metal Performance Shaders |
| Hardware | CPU | GPU |

There are additional layers too; iOS 11 has introduced and extended domain-specific layers that further abstract a lot of the common tasks you may use when working with image and text data, such as face detection, object tracking, language translation, and **named entity recognition** (**NER**). These domain-specific layers are encapsulated in the **Vision** and **natural language processing** (**NLP**) frameworks; we won't be going into any details of these frameworks here, but you will get a chance to use them in later chapters:

| | | |
|---|---|---|
| | App | |
| Domain Specific Frameworks | Vision | NLP |
| | CoreML | |
| ML Performance Primitives | Accelerate | Metal Performance Shaders |
| Hardware | CPU | GPU |

It's worth noting that these layers are not mutually exclusive and it is common to find yourself using them together, especially the domain-specific frameworks that provide useful preprocessing methods we can use to prepare our data before sending to a Core ML model.

So what exactly is Core ML? You can think of Core ML as a suite of tools used to facilitate the process of bringing ML models to iOS and wrapping them in a standard interface so that you can easily access and make use of them in your code. Let's now take a closer look at the typical workflow when working with Core ML.

# Workflow

As described previously, the two main tasks of a ML workflow consist of **training** and **inference**. Training involves obtaining and preparing the data, defining the model, and then the real training. Once your model has achieved satisfactory results during training and is able to perform adequate predictions (including on data it hasn't seen before), your model can then be deployed and used for inference using data outside of the training set. Core ML provides a suite of tools to facilitate getting a trained model into iOS, one being the Python packaged released called **Core ML Tools**; it is used to take a model (consisting of the architecture and weights) from one of the many popular packages and exporting a `.mlmodel` file, which can then be imported into your Xcode project.

Once imported, Xcode will generate an interface for the model, making it easily accessible via code you are familiar with. Finally, when you build your app, the model is further optimized and packaged up within your application. A summary of the process of generating the model is shown in the following diagram:

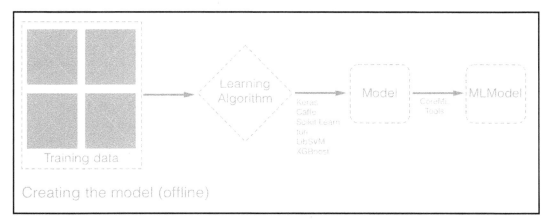

The previous diagram illustrates the process of creating the `.mlmodel;`, either using an existing model from one of the supported frameworks, or by training it from scratch. Core ML Tools supports most of the frameworks, either internal or as third party plug-ins, including Keras, turi, Caffe, scikit-learn, LibSVN, and XGBoost frameworks. Apple has also made this package open source and modular for easy adaption for other frameworks or by yourself. The process of importing the model is illustrated in this diagram:

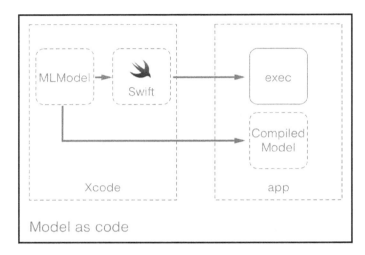

In addition; there are frameworks with tighter integration with Core ML that handle generating the Core ML model such as **Turi Create, IBM Watson Services for Core ML,** and **Create ML.**

We will be introducing Create ML in chapter 10; for those interesting in learning more about Turi Create and IBM Watson Services for Core ML then please refer to the official webpages via the following links:
Turi Create; `https://github.com/apple/turicreate`
IBM Watson Services for Core ML; `https://developer.apple.com/ibm/`

Once the model is imported, as mentioned previously, Xcode generates an interface that wraps the **model**, model **inputs**, and **outputs**. You will get acquainted with these throughout the rest of this book, so we won't go into any further details here.

In the previous diagrams we have seen the workflow of training and importing a **model** - let's now delve into the details of what this model is and what Core ML currently supports.

# Learning algorithms

In `Chapter 1`, *Introduction to Machine Learning*, we saw many different types of learning algorithms and learned that ML is really a process of automatically discovering rules given a set of examples. The main components required for this process, specifically for supervised learning, include:

- **Input data points**: For image classification, we would require images of the domain we want to classify, for example, animals.
- **The expected outputs for these inputs**: Continuing from our previous example of image classification of animals, the expected outputs could be labels associated with each of the images, for example, cat, dog, and many more.
- **A ML algorithm**: This is the algorithm used to automatically learn how to transform the input data points into a meaningful output. These derived sets of rules are what we call the model, derived through a process of learning called **training**.

Let's make these concepts more concrete by working through a simple example.

# Auto insurance in Sweden

If you haven't done so already, navigate to the repository at `https://github.com/joshnewnham/MachineLearningWithCoreML` and download the latest code. Once downloaded, navigate to the directory `Chapter2/Start/` and open the playground `LinearRegression.playground`.

We will be creating a model that will predict the total payments for all claims (y) given the number of claims (x); the dataset we will be working with is auto insurance claims in Sweden. It consists of 2 columns and 64 rows, the first column containing the number of claims, and the second containing the total payments for all claims. Here is an extract from the dataset:

| Number of claims | Total payments for all claims in thousands of Swedish Kronor |
|---|---|
| 108 | 329.5 |
| 19 | 46.2 |
| 13 | 15.7 |
| 124 | 422.2 |
| ... | ... |

For more details, visit the source website: `http://college.cengage.com/ mathematics/brase/understandable_statistics/7e/students/ datasets/slr/frames/slr06.html`.

In the playground script, you will see that we are creating a view of the type `ScatterPlotView` and assigning it to the playground's live view. We will use this view to visualize the data and the predictions from our model:

```
let view = ScatterPlotView(frame: CGRect(x: 20, y: 20, width: 300, height:
300))

PlaygroundPage.current.liveView = view
```

By using this view, we can plot an array of data points using the `view.scatter(dataPoints:)` method and draw a line using the `view.line(pointA:,pointB)` method. Let's load the raw data and visualize it:

```
let csvData = parseCSV(contents:loadCSV(file:"SwedishAutoInsurance"))

let dataPoints = extractDataPoints(data: csvData, xKey: "claims", yKey:
"payments")

view.scatter(dataPoints)
```

In the previous code snippet, we first load the data into the `csvData` variable and then cast it into a strongly typed array of `DataPoint` (a strongly typed data object, which our view is expecting). Once loaded, we pass our data to the view via the `scatter` method, which renders the following output:

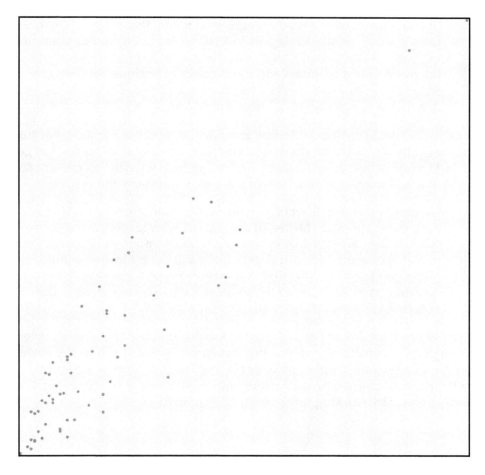

Each dot represents a single datapoint plotted against the number of claims (*x* axis) and total payments for all claims (*y* axis). From this visualization, we can infer some linear relationship between the **number of claims** and **total payments for all claims**; that is, an increase in **number of claims** increases the **total payments for all claims**. Using this intuition, we will attempt to model the data according to a linear model, one that, when given the **number of claims**, is able to predict the **total payments for all claims**. What we are describing here is a type of algorithm known as **simple linear regression**; in essence, this is just finding a straight line that best fits our data. It can be described with the function $y = w * x + b$, where *y* is the **total payments for all claims**, *x* is the **number of claims**, *w* is the relationship between *y* and *x*, and *b* is the intercept.

Linear regression is a type of regression model that maps a linear function from a set of continuous inputs to a continuous output. For example, you may want to model and predict **house prices**; here, your inputs may be the **number of bedrooms** and the **number of bathrooms**. Using these two features, you'd want to find a function that can predict the house price, one that assumes there is a linear correlation.

Simple enough! Our next problem is finding this line that best fits our data. For this, we are going to use an approach called **gradient descent**; there are plenty of books that go into the theoretical and technical details of gradient descent, so here we will just present some intuition behind it and leave it to you, the curious reader, to study the details.

 Gradient descent is a set of algorithms that minimize a function; in our case, they minimize the loss of our output with respect to the actual output. They achieve this by starting with an initial set of parameters (weights or coefficients) and iteratively adjusting these to minimize the calculated loss. The direction and magnitude of these adjustments are determined by how far off the predicted value is compared to the expected error and the parameters' contribution.

You can think of gradient descent as a search for some minimum point; what determines this minimum point is something called a **loss function**. For us, it will be the absolute error between our prediction and actual number of claims. The algorithm is steered by calculating the relative contribution of each of our variables (here it is $w$ and $b$). Let's see how this looks in code by working through the `train` method:

```
func train(
    x:[CGFloat],
    y:[CGFloat],
    b:CGFloat=0.0,
    w:CGFloat=0.0,
    learningRate:CGFloat=0.00001,
    epochs:Int=100,
    trainingCallback: ((Int, Int, CGFloat, CGFloat) -> Void)? = nil) ->
(b:CGFloat, w:CGFloat){
    var B = b // bias
    var W = w // weight
    let N = CGFloat(x.count) // number of data points
    for epoch in 0...epochs{
        // TODO: create variable to store this epoch's gradient for b
and w
        for i in 0..<x.count{
            // TODO: make a prediction (using the linear equation y = b
+ x * w
```

```
                // TODO: calculate the absolute error (prediction - actual
value)
                // TODO: calculate the gradient with respect to the error
and b (); adding it to the epochs bias gradient
                // TODO: calculate the gradient with respect to the error
and w (); adding it to the epochs weight gradient
            }
        // TODO: update the bias (B) using the learningRate
        // TODO: update the weight (W) using the learningRate
        if let trainingCallback = trainingCallback{
            trainingCallback(epoch, epochs, W, B)
        }
    }
    return (b:B, w:W)
}
```

Our `train` method takes in these arguments:

- `x`: An array of `DataPoint` containing the number of claims
- `y`: An array of `DataPoint` containing the total number of payments
- `b`: This is a random value used in our linear function to start our search
- `w`: Another random value used in our linear function to start our search
- `learningRate`: How quickly we adjust the weights
- `epochs`: The number of times we iterate, that is, make a prediction, and adjust our coefficients based on the difference between the prediction and expected value
- `trainingCallback`: This function is called after each epoch to report the progress

We next create some variables that will be used throughout training and begin our search (`for epoch in 0...epochs`). Let's step through each `TODO` and replace them with their respective code.

First, we start by creating two variables to hold the gradients for our variables b and w (these are the adjustments we need to make to their respective coefficients to minimize the loss, also known as **absolute error**):

```
// TODO: create variable to store this epoch's gradient for b and w
var bGradient : CGFloat = 0.0
var wGradient : CGFloat = 0.0
```

Next, we iterate over each data point, and for each data point, make a prediction and calculate the absolute error:

```
// TODO: make a prediction (using the linear equation y = b + x * w
let yHat = W * x[i] + B
// TODO: calculate the absolute error (prediction - actual value)
let error = y[i] - yHat
```

Now calculate the partial derivative with respect to the error. Think of this as a way to steer the search in the right direction, that is, calculating this gives us the **direction** and **magnitude** that we need to change b and w to minimize our error:

 Note that this is done after iterating through all data points; that is, it is influenced by all data points. Alternatives are to perform this update per data point or over a subset, known as a **batch**.

```
// TODO: calculate the gradient with respect to the error and b (); adding
it to the epochs bias gradient
B = B - (learningRate * bGradient)
// TODO: calculate the gradient with respect to the error and w (); adding
it to the epochs weight gradient
W = W - (learningRate * wGradient)
```

After iterating over each data point, we adjust the coefficients B and W using their accumulated gradients.

After each epoch, `trainingCallback` is called to draw a line using the current model's coefficients (its current best fit line that fits the data); the progress of this is shown in the following diagram:

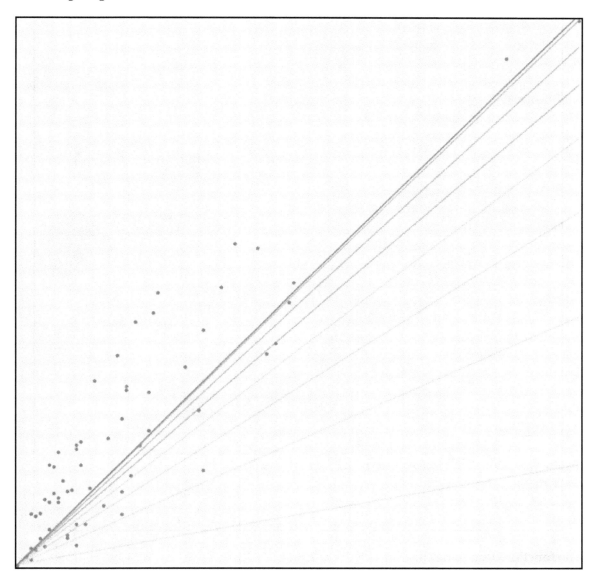

Admittedly, this is difficult to interpret without a key! But the pattern will hopefully be obvious; with each iteration, our line better fits the data. After 100 epochs, we end up with this model:

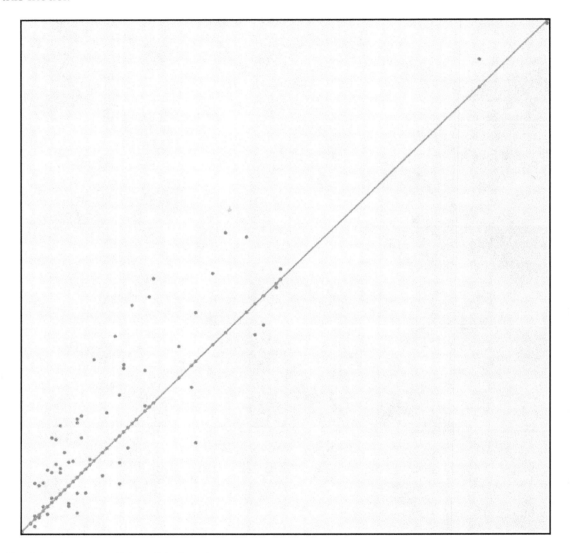

The function describing this line is y = 0.733505317339142 + 3.4474988368438 * x. Using this model, we can predict the **total payments for all claims** given the **number of claims** (by simply substituting *x* with the **number of claims**).

# Supported learning algorithms

In the previous example, we used **linear regression** (algorithm) to build a model that predicts the total payments for all claims (output) given the number of claims (input). This is one of many algorithms available for ML; a few of them are plotted in the following diagram, grouped into **unsupervised** or **supervised**, and **continuous** or **categorical**:

Machine Learning Algorithms

|  | Unsupervised | Supervised |
|---|---|---|
| **Continuous** | Clustering & Dimensionality Reduction<br>SVD<br>PCA<br>K-Means | Regression<br>Linear<br>Polynomial<br>Decision Trees<br>Random Forests<br>Nerual Networks |
| **Categorical** | Association Analysis<br>Apriori<br>FP-Growth<br>Hidden Markov Model | Classification<br>KNN<br>Trees<br>Logistic Regression<br>Naive-Bayes<br>SVN<br>Nerual Networks |

The process of creating Core ML models involves translating the model from the source framework into something that can be run on iOS. The following diagram shows which learning algorithms Core ML currently supports:

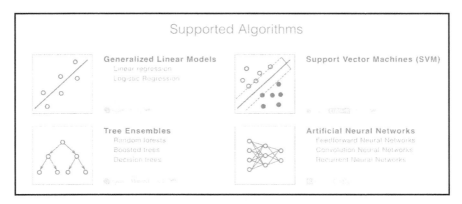

Supported Algorithms

**Generalized Linear Models**
Linear regression
Logistic Regression

**Support Vector Machines (SVM)**

**Tree Ensembles**
Random forests
Boosted trees
Decision trees

**Artificial Neural Networks**
Feedforward Neural Networks
Convolution Neural Networks
Recurrent Neural Networks

The supported algorithms and neural networks should be versatile enough for most ML tasks but given how fast this field is moving, it's inevitable that you will encounter one that is not supported. Apple have anticipated this and provides two protocols for extending the framework; `MLCustomLayer` can be used to create custom layers (which we cover in later chapters) and `MLCustomModel` for creating custom models.

This has hopefully given you some idea of where Core ML fits in the general ML workflow and why Apple has made the design decisions it has. We will finish this chapter by looking at a few high-level considerations when dealing with ML on an iOS device, or, more generally, the edge before wrapping up.

# Considerations

When performing ML on the edge, you lose some of the luxuries you tend to have when running on a more powerful device (albeit this is shifting all the time). Here is a list of considerations to keep in mind:

- **Model size**: Previously, we walked through building a simple linear regression model. The model itself consists of two floats (bias and weight coefficients), which of course are negligible in terms of memory requirements. But, as you dive into the world of deep learning, it's common to find models hundreds of megabytes in size. For example, the VGG16 model is a 16-layer conventional neural network architecture trained on the ImageNet dataset used for image classification, available on Apple's site. It is just over 500 megabytes. Currently, Apple allows apps 2 gigabytes in size, but asking your user to download such a large file may well put them off.
- **Memory**: It's not just the executable size that you need to be mindful of, but also the amount of working memory available. It's common for desktop machines to have memory in the range of 16-32 gigabytes, but the memory for the latest iPhone (iPhone 8) is just 2 gigabytes—impressive for a mobile device, but quite a difference from its counterpart. This constraint is likely to dictate what model you choose, more so than how much memory it takes on disk. It is also worth mentioning that it's not just the model weights you'll need to load into the memory; you will also need to load in any label data and, of course, the input data you are performing inference on.

- **Speed**: This, of course, is correlated to the model size (in normal circumstances) and relevant to your specific use case. Just keep in mind that performing inference is only one part of the workflow. You have pre-processing and post-processing tasks that also need to be taken into account, such as loading and pre-processing the input data. In some cases, you may have to trade off accuracy with performance and size.
- **Supported algorithms and data types**: In the previous section, we presented the current algorithms that Core ML supports. Along with these, Core ML supports a subset of data types, summarized in the following table for convenience:

| Input type | Data type |
|------------|-----------|
| Numeric | Double, Int64 |
| Categories | String, Int64 |
| Images | CVPixelBuffer |
| Arrays | MLMultiArray |
| Dictionaries | [String : Double], [Int64, Double] |

Here, we have presented just a few of the considerations at a high level when performing ML on a mobile device. The specifics will be dependent on your use case and models available, but it's worth keeping these in the back of your mind and reminding yourself that these, albeit very powerful devices, are still mobile devices. They run on a battery and are therefore subject to the typical considerations and optimizations normally required for a mobile project. These considerations are even more applicable to those who plan to create their own model, which should be most of you if you plan to take advantage of ML.

# Summary

In this chapter, we discussed the difference between training and inference, along with the typical ML workflow and where Core ML fits in. We also saw how Core ML is not just a single framework, but rather a suite of tools that facilitate getting pretrained models into the iOS platform and making them available to your application via a familiar and simple interface. Thus, it democratizes ML and puts it into the hands of many iOS app developers.

It has been suggested that the explosion in diverse apps contributed to the success of the adoption of smartphones; if this is true, then prepare yourself for the next explosion of AI-enhanced apps. And take comfort knowing that you are in the perfect place to begin and lead this journey, where we will explore many concepts and examples related to computer vision using Core ML, including these:

- Recognizing objects through the video feed of your camera
- Leveraging object detection to build intelligent image search, allowing you to search for images with specific objects and their position relative to one another
- Recognizing facial expressions and inferring the emotional state of a person
- Recognizing hand-drawn sketches using convolutional neural networks and then with recurrent neural networks
- Learning the secrets behind Prisma's style transfer and implementing your own version
- Finally, using image segmentation to create the action shot effect

There is plenty to get through, so let's get started!

# Recognizing Objects in the World 3

In this chapter, we will immerse ourselves in the world of **machine learning** (**ML**) and Core ML by working through what could be considered the 101 Core ML application. We will be using an image classification model to allow the user to point their iPhone at anything and have the app classify the most dominant object in the view.

We will start off by first discussing the concept of **convolutional neural networks** (**ConvNets** or **CNNs**), a category of neural networks well suited to image classification, before jumping into implementation. Starting from a skeleton project, you will soon discover just how easy it is to integrate ML into your apps with the help of Core ML.

In this chapter, we will cover the following topics:

- Gaining some intuition on how machines understand images
- Building out the example application for this chapter
- Capturing photo frames and preprocessing them before passing them to the Core ML model
- Using the Core ML model to perform inference and interpreting the result

 Convolutional neural networks are commonly referred to as either CNNs or ConvNets, and these terms are used interchangeably throughout this book.

# Understanding images

As mentioned previously, it's not my intention to give you a theoretical or deep understanding of any particular ML algorithm, but rather gently introduce you to some of the main concepts. This will help you to gain an intuitive understanding of how they work so that you know where and how to apply them, as well as give you a platform to dive deeper into the particular subject, which I strongly encourage you to do.

 For a good introductory text on deep learning, I strongly recommend Andrew Trask's book *Grokking Deep Learning*. For a general introduction to ML, I would recommend Toby Segaran's book *Programming Collective Intelligence: Building Smart Web 2.0 Applications*.

In this section, we will be introducing CNNs, specifically introducing what they are and why they are well suited for spatial data, that is, images. But before discussing CNNs, we will start by inspecting the data; then we'll see why CNNs perform better than their counterpart, fully connected neural networks (or just neural networks).

For the purpose of illustrating these concepts, consider the task of classifying the following digits, where each digit is represented as a 5 x 5 matrix of pixels. The dark gray pixels have a value of 1 and light gray pixels have a value of 0:

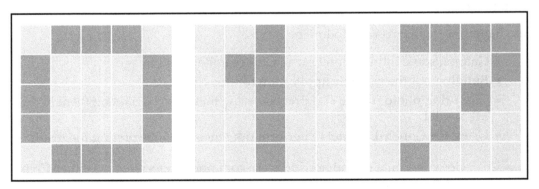

Using a fully connected neural network (single hidden layer), our model would learn the joint probability of each pixel with respect to their associated label; that is, the model will assign positive weights to pixels that correlate with the label and using the output with the highest likelihood to be the most probable label. During training, we take each image and flatten it before feeding into our network, as shown in the following diagram:

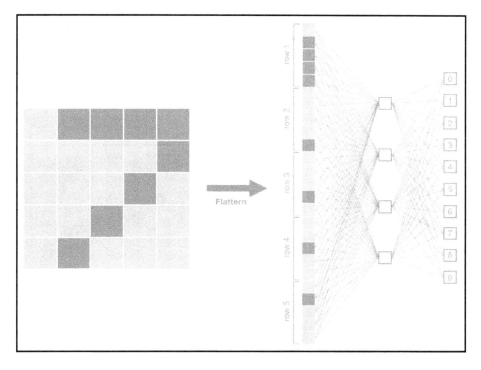

This works remarkably well, and if you have experience with ML, particularly deep learning, you would have likely come across the MNIST dataset. It's a dataset consisting of labeled handwritten digits, where each digit is centrally rendered to a 28 x 28 gray scale (single channel with the pixel value ranging from 0-255) image. Using a single-layer fully connected network will likely result in a validation accuracy close to 90%. But what happens if we introduce some complexities such as moving the image around a larger space, as illustrated in the following diagram?

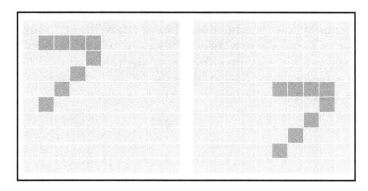

The fully connected network has no concept of space or local relationships; in this case, the model would need to learn all variants of each digit at each possible location. To further emphasize the importance of being able to capture the relationship of spatial data, consider the need to learn more complex images, such as classifying dogs and cats using a network that discards 2D information. Individual pixels alone are unable to portray complex shapes such as eyes, a nose, or ears; it's only when you consider neighboring pixels that you can describe these more complex shapes:

Images taken from the Kaggle competition cats vs dogs (https://www.kaggle.com/c/dogs-vs-cats)

We need something that can abstract away from the raw pixels, something that can describe images using high-level features. Let's return to our digits dataset and investigate how we might go about extracting higher-level features for the task of classification. As alluded to in an earlier example, we need a set of features that abstracts away from the raw pixels, is unaffected by position, and preserves 2D spatial information. If you're familiar with image processing, or even image processing tools, you would have most probably come across the idea and results of **edge detection** or **edge filters**; in simplest terms, these work by passing a set of kernels across the whole image, where the output is the image with its edges emphasized. Let's see how this looks diagrammatically. First, we have our set of kernels; each one extracts a specific feature of the image, such the presence of horizontal edges, vertical edges, or edges at a 45 degree angle:

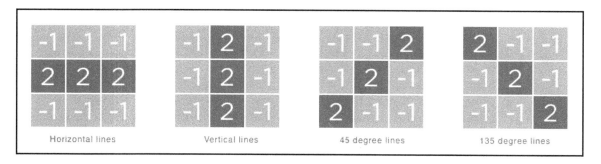

For each of these filters, we pass them over our image, extracting each of the features; to help illustrate this, let's take one digit and pass the vertical kernel over it:

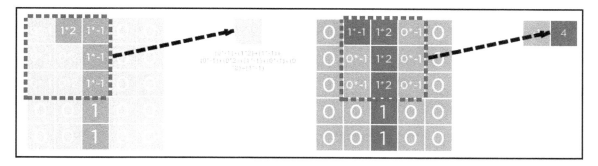

As illustrated in the previous diagram, we slide the horizontal kernel across the image, producing a new image using the values of the image and kernel. We continue until we have reached the bounds of the image, as shown in the following diagram:

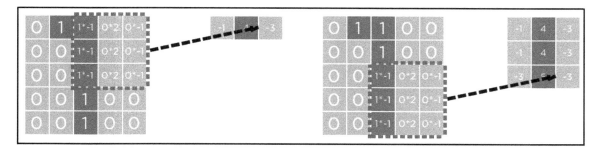

The output of this is a map showing the presence of vertical lines detected within the image. Using this and the other kernels, we can now describe each class by its dominant gradients rather than using pixel positions. This higher level abstraction allows us to recognize classes independent of their location as well as describe more complex objects.

Two useful things to be aware of when dealing with kernels are the **stride value** and **padding**. Strides determines how large your step size is when sliding your kernel across the image. In the preceding example, our stride is set to 1; that is, we're sliding only by a single value. Padding refers to how you deal with the boundaries; here, we are using **valid**, where we only process pixels within valid ranges. **same** would mean adding a border around the image to ensure that the output remains the same size as the input.

What we have performed here is known as **feature engineering** and something neural networks perform automatically; in particular, this is what CNNs do. They create a series of kernels (or convolution matrices) that are used to convolve the image to extract local features from neighboring pixels. Unlike our previous engineered example, these kernels are learned during training. Because they are learned automatically, we can afford to create many filters that can extract granular nuances of the image as well, allowing us to effectively stack convolution layers on top of each other. This allows for increasingly higher levels of abstraction to learn. For example, your first layer may learn to detect simple edges, and your second layer (operating on the previous extracted features) may learn to extract simple shapes. The deeper we go, the higher the level achieved by our features, as illustrated in the diagram:

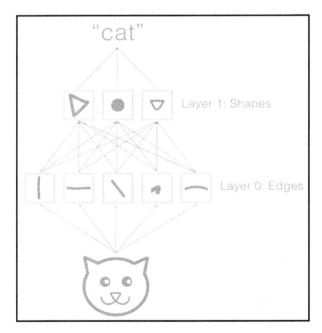

And there we have it! An architecture capable of understanding the world by learning features and layers of abstraction to efficiently describe it. Let's now put this into practice using a pretrained model and Core ML to get our phone to recognize the objects it sees.

# Recognizing objects in the world

To recap, our goal in this chapter is to create an application that will recognize what it sees. We will start by first capturing video frames, prepare these frames for our model, and finally feed them into a Core ML model to perform inference. Let's get started.

## Capturing data

If you haven't done it already, download the latest code from the accompanying repository: https://github.com/packtpublishing/machine-learning-with-core-ml. Once downloaded, navigate to the directory Chapter3/Start/ObjectRecognition/ and open the project ObjectRecognition.xcodeproj. Once loaded, you will see the skeleton project for this chapter, as shown in the following screenshot:

To help you navigate around the project, here is a list of core files/classes and their main functions:

- `VideoCapture` will be responsible for the management and handling of the camera, including capturing video frames
- `CaptureVideoPreviewView.swift` contains the class `CapturePreviewView`, which will be used to present the captured frames
- `CIImage` provides convenient extensions to the class `CIImage`, used for preparing the frame for the Core ML model
- `VideoController`, as you would expect, is the controller for the application and is responsible for interfacing with the imported Core ML model

We will be making changes to each of these in the following sections in order to realize the desired functionality. Our first task will be to get access to the camera and start capturing frames; to do this, we will be making use of Apple's iOS frameworks **AVFoundation** and **CoreVideo**.

The AVFoundation framework encompasses classes for handing capturing, processing, synthesizing, controlling, importing, and exporting of audiovisual media on iOS and other platforms. In this chapter, we are most interested in a subset of this framework for dealing with cameras and media capture, but you can learn more about the AVFoundation framework on Apple's official documentation site at `https://developer.apple.com/documentation/avfoundation`.

CoreVideo provides a pipeline-based API for manipulating digital videos, capable of accelerating the process using support from both Metal and OpenGL.

We will designate the responsibility of setting up and capturing frames from the camera to the class `VideoCapture`; let's jump into the code now. Select `VideoCapture.swift` from the left-hand side panel to open in the editing window. Before making amendments, let's inspect what is already there and what's left to do.

At the top of the class, we have the protocol `VideoCaptureDelegate` defined:

```
public protocol VideoCaptureDelegate: class {
    func onFrameCaptured(
      videoCapture: VideoCapture,
      pixelBuffer:CVPixelBuffer?,
      timestamp:CMTime)
}
```

`VideoCapture` will pass through the captured frames to a registered delegate, thus allowing the `VideoCapture` class to focus solely on the task of capturing the frames. What we pass to the delegate is a reference to itself, the image data (captured frame) of type `CVPixelBuffer` and the timestamp as type `CMTime`. `CVPixelBuffer` is a CoreVideo data structure specifically for holding pixel data, and the data structure our Core ML model is expecting (which we'll see in a short while). `CMTTime` is just a struct for encapsulating a timestamp, which we'll obtain directly from the video frame.

Under the protocol, we have the skeleton of our `VideoCapture` class. We will be walking through it in this section, along with an extension to implement the `AVCaptureVideoDataOutputSampleBufferDelegate` protocol, which we will use to capture frames:

```
public class VideoCapture : NSObject{
    public weak var delegate: VideoCaptureDelegate?
    public var fps = 15
    var lastTimestamp = CMTime()
    override init() {
        super.init()
    }
    private func initCamera() -> Bool
    {
        return true
    }
    public func asyncStartCapturing(
        completion: (() -> Void)? = nil)
        {
        }
    public func asyncStopCapturing(
        completion: (() -> Void)? = nil)
        {
        }
}
```

Most of this should be self-explanatory, so I will only highlight the not-so-obvious parts, starting with the variables `fps` and `lastTimestamp`. We use these together to throttle how quickly we pass frames back to the delegate; we do this as it's our assumption that we capture frames far quicker than we can process them. And to avoid having our camera lag or jump, we explicitly limit how quickly we pass frames to the delegate. **Frames per second (fps)** sets this frequency while `lastTimestamp` is used in conjunction to calculate the elapsed time since the last processing of a frame.

The only other part of the code I will highlight here is the `asyncStartCapturing` and `asyncStopCapturing` methods; these methods, as the names imply, are responsible for starting and stopping the capture session respectively. Because they both will be using blocking methods, which can take some time, we will dispatch the task off the main thread to avoid blocking it and affecting the user's experience.

Finally, we have the extension; it implements the `AVCaptureVideoDataOutputSampleBufferDelegate` protocol:

```
extension VideoCapture : AVCaptureVideoDataOutputSampleBufferDelegate{
    public func captureOutput(_ output: AVCaptureOutput,
                              didOutput sampleBuffer: CMSampleBuffer,
                              from connection: AVCaptureConnection)
    {
    }
}
```

We will discuss the details shortly, but essentially it is the delegate that we assign to the camera for handling incoming frames of the camera. We will then proxy it through to the `VideoCaptureDelegate` delegate assigned to this class.

Let's now walk through implementing the methods of this class, starting with `initCamera`. In this method, we want to set up the pipeline that will grab the frames from the physical camera of the device and pass them onto our delegate method. We do this by first getting a reference to the physical camera and then wrapping it in an instance of the `AVCaptureDeviceInput` class, which takes care of managing the connection and communication with the physical camera. Finally, we add a destination for the frames, which is where we use an instance of `AVCaptureVideoDataOutput`, assigning ourselves as the delegate for receiving these frames. This pipeline is wrapped in something called `AVCaptureSession`, which is responsible for coordinating and managing this pipeline.

Let's now define some instance variables we'll need; inside the class `VideoCapture`, add the following variables:

```
let captureSession = AVCaptureSession()
let sessionQueue = DispatchQueue(label: "session queue")
```

We mentioned the purpose of `captureSession` previously, but also introduced a `DispatchQueue`. When adding a delegate to `AVCaptureVideoDataOutput` (for handling the arrival of new frames), you also pass in a `DispatchQueue`; this allows you to control which queue the frames are managed on. For our example, we will be handling the processing of the images off the main thread so as to avoid impacting the performance of the user interface.

With our instance variables now declared, we will turn our attention to the `initCamera` method, breaking it down into small snippets of code. Add the following within the body of the method:

```
captureSession.beginConfiguration()
captureSession.sessionPreset = AVCaptureSession.Preset.medium
```

We signal to the `captureSession` that we want to batch multiple configurations by calling the method `beginConfiguration`; these changes won't be made until we commit them by calling the session's `commitConfiguration` method. Then, in the next line of code, we set the desired quality level:

```
guard let captureDevice = AVCaptureDevice.default(for: AVMediaType.video)
else {
    print("ERROR: no video devices available")
    return false
}

guard let videoInput = try? AVCaptureDeviceInput(device: captureDevice)
else {
    print("ERROR: could not create AVCaptureDeviceInput")
    return false
}

if captureSession.canAddInput(videoInput) {
    captureSession.addInput(videoInput)
}
```

In the next snippet, we obtain the physical device; here, we are obtaining the default device capable of recording video, but you can just as easily search for one with specific capabilities, such as the front camera. After successfully obtaining the device, we wrap it in an instance of `AVCaptureDeviceInput` that will be responsible for capturing data from the physical camera and finally adding it to the session.

We now have to add the destination for these frames; again, add the following snippet to the `initCamera` method where you left off:

```
let videoOutput = AVCaptureVideoDataOutput()

let settings: [String : Any] = [
    kCVPixelBufferPixelFormatTypeKey as String: NSNumber(value:
kCVPixelFormatType_32BGRA)
]
videoOutput.videoSettings = settings
videoOutput.alwaysDiscardsLateVideoFrames = true
videoOutput.setSampleBufferDelegate(self, queue: sessionQueue)
```

```
if captureSession.canAddOutput(videoOutput) {
    captureSession.addOutput(videoOutput)
}

videoOutput.connection(with: AVMediaType.video)?.videoOrientation =
.portrait
```

In the previous code snippet, we create, set up, and added our output. We start by instantiating an instance of `AVCaptureVideoDataOutput`, before defining what data we want. Here, we are requesting full color (`kCVPixelFormatType_32BGRA`), but depending on your model, it may be more efficient to request images in grayscale (`kCVPixelFormatType_8IndexedGray_WhiteIsZero`).

Setting `alwaysDiscardsLateVideoFrames` to true means any frames that arrive while the dispatch queue is busy will be discarded—a desirable feature for our example. We then assign ourselves along with our dedicated dispatch queue as the delegate for handing incoming frames using the method `videoOutput.setSampleBufferDelegate(self, queue: sessionQueue)`. Once we have configured our output, we are ready to add it to our session as part of our configuration request. To prevent our images from being rotated by 90 degrees, we then request that our images are in portrait orientation.

Add the final statement to commit these configurations; it's only after we do this that these changes will take effect:

```
captureSession.commitConfiguration()
```

This now completes our `initCamera` method; let's swiftly (excuse the pun) move onto the methods responsible for starting and stopping this session. Add the following code to the body of the `asyncStartCapturing` method:

```
sessionQueue.async {
    if !self.captureSession.isRunning{
        self.captureSession.startRunning()
    }

    if let completion = completion{
        DispatchQueue.main.async {
            completion()
        }
    }
}
```

As mentioned previously, the `startRunning` and `stopRunning` methods both block the main thread and can take some time to complete; for this reason, we execute them off the main thread, again to avoid affecting the responsiveness of the user interface. Invoking `startRunning` will start the flow of data from the subscribed inputs (camera) to the subscribed outputs (delegate).

 Errors, if any, are reported through the notification `AVCaptureSessionRuntimeError`. You can subscribe to listen to it using the default `NotificationCenter`. Similarly, you can subscribe to listen when the session starts and stops with the notifications `AVCaptureSessionDidStartRunning` and `AVCaptureSessionDidStopRunning`, respectively.

Similarly, add the following code to the method `asyncStopCapturing`, which will be responsible for stopping the current session:

```
sessionQueue.async {
    if self.captureSession.isRunning{
        self.captureSession.stopRunning()
    }

    if let completion = completion{
        DispatchQueue.main.async {
            completion()
        }
    }
}
```

Within the `initCamera` method, we subscribed ourselves as the delegate to handle arriving frames using the statement `videoOutput.setSampleBufferDelegate(self, queue: sessionQueue)`; let's now turn our attention to handling this. As you may recall, we included an extension of the `VideoCapture` class to implement the `AVCaptureVideoDataOutputSampleBufferDelegate` protocol within the `captureOutput` method. Add the following code:

```
guard let delegate = self.delegate else{ return }

let timestamp = CMSampleBufferGetPresentationTimeStamp(sampleBuffer)

let elapsedTime = timestamp - lastTimestamp
if elapsedTime >= CMTimeMake(1, Int32(fps)) {

lastTimestamp = timestamp
```

```
let imageBuffer = CMSampleBufferGetImageBuffer(sampleBuffer)

delegate.onFrameCaptured(videoCapture: self,
pixelBuffer:imageBuffer,
timestamp: timestamp)
}
```

Before walking through this code snippet, it's worth mentioning what parameters this method is passed and how we use them. The first parameter, `output`, is of the type `AVCaptureVideoDataOutput` and references the associated output that this frame originated from. The next parameter, `sampleBuffer`, is of the type `CMSampleBuffer` and this is what we will use to access data of the current frame. Along with the frames, the duration, format, and timestamp associated with each frame can also be obtained. The final parameter, `connection`, is of the type `AVCaptureConnection` and provides a reference to the connection associated with the received frame.

Now, walking through the code, we start by guarding against any occurrences where no delegate is assigned, and returning early if so. Then we determine whether enough time has elapsed since the last time we processed a frame, remembering that we are throttling how frequently we process a frame to ensure a seamless experience. Here, instead of using the systems clock, we obtain the time associated with the latest frame via the statement `let timestamp = CMSampleBufferGetPresentationTimeStamp(sampleBuffer)`; this ensures that we are measuring against the relative time with respect to the frame rather than absolute time of the system. Given that enough time has passed, we proceed to get a reference to the sample's image buffer via the statement `CMSampleBufferGetImageBuffer(sampleBuffer)`, finally passing it over to the assigned delegate.

This now completes our `VideoCapture` class; let's move on to hooking it up to our view using the `ViewController`. But before jumping into the code, let's inspect the interface via the storyboard to better understand where we'll be presenting the video stream. Within Xcode, select `Main.storyboard` from the **Project Navigator** panel on the left to open up interface builder; when opened, you will be presented with a layout similar to the following screenshot:

Nothing complicated; we have a label to present our results and a view to render our video frames onto. If you select the **VideoPreview** view and inspect the class assigned to it, you will see we have a custom class to handle the rendering called, appropriately, **CapturePreviewView**. Let's jump into the code for this class and make the necessary changes:

```
import AVFoundation
 import UIKit

 class CapturePreviewView: UIView {

 }
```

Fortunately, AVFoundation makes available a subclass of CALayer specifically for rendering frames from the camera; all that remains for us to do is to override the view's layerClass property and return the appropriate class. Add the following code to the CapturePreviewView class:

```
override class var layerClass: AnyClass {
    return AVCaptureVideoPreviewLayer.self
}
```

This method is called early during the creation of the view and is used to determine what CALayer to instantiate and associate with this view. As previously mentioned, the AVCaptureVideoPreviewLayer is—as the name suggests—specifically for handling video frames. In order to get the frames rendered, we simply assign AVCaptureSession with the AVCaptureVideoPreviewLayer.session property. Let's do that now; first open up the ViewController class in **Xcode** and add the following variable (in bold):

```
@IBOutlet var previewView:CapturePreviewView!
@IBOutlet var classifiedLabel:UILabel!

let videoCapture : VideoCapture = VideoCapture()
```

The previewView and classifiedLabel are existing variables associated with the interface via the **Interface Builder**. Here, we are creating an instance of VideoCapture, which we had implemented earlier. Next, we will set up and start the camera using the VideoCapture instance, before assigning the session to our previewView layer. Add the following code within the ViewDidLoad method under the statement super.viewDidLoad():

```
if self.videoCapture.initCamera(){
  (self.previewView.layer as! AVCaptureVideoPreviewLayer).session =
self.videoCapture.captureSession

  (self.previewView.layer as! AVCaptureVideoPreviewLayer).videoGravity =
AVLayerVideoGravity.resizeAspectFill

  self.videoCapture.asyncStartCapturing()
  } else{
  fatalError("Failed to init VideoCapture")
  }
```

Most of the code should look familiar to you as a lot of it is using the methods we have just implemented. First we initialize the camera, calling the `initCamera` method of the `VideoCamera` class. Then, if successful, we assign the created `AVCaptureSession` to the layer's session. We also hint to the layer how we want it to handle the content, in this case filling the screen whilst respecting its aspect ratio. Finally, we start the camera by calling `videoCapture.asyncStartCapturing()`.

With that now completed, it's a good time to test that everything is working correctly. If you build and deploy on an iOS 11+ device, you should see the video frames being rendered on your phone's screen.

In the next section, we will walk through how to capture and process them for our model before performing inference (recognition).

# Preprocessing the data

At this stage, we have the app rendering the frames from the camera, but we are not yet receiving any frames. To do this, we will assign ourselves to receive these frames, as implemented in the previous section. The existing `ViewController` class already has an extension implementing the `VideoCaptureDelegate` protocol. What's left to do is to assign ourselves as the delegate of the `VideoCapture` instance and implement the details of the callback method; the following is the code for `extension`:

```
extension ViewController : VideoCaptureDelegate{
    func onFrameCaptured(videoCapture: VideoCapture,
    pixelBuffer:CVPixelBuffer?,
    timestamp:CMTime){
    }
}
```

 Depending on your coding style, you can just as easily implement the protocols inside the main class. I tend to make use of extensions to implement the protocols—a personal preference.

First, let's assign ourselves as the delegate to start receiving the frames; within the `ViewDidLoad` method of the `ViewController` class, we add the following statement just before we initialize the camera:

```
self.videoCapture.delegate = self
```

Now that we have assigned ourselves as the delegate, we will receive frames (at the defined frame rate) via the callback:

```
func onFrameCaptured(videoCapture: VideoCapture,
 pixelBuffer:CVPixelBuffer?,
 timestamp:CMTime){
 // TODO
 }
```

It's within this method that we will prepare and feed the data to the model to classify the dominant object within the frame. What the model is expecting is dependent on the model, so to get a better idea of what we need to pass it, let's download the trained model we will be using for this example and import it into our project.

Trained models can be obtained from a variety of sources; in some instances, you will need to convert them, and in other cases, you will need to train the model yourself. But in this instance, we can make use of the models Apple has made available; open up your web browser and navigate to `https://developer.apple.com/machine-learning/`:

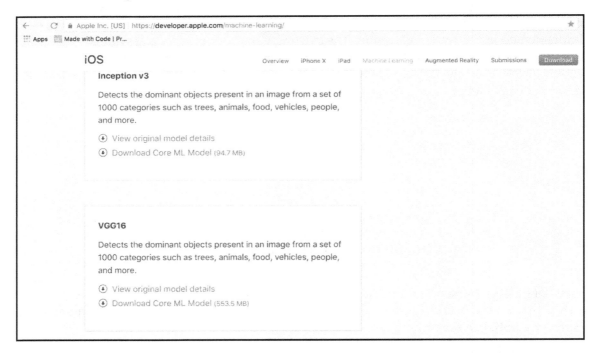

You will be taken to a web page where Apple has made available a range of pretrained and converted models. Conveniently, most of the available models are specifically for object classification; given our use case, we're particularly interested in the models trained on a large array of objects. Our options include **MobileNet**, **SqueezeNet**, **ResNet50**, **Inception v3**, and **VGG16**. Most of these have been trained on the ImageNet dataset, a dataset with reference to over 10 million URLs' images that have been manually assigned to one of 1,000 classes. References to the original research papers and performance can be obtained via the **View original model details** link. For this example, we'll use **Inception v3**, a good balance between size and accuracy.

 Here, we are using the **Inception v3** model, but the effort to swap the model is minimal; it requires updating the references as the generated classes are prefixed with the model's name, as you will soon see, and ensuring that you are conforming to the expected inputs of the model (which can be alleviated by using the Vision framework, as you will see in future chapters).

Click on the **Download Core ML Model link** to proceed to download and, once downloaded, drag the `Inceptionv3.mlmodel` file onto the **Project Navigator** panel on the left of Xcode, checking **Copy items if needed** if desired or else leaving everything as default. Select the `Inceptionv3.mlmodel` file from the **Project Navigator** panel on the left to bring up the details within the **Editor area**, as shown in the following screenshot:

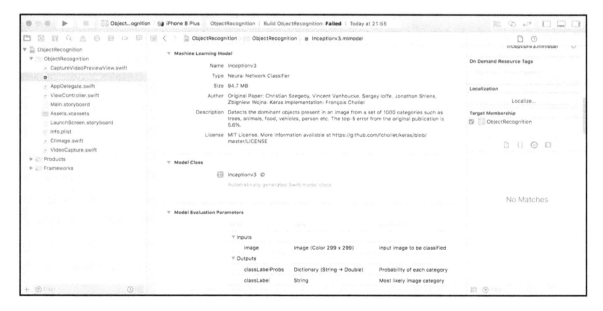

It is important to ensure that the model is correctly assigned to the appropriate target; in this example, this means verifying that the **ObjectRecognition** target is checked, as seen here on the **Utilities panel** to the right. Also worth noting are the expected inputs and outputs of the model. Here, the model is expecting a color image of size 299 x 299 for its input, and it returns a single class label as a string and a dictionary of string-double pairs of probabilities of all the classes.

When a .mlmodel file is imported, Xcode will generate a wrapper for the model itself and the input and output parameters to interface with the model; this is illustrated here:

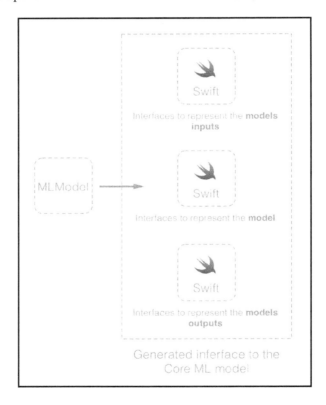

You can easily access this by tapping on the arrow button next to the Inceptionv3 label within the **Model Class** section; when tapped, you will see the following code (separated into three distinct blocks to make it more legible):

```
@available(macOS 10.13, iOS 11.0, tvOS 11.0, watchOS 4.0, *)
class Inceptionv3Input : MLFeatureProvider {

    /// Input image to be classified as color (kCVPixelFormatType_32BGRA)
```

```
image buffer, 299 pixels wide by 299        pixels high
 var image: CVPixelBuffer

 var featureNames: Set<String> {
     get {
         return ["image"]
     }
 }

 func featureValue(for featureName: String) -> MLFeatureValue? {
     if (featureName == "image") {
         return MLFeatureValue(pixelBuffer: image)
     }
     return nil
 }

 init(image: CVPixelBuffer) {
     self.image = image
     }
 }
```

The first block of the preceding code is the input for our model. This class implements
the MLFeatureProvider protocol, a protocol representing a collection of feature values for
the model, in this case, the image feature. Here, you can see the expected data
structure, CVPixelBuffer, along with the specifics declared (handily) in the comments.
Let's continue on with our inspection of the generated classes by looking at the binding for
the output:

```
@available(macOS 10.13, iOS 11.0, tvOS 11.0, watchOS 4.0, *)
 class Inceptionv3Output : MLFeatureProvider {

 /// Probability of each category as dictionary of strings to doubles
 let classLabelProbs: [String : Double]

 /// Most likely image category as string value
 let classLabel: String

 var featureNames: Set<String> {
     get {
         return ["classLabelProbs", "classLabel"]
     }
 }

 func featureValue(for featureName: String) -> MLFeatureValue? {
     if (featureName == "classLabelProbs") {
         return try! MLFeatureValue(dictionary: classLabelProbs as
[NSObject : NSNumber])
```

```
        }
        if (featureName == "classLabel") {
            return MLFeatureValue(string: classLabel)
        }
        return nil
    }

    init(classLabelProbs: [String : Double], classLabel: String) {
        self.classLabelProbs = classLabelProbs
        self.classLabel = classLabel
        }
    }
```

As previously mentioned, the output exposes a directory of probabilities and a string for the dominated class, each exposed as properties or accessible using the getter method `featureValue(for featureName: String)` by passing in the feature's name. Our final extract for the generated code is the model itself; let's inspect that now:

```
@available(macOS 10.13, iOS 11.0, tvOS 11.0, watchOS 4.0, *)
class Inceptionv3 {
var model: MLModel

/**
Construct a model with explicit path to mlmodel file
- parameters:
- url: the file url of the model
- throws: an NSError object that describes the problem
*/
init(contentsOf url: URL) throws {
self.model = try MLModel(contentsOf: url)
}

/// Construct a model that automatically loads the model from the app's
bundle
convenience init() {
let bundle = Bundle(for: Inceptionv3.self)
let assetPath = bundle.url(forResource: "Inceptionv3",
withExtension:"mlmodelc")
try! self.init(contentsOf: assetPath!)
}

/**
Make a prediction using the structured interface
- parameters:
- input: the input to the prediction as Inceptionv3Input
- throws: an NSError object that describes the problem
- returns: the result of the prediction as Inceptionv3Output
```

```
*/
func prediction(input: Inceptionv3Input) throws -> Inceptionv3Output {
let outFeatures = try model.prediction(from: input)
let result = Inceptionv3Output(classLabelProbs:
outFeatures.featureValue(for: "classLabelProbs")!.dictionaryValue as!
[String : Double], classLabel: outFeatures.featureValue(for:
"classLabel")!.stringValue)
return result
}

/**
Make a prediction using the convenience interface
- parameters:
- image: Input image to be classified as color (kCVPixelFormatType_32BGRA)
image buffer, 299 pixels wide by 299 pixels high
- throws: an NSError object that describes the problem
- returns: the result of the prediction as Inceptionv3Output
*/
func prediction(image: CVPixelBuffer) throws -> Inceptionv3Output {
let input_ = Inceptionv3Input(image: image)
return try self.prediction(input: input_)
}
}
```

This class wraps the model class and provides strongly typed methods for performing inference via the `prediction(input: Inceptionv3Input)` and `prediction(image: CVPixelBuffer)` methods, each returning the output class we saw previously—`Inceptionv3Output`. Now, knowing what our model is expecting, let's continue to implement the preprocessing functionality required for the captured frames in order to feed them into the model.

 Core ML 2 introduced a the ability to work with batches; if your model was compiled with Xcode 10+ then you will also see the additional method `<CODE>func predictions(from: MLBatchProvider, options: MLPredictionOptions)</CODE>` allowing you to perform inference on a batch of inputs.

At this stage, we know that we are receiving the correct data type (`CVPixelBuffer`) and image format (explicitly defined in the settings when configuring the capture video output instance `kCVPixelFormatType_32BGRA`) from the camera. But we are receiving an image significantly larger than the expected size of 299 x 299. Our next task will be to create some utility methods to perform resizing and cropping.

For this, we will be extending CIImage to wrap and process the pixel data we receive along with making use of CIContext to obtain the raw pixels again. If you're unfamiliar with the CoreImage framework, then it suffices to say that it is a framework dedicated to efficiently processing and analyzing images. CIImage can be considered the base data object of this framework that is often used in conjunction with other CoreImage classes such as CIFilter, CIContext, CIVector, and CIColor. Here, we are interested in CIImage as it provides convenient methods for manipulating images along with CIContext to extract the raw pixel data from CIImage (CVPixelBuffer).

Back in Xcode, select the CIImage.swift file from the **Project navigator** to open it up in the **Editor area**. In this file, we have extended the CIImage class with a method responsible for rescaling and another for returning the raw pixels (CVPixelBuffer), a format required for our Core ML model:

```
extension CIImage{

    func resize(size: CGSize) -> CIImage {
        fatalError("Not implemented")
    }

    func toPixelBuffer(context:CIContext,
    size insize:CGSize? = nil,
        gray:Bool=true) -> CVPixelBuffer?{
            fatalError("Not implemented")
        }
}
```

Let's start by implementing the resize method; this method is passed in the desired size, which we'll use to calculate the relative scale; then we'll use this to scale the image uniformly. Add the following code snippet to the resize method, replacing the fatalError("Not implemented") statement:

```
let scale = min(size.width,size.height) / min(self.extent.size.width,
self.extent.size.height)

let resizedImage = self.transformed(
by: CGAffineTransform(
scaleX: scale,
y: scale))
```

Unless the image is a square, we are likely to have an overflow either vertically or horizontally. To handle this, we will simply center the image and crop it to the desired size; do this by appending the following code to the `resize` method (beneath the code written in the preceding snippet):

```
let width = resizedImage.extent.width
 let height = resizedImage.extent.height
 let xOffset = (CGFloat(width) - size.width) / 2.0
 let yOffset = (CGFloat(height) - size.height) / 2.0
 let rect = CGRect(x: xOffset,
 y: yOffset,
 width: size.width,
 height: size.height)

 return resizedImage
 .clamped(to: rect)
 .cropped(to: CGRect(
 x: 0, y: 0,
 width: size.width,
 height: size.height))
```

We now have the functionality to rescale the image; our next piece of functionality is to obtain a `CVPixelBuffer` from the `CIImage`. Let's do that by implementing the body of the `toPixelBuffer` method. Let's first review the method's signature and then briefly talk about the functionality required:

```
func toPixelBuffer(context:CIContext, gray:Bool=true) -> CVPixelBuffer?{
    fatalError("Not implemented")
 }
```

This method is expecting a `CIContext` and flag indicating whether the image should be grayscale (single channel) or full color; `CIContext` will be used to render the image to a pixel buffer (our `CVPixelBuffer`). Let's now flesh out the implementation for `toPixelBuffer` piece by piece.

The preprocessing required on the image (resizing, grayscaling, and normalization) is dependent on the Core ML model and the data it was trained on. You can get a sense of these parameters by inspecting the Core ML model in Xcode. If you recall, the expected input to our model is (image color 299 x 299); this tells us that the Core ML model is expecting the image to be color (three channels) and 299 x 299 in size.

We start by creating the pixel buffer we will be rendering our image to; add the following code snippet to the body of the `toPixelBuffer` method, replacing the `fatalError("Not implemented")` statement:

```
let attributes = [
kCVPixelBufferCGImageCompatibilityKey:kCFBooleanTrue,
kCVPixelBufferCGBitmapContextCompatibilityKey:kCFBooleanTrue
] as CFDictionary

var nullablePixelBuffer: CVPixelBuffer? = nil
let status = CVPixelBufferCreate(kCFAllocatorDefault,
Int(self.extent.size.width),
Int(self.extent.size.height),
gray ? kCVPixelFormatType_OneComponent8 : kCVPixelFormatType_32ARGB,
attributes,
&nullablePixelBuffer)

guard status == kCVReturnSuccess, let pixelBuffer = nullablePixelBuffer
else { return nil }
```

We first create an array to hold the attributes defining the compatibility requirements for our pixel buffer; here, we specify that we want our pixel buffer to be compatible with `CGImage` **types** (`kCVPixelBufferCGImageCompatibilityKey`) and compatible with CoreGraphics bitmap contexts (`kCVPixelBufferCGBitmapContextCompatibilityKey`).

We then proceed to create a pixel buffer, passing in our compatibility attributes, the format (either grayscale or full color depending on the value of `gray`), width, height, and pointer to the variable. Next, we unwrap the nullable pixel buffer as well as ensure that the call was successful; if either of these is `false`, we return NULL. Otherwise, we're ready to render our `CIImage` into the newly created pixel buffer. Append the following code to the `toPixelBuffer` method:

```
CVPixelBufferLockBaseAddress(pixelBuffer, CVPixelBufferLockFlags(rawValue:
0))

context.render(self,
to: pixelBuffer,
bounds: CGRect(x: 0,
y: 0,
width: self.extent.size.width,
height: self.extent.size.height),
colorSpace:gray ?
CGColorSpaceCreateDeviceGray() :
self.colorSpace)

CVPixelBufferUnlockBaseAddress(pixelBuffer,
```

```
CVPixelBufferLockFlags(rawValue: 0))

   return pixelBuffer
```

Before drawing, we lock the address of the pixel buffer via `CVPixelBufferLockBaseAddress` and then unlock once we've finished using the `CVPixelBufferUnlockBaseAddress` method. We are required to do this when accessing pixel data from the CPU, which we are doing here.

Once locked, we simply use the `CIContext` to render the scaled image to the buffer, passing in the destination rectangle (in this case, the full size of the pixel buffer) and destination color space, which is full color or grayscale depending on the value of `gray` as mentioned previously. After unlocking the pixel buffer, as described earlier, we return our newly created pixel buffer.

We have now extended the `CIImage` with two convenient methods, one responsible for rescaling and the other for creating a pixel buffer representation of itself. We will now return to the `ViewController` class to handle the preprocessing steps required before passing our data into the model. Select the `ViewController.swift` file from the **Projector navigator** panel within Xcode to bring up the source code, and within the body of the `ViewController` class, add the following variable:

```
let context = CIContext()
```

As previously discussed, we will be passing this to our `CIImage.toPixelBuffer` method for rendering the image to the pixel buffer. Now return to the `onFrameCaptured` method and add the following code, to make use of the methods we've just created for preprocessing:

```
guard let pixelBuffer = pixelBuffer else{ return }

  // Prepare our image for our model (resizing)
  guard let scaledPixelBuffer = CIImage(cvImageBuffer: pixelBuffer)
  .resize(size: CGSize(width: 299, height: 299))
  .toPixelBuffer(context: context) else{ return }
```

We first unwrap the `pixelBuffer`, returning if it is `NULL`; then we create an instance of `CIImage`, passing in the current frame and then chaining our extension methods to perform rescaling (299 x 299) and rendering out to a pixel buffer (setting the gray parameter to false as the model is expecting full color images). If successful, we are returned a image ready to be passed to our model for inference, the focus of the next section.

# Performing inference

This may come as a bit of an anticlimax for someone expecting some hardcore coding, but its simplicity definitely pays tribute to the effort of Apple's engineers in making this framework one of the most accessible ways to work with a ML model. Without further ado, let's put the final pieces together; we start by instantiating an instance of our model we had imported in the previous section.

Near the top, but within the body of the `ViewController` class, add the following line:

```
let model = Inceptionv3()
```

Our model is now ready; we return to the `onFrameCaptured` method, starting from where we previously left off, and add the following code snippet:

```
let prediction = try? self.model.prediction(image:scaledPixelBuffer)

// Update label
DispatchQueue.main.sync {
classifiedLabel.text = prediction?.classLabel ?? "Unknown"
}
```

In case you have missed it, I have made the statement performing inference in bold. That's it!

After performing inference, we simply assign the `classLabel` property (the class with the highest probability) to our `UILabel`, `classifiedLabel`.

With the final piece put in place, we build and deploy. And see how well our app performs, recognizing some objects we have lying nearby. Once you're done surveying your space, return here, where we will wrap up this chapter and move on to greater and more impressive examples.

# Summary

In this chapter, we introduced object recognition, the 101 project for ML with Core ML. We spent some time introducing CNNs or ConvNets, a category of neural networks well suited for extracting patterns from images. We discussed how they build increasing levels of abstraction with each convolutional layer. We then proceeded to make use of our newfound knowledge by implementing the functionality that allowed our application to recognize the physical world through its camera. We saw firsthand that the majority of the work wasn't performing inference but rather implementing the functionality to facilitate and make use of it. This is the take-away; intelligence by itself is not useful. What we are interested in exploring in this book is the application of trained models to deliver intuitive and intelligent experiences. For instance, this example can easily be turned into a language tutor assistant, allowing the user to learn a new language by observing the world around them.

In the next chapter, we will continue our journey into the world of computer vision with Core ML by looking at how we can infer the emotional state of someone by recognizing their facial expressions. Let's get to it.

# Emotion Detection with CNNs

**4**

Up until recently, interacting with a computer was not too dissimilar from interacting with, say, a power tool; we pick it up, turn it on, manually control it, and then put it down until the next time we require it for that specific task. But recently, we are seeing signs that this is about to change; computers allow natural forms of interaction and are becoming more ubiquitous, more capable, and more ingrained in our daily lives. They are becoming less like heartless dumb tools and more like friends, able to entertain us, look out for us, and assist us with our work.

With this shift comes a need for computers to be able to understand our emotional state. For example, you don't want your social robot cracking a joke after you arrive back from work having lost your job (to an AI bot!). This is a field of computer science known as **affective computing** (also referred to as **artificial emotional intelligence** or **emotional AI**), a field that studies systems that can recognize, interpret, process, and simulate human emotions. The first stage of this is being able to recognize emotional state, which is the topic of this chapter. We will first introduce the data and model we will be using, and then walk through how we approach the problem of expression recognition on the iPhone and how to appropriately preprocess the data for inference.

By the end of of this chapter, you will have achieved the following:

- Built a simple application that will infer your mood in real time using the front camera feed
- Gained hands-on experience using the `Vision` framework
- Developed a deeper understanding and intuition of how **convolutional neural networks** (**CNNs**) work and how they can be applied at the edge

Let's start by introducing the data and model we will be using.

# Facial expressions

Our face is one of the strongest indicators of emotions; as we laugh or cry, we put our emotions on display, allowing others to glimpse into our minds. It's a form of nonverbal communication that, apparently, accounts for over 50% of our communication with others. Forty independently controlled muscles make the face one of the most complex systems we possess, which could be the reason we use it as a medium for communicating something so important as our current emotional state. But can we classify it?

In 2013, the **International Conference on Machine Learning** (**ICML**) ran a competition inviting contestants to build a facial expression classifier using a training dataset of over 28,000 grayscale images. They were labeled as either anger, disgust, fear, happiness, sadness, surprise, or neutral. The following are a few samples of this training data (available at `https://www.kaggle.com/c/challenges-in-representation-learning-facial-expression-recognition-challenge`):

As previously mentioned, the training dataset consists of 28,709 grayscale images of faces in 48 x 48 pixels, where each face is centered and associated with a label defining the assigned emotion. This emotion can be one of the following labels (textual description was added for legibility):

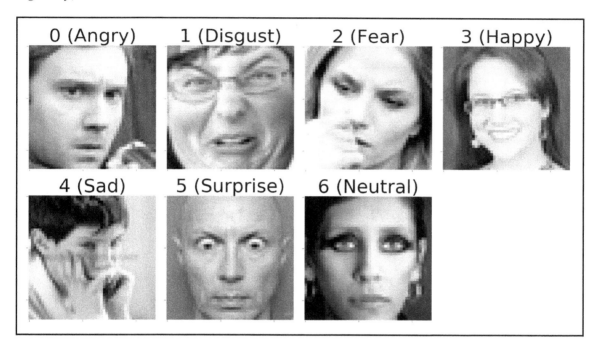

Neural networks (or any other machine learning algorithm) can't really do anything by themselves. All a neural network does is find a direct or indirect correlation between two datasets (inputs and their corresponding outputs). In order for a neural network to learn, we need to present it with two meaningful datasets where some true correlation exists between the inputs and outputs. A good practice when tackling any new data problem is to come up with a predictive theory of how you might approach it or search for correlation using techniques such as data visualization or some other explorational data analysis technique. In doing so, we also better understand how we need to prepare our data to align it with the training data.

Let's look at the results of a data visualization technique that can be performed on the training data; here, it's our assumption that some pattern exists between each expression (happy, sad, angry, and so on). One way of visually inspecting this is by averaging each expression and the associated variance. This can be achieved simply by finding the mean and standard deviation across all images for their respective class (expression example, happy, angry, and so on). The results of some of the expressions can be seen in the following image:

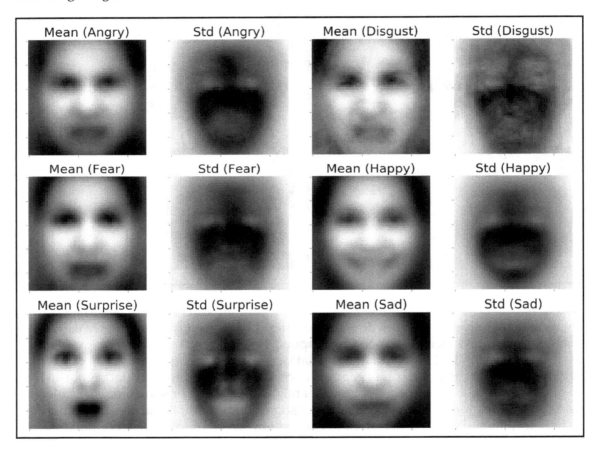

After you get over the creepiness of the images, you get a sense that a pattern does exist, and you understand what our model needs to learn to be able to recognize facial expressions. Some other notable, and fairly visible, takeaways from this exercise include the amount of variance with the disgust expression; this hints that our model might find it difficult to effectively learn to recognize this expression. The other observation - and the one more applicable to our task in this chapter - is that the training data consists of forward-facing faces with little padding beyond the face, therefore highlighting what the model expects for its input. Now that we have a better sense of our data; let's move on and introduce the model we will be using in this chapter.

In `chapter 3`, *Recognising Objects in the World,* we presented the intuition behind CNNs or ConvNets. So, given that we won't be introducing any new concepts in this chapter, we will omit any discussion on the details of the model and just present it here for reference, with some commentary about its architecture and the format of the data it is expecting for its input:

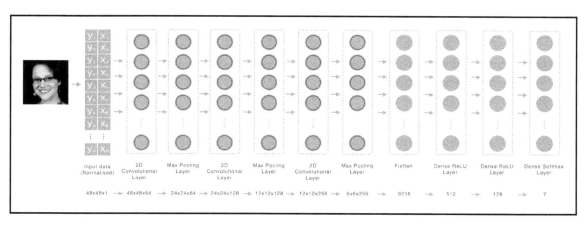

The preceding figure is a visualization of the architecture of the model; it's your typical CNN, with a stack of convolutional and pooling layers before being flattened and fed into a series of fully connected layers. Finally, it is fed into a softmax activation layer for multi-class classification. As mentioned earlier, the model is expecting a 3D tensor with the dimensions 48 x 48 x 1 (width, height, channels). To avoid feeding our model with large numbers (0 - 255), the input has been normalized (dividing each pixel by 255, which gives us a range of 0.0 - 1.0). The model outputs the probability of a given input with respect to each class, that is, seven outputs with each class representing the probability of how likely it is correlated for the given input. To make a prediction, we simply take the class with the largest probability.

This model was trained on 22,967 samples, reversing the other 5,742 samples for validation. After 15 epochs, the model achieved approximately 59% accuracy on the validation set, managing to squeeze into the 13th place of the Kaggle competition (at the time of writing this chapter). The following graphs show the training accuracy and loss during training:

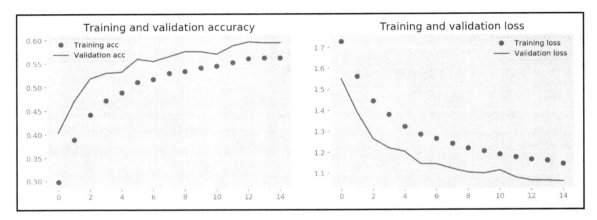

This concludes our brief introduction of the data and model we will be using for this chapter. The two main takeaways are an appreciation of what data the model has been fed during training, and the fact that our model achieved just 59% accuracy.

The former dictates how we approach obtaining and process the data before feeding it into the model. The latter poses an opportunity for further investigation to better understand what is pulling the accuracy down and how to improve it; it also can be seen as a design challenge—a design to be made around this constraint.

In this chapter, we are mainly concerned with the former so, in the next section, we will explore how to obtain and preprocess the data before feeding it to the model. Let's get started.

# Input data and preprocessing

In this section, we will implement the preprocessing functionality required to transform images into something the model is expecting. We will build up this functionality in a playground project before migrating it across to our project in the next section.

If you haven't done so already, pull down the latest code from the accompanying repository: https://github.com/packtpublishing/machine-learning-with-core-ml. Once downloaded, navigate to the directory Chapter4/Start/ and open the Playground project ExploringExpressionRecognition.playground. Once loaded, you will see the playground for this chapter, as shown in the following screenshot:

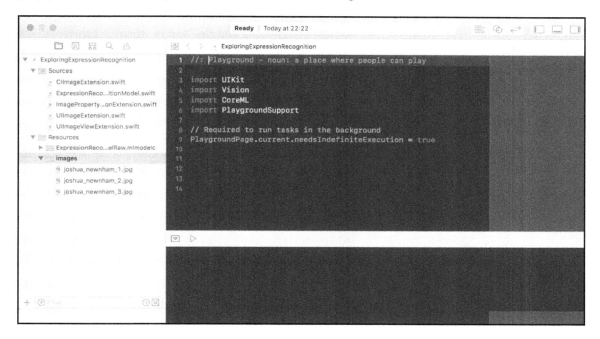

Before starting, to avoid looking at images of me, please replace the test images with either personal photos of your own or royalty free images from the internet, ideally a set expressing a range of emotions.

Along with the test images, this playground includes a compiled Core ML model (we introduced it in the previous image) with its generated set of wrappers for inputs, outputs, and the model itself. Also included are some extensions for UIImage, UIImageView, CGImagePropertyOrientation, and an empty CIImage extension, to which we will return later in the chapter. The others provide utility functions to help us visualize the images as we work through this playground.

Before jumping into the code, let's quickly discuss the approach we will take in order to determine what we actually need to implement.

Up to this point, our process of performing machine learning has been fairly straightforward; apart from some formatting of input data, our model didn't require too much work. This is not the case here. A typical photo of someone doesn't normally have just a face, nor is their face nicely aligned to the frame unless you're processing passport photos. When developing machine learning applications, you have two broad paths.

The first, which is becoming increasingly popular, is to use an end-to-end machine learning model capable of just being fed the raw input and producing adequate results. One particular field that has had great success with end-to-end models is speech recognition. Prior to end-to-end deep learning, speech recognition systems were made up of many smaller modules, each one focusing on extracting specific pieces of data to feed into the next module, which was typically manually engineered. Modern speech recognition systems use end-to-end models that take the raw input and output the result. Both of the described approaches can been seen in the following diagram:

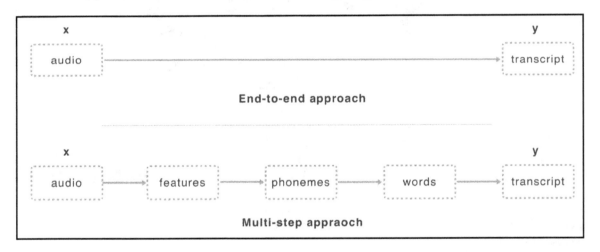

Obviously, this approach is not constrained to speech recognition and we have seen it applied to image recognition tasks, too, along with many others. But there are two things that make this particular case different; the first is that we can simplify the problem by first extracting the face. This means our model has less features to learn and offers a smaller, more specialized model that we can tune. The second thing, which is no doubt obvious, is that our training data consisted of only faces and not natural images. So, we have no other choice but to run our data through two models, the first to extract faces and the second to perform expression recognition on the extracted faces, as shown in this diagram:

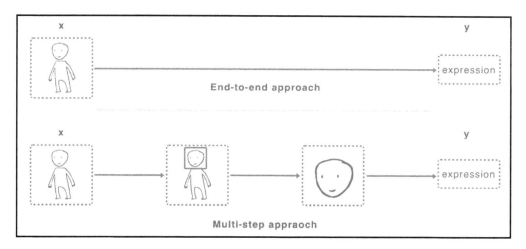

Luckily for us, Apple has mostly taken care of our first task of detecting faces through the Vision framework it released with iOS 11. The Vision framework provides performant image analysis and computer vision tools, exposing them through a simple API. This allows for face detection, feature detection and tracking, and classification of scenes in images and video. The latter (expression recognition) is something we will take care of using the Core ML model introduced earlier.

Prior to the introduction of the Vision framework, face detection would typically be performed using the Core Image filter. Going back further, you had to use something like OpenCV. You can learn more about Core Image here: https://developer.apple.com/library/content/documentation/GraphicsImaging/Conceptual/CoreImaging/ci_detect_faces/ci_detect_faces.html.

Now that we have got a bird's-eye view of the work that needs to be done, let's turn our attention to the editor and start putting all of this together. Start by loading the images; add the following snippet to your playground:

```
var images = [UIImage]()
for i in 1...3{
    guard let image = UIImage(named:"images/joshua_newnham_\(i).jpg")
        else{ fatalError("Failed to extract features") }
    images.append(image)
}

let faceIdx = 0
let imageView = UIImageView(image: images[faceIdx])
imageView.contentMode = .scaleAspectFit
```

In the preceding snippet, we are simply loading each of the images we have included in our resources' `Images` folder and adding them to an array we can access conveniently throughout the playground. Once all the images are loaded, we set the constant `faceIdx`, which will ensure that we access the same images throughout our experiments. Finally, we create an `ImageView` to easily preview it. Once it has finished running, click on the eye icon in the right-hand panel to preview the loaded image, as shown in the following screenshot:

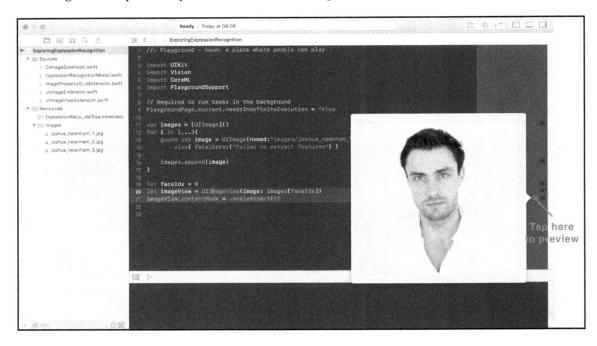

Next, we will take advantage of the functionality available in the `Vision` framework to detect faces. The typical flow when working with the `Vision` framework is **defining a request,** which determines what analysis you want to perform, and **defining the handler,** which will be responsible for executing the request and providing means of obtaining the results (either through delegation or explicitly queried). The result of the analysis is a collection of observations that you need to cast into the appropriate observation type; concrete examples of each of these can be seen here:

As illustrated in the preceding diagram, the request determines what type of image analysis will be performed; the handler, using a request or multiple requests and an image, performs the actual analysis and generates the results (also known as **observations**). These are accessible via a property or delegate if one has been assigned. The type of observation is dependent on the request performed; it's worth highlighting that the Vision framework is tightly integrated into Core ML and provides another layer of abstraction and uniformity between you and the data and process. For example, using a classification Core ML model would return an observation of type VNClassificationObservation. This layer of abstraction not only simplifies things but also provides a consistent way of working with machine learning models.

In the previous figure, we showed a request handler specifically for static images. Vision also provides a specialized request handler for handling sequences of images, which is more appropriate when dealing with requests such as tracking. The following diagram illustrates some concrete examples of the types of requests and observations applicable to this use case:

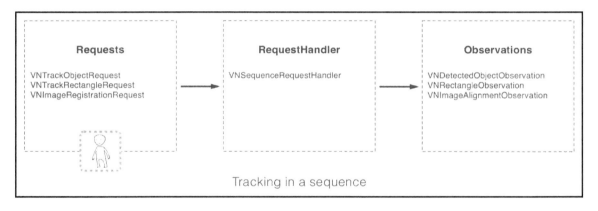

Tracking in a sequence

So, when do you use VNImageRequestHandler and VNSequenceRequestHandler? Though the names provide clues as to when one should be used over the other, it's worth outlining some differences.

The image request handler is for interactive exploration of an image; it holds a reference to the image for its life cycle and allows optimizations of various request types. The sequence request handler is more appropriate for performing tasks such as tracking and does not optimize for multiple requests on an image.

Let's see how this all looks in code; add the following snippet to your playground:

```
let faceDetectionRequest = VNDetectFaceRectanglesRequest()
let faceDetectionRequestHandler = VNSequenceRequestHandler()
```

Here, we are simply creating the request and handler; as discussed in the preceding code, the request encapsulates the type of image analysis while the handler is responsible for executing the request. Next, we will get `faceDetectionRequestHandler` to run `faceDetectionRequest`; add the following code:

```
try? faceDetectionRequestHandler.perform(
    [faceDetectionRequest],
    on: images[faceIdx].cgImage!,
    orientation:
CGImagePropertyOrientation(images[faceIdx].imageOrientation))
```

The `perform` function of the handler can throw an error if it fails; for this reason, we wrap the call with `try?` at the beginning of the statement and can interrogate the `error` property of the handler to identify the reason for failing. We pass the handler a list of requests (in this case, only our `faceDetectionRequest`), the image we want to perform the analysis on, and, finally, the orientation of the image that can be used by the request during analysis.

Once the analysis is done, we can inspect the observation obtained through the `results` property of the request itself, as shown in the following code:

```
if let faceDetectionResults = faceDetectionRequest.results as?
[VNFaceObservation]{
    for face in faceDetectionResults{
        // ADD THE NEXT SNIPPET OF CODE HERE
    }
}
```

The type of observation is dependent on the analysis; in this case, we're expecting a VNFaceObservation. Hence, we cast it to the appropriate type and then iterate through all the observations.

Next, we will take each recognized face and extract the bounding box. Then, we'll proceed to draw it in the image (using an extension method of UIImageView found within the UIImageViewExtension.swift file). Add the following block within the for loop shown in the preceding code:

```
if let currentImage = imageView.image{
    let bbox = face.boundingBox
    let imageSize = CGSize(
        width:currentImage.size.width,
        height: currentImage.size.height)
    let w = bbox.width * imageSize.width
    let h = bbox.height * imageSize.height
    let x = bbox.origin.x * imageSize.width
    let y = bbox.origin.y * imageSize.height
    let faceRect = CGRect(
        x: x,
        y: y,
        width: w,
        height: h)
    let invertedY = imageSize.height - (faceRect.origin.y +
faceRect.height)
    let invertedFaceRect = CGRect(
        x: x,
        y: invertedY,
        width: w,
        height: h)
    imageView.drawRect(rect: invertedFaceRect)
}
```

We can obtain the bounding box of each face via the let boundingBox property; the result is normalized, so we then need to scale this based on the dimensions of the image. For example, you can obtain the width by multiplying boundingBox with the width of the image: bbox.width * imageSize.width.

Next, we invert the $y$ axis as the coordinate system of Quartz 2D is inverted with respect to that of UIKit's coordinate system, as shown in this diagram:

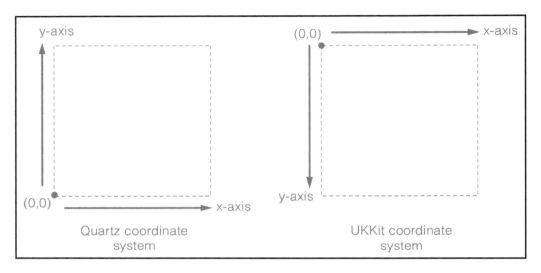

We invert our coordinates by subtracting the bounding box's origin and height from height of the image and then passing this to our `UIImageView` to render the rectangle. Click on the eye icon in the right-hand panel in line with the statement `imageView.drawRect(rect: invertedFaceRect)` to preview the results; if successful, you should see something like the following:

An alternative to inverting the face rectangle would be to use an `AfflineTransform`, such as:
```
var transform = CGAffineTransform(scaleX: 1, y: -1)
transform = transform.translatedBy(x: 0, y: -
imageSize.height)
let invertedFaceRect = faceRect.apply(transform)
```

This approach leads to less code and therefore less chances of errors. So, it is the recommended approach. The long approach was taken previously to help illuminate the details.

Let's now take a quick detour and experiment with another type of request; this time, we will analyze our image using `VNDetectFaceLandmarksRequest`. It is similar to `VNDetectFaceRectanglesRequest` in that this request will detect faces and expose their bounding boxes; but, unlike `VNDetectFaceRectanglesRequest`, `VNDetectFaceLandmarksRequest` also provides detected facial landmarks. A landmark is a prominent facial feature such as your eyes, nose, eyebrow, face contour, or any other feature that can be detected and describes a significant attribute of a face. Each detected facial landmark consists of a set of points that describe its contour (outline). Let's see how this looks; add a new request as shown in the following code:

```
imageView.image = images[faceIdx]

let faceLandmarksRequest = VNDetectFaceLandmarksRequest()

try? faceDetectionRequestHandler.perform(
    [faceLandmarksRequest],
    on: images[faceIdx].cgImage!,
    orientation:
CGImagePropertyOrientation(images[faceIdx].imageOrientation))
```

The preceding snippet should look familiar to you; it's almost the same as what we did previously, but this time replacing `VNDetectFaceRectanglesRequest` with `VNDetectFaceLandmarksRequets`. We have also refreshed the image in our image view with the statement `imageView.image = images[faceIdx]`. As we did before, let's iterate through each of the detected observations and extract some of the common landmarks. Start off by creating the outer loop, as shown in this code:

```
if let faceLandmarkDetectionResults = faceLandmarksRequest.results as?
[VNFaceObservation]{
    for face in faceLandmarkDetectionResults{
        if let currentImage = imageView.image{
            let bbox = face.boundingBox
            let imageSize = CGSize(width:currentImage.size.width,
```

```
                                          height: currentImage.size.height)
            let w = bbox.width * imageSize.width
            let h = bbox.height * imageSize.height
            let x = bbox.origin.x * imageSize.width
            let y = bbox.origin.y * imageSize.height
            let faceRect = CGRect(x: x,
                                  y: y,
                                  width: w,
                                  height: h)
        }
    }
}
```

Up to this point, the code will look familiar; next, we will look at each of the landmarks. But first, let's create a function to handle the transformation of our points from the Quartz 2D coordinate system to UIKit's coordinate system. We add the following function but within the same block as our `faceRect` declaration:

```
func getTransformedPoints(
    landmark:VNFaceLandmarkRegion2D,
    faceRect:CGRect,
    imageSize:CGSize) -> [CGPoint]{
    return landmark.normalizedPoints.map({ (np) -> CGPoint in
        return CGPoint(
            x: faceRect.origin.x + np.x * faceRect.size.width,
            y: imageSize.height - (np.y * faceRect.size.height +
faceRect.origin.y))
    })
}
```

As mentioned before, each landmark consists of a set of points that describe the contour of that particular landmark, and, like our previous feature, the points are normalized between 0.0 - 1.0. Therefore, we need to scale them based on the associated face rectangle, which is exactly what we did in the preceding example. For each point, we are scaling and transforming it into the appropriate coordinate space, and then returning the mapped array to the caller.

Let's now define some constants that we will use to visualize each landmark; we add the following two constants in the function we implemented just now, `getTransformedPoints`:

```
let landmarkWidth : CGFloat = 1.5
let landmarkColor : UIColor = UIColor.red
```

We will now step through a few of the landmarks, showing how we extract the features and occasionally showing the result. Let's start with the left eye and right eye; continue adding the following code just after the constants you just defined:

```
if let landmarks = face.landmarks?.leftEye {
    let transformedPoints = getTransformedPoints(
        landmark: landmarks,
        faceRect: faceRect,
        imageSize: imageSize)
    imageView.drawPath(pathPoints: transformedPoints,
                       closePath: true,
                       color: landmarkColor,
                       lineWidth: landmarkWidth,
                       vFlip: false)
    var center = transformedPoints
        .reduce(CGPoint.zero, { (result, point) -> CGPoint in
        return CGPoint(
            x:result.x + point.x,
            y:result.y + point.y)
    })
    center.x /= CGFloat(transformedPoints.count)
    center.y /= CGFloat(transformedPoints.count)
    imageView.drawCircle(center: center,
                         radius: 2,
                         color: landmarkColor,
                         lineWidth: landmarkWidth,
                         vFlip: false)
}

if let landmarks = face.landmarks?.rightEye {
    let transformedPoints = getTransformedPoints(
        landmark: landmarks,
        faceRect: faceRect,
        imageSize: imageSize)
    imageView.drawPath(pathPoints: transformedPoints,
                       closePath: true,
                       color: landmarkColor,
                       lineWidth: landmarkWidth,
                       vFlip: false)
    var center = transformedPoints.reduce(CGPoint.zero, { (result, point)
-> CGPoint in
        return CGPoint(
            x:result.x + point.x,
            y:result.y + point.y)
    })
    center.x /= CGFloat(transformedPoints.count)
    center.y /= CGFloat(transformedPoints.count)
```

```
imageView.drawCircle(center: center,
                radius: 2,
                color: landmarkColor,
                lineWidth: landmarkWidth,
                vFlip: false)
}
```

Hopefully, as is apparent from the preceding code snippet, we get a reference to each of the landmarks by interrogating the face observations landmark property, which itself references the appropriate landmark. In the preceding code, we get reference to the landmarks `leftEye` and `rightEye`. And for each, we first render the contour of the eye, as shown in this screenshot:

Next, we iterate through each of the points to find the center of the eye and render a circle using the following code:

```
var center = transformedPoints
    .reduce(CGPoint.zero, { (result, point) -> CGPoint in
    return CGPoint(
        x:result.x + point.x,
        y:result.y + point.y)
})

center.x /= CGFloat(transformedPoints.count)
center.y /= CGFloat(transformedPoints.count)
imageView.drawCircle(center: center,
                radius: 2,
                color: landmarkColor,
                lineWidth: landmarkWidth,
                vFlip: false)
```

This is slightly unnecessary as one of the landmarks available is `leftPupil`, but I wanted to use this instance to highlight the importance of inspecting the available landmarks. The next half of the block is concerned with performing the same tasks for the right eye; by the end of it, you should have an image resembling something like the following, with both eyes drawn:

Let's continue highlighting some of the landmarks available. Next, we will inspect the face contour and nose; add the following code:

```
if let landmarks = face.landmarks?.faceContour {
    let transformedPoints = getTransformedPoints(
        landmark: landmarks,
        faceRect: faceRect,
        imageSize: imageSize)
    imageView.drawPath(pathPoints: transformedPoints,
                    closePath: false,
                    color: landmarkColor,
                    lineWidth: landmarkWidth,
                    vFlip: false)
}

if let landmarks = face.landmarks?.nose {
    let transformedPoints = getTransformedPoints(
        landmark: landmarks,
        faceRect: faceRect,
        imageSize: imageSize)
    imageView.drawPath(pathPoints: transformedPoints,
                    closePath: false,
                    color: landmarkColor,
```

```
                              lineWidth: landmarkWidth,
                              vFlip: false)
    }

    if let landmarks = face.landmarks?.noseCrest {
        let transformedPoints = getTransformedPoints(
            landmark: landmarks,
            faceRect: faceRect,
            imageSize: imageSize)
        imageView.drawPath(pathPoints: transformedPoints,
                           closePath: false,
                           color: landmarkColor,
                           lineWidth: landmarkWidth,
                           vFlip: false)
    }
```

The patterns should be obvious now; here we can draw the landmarks `faceContour`, `nose`, and `noseCrest`; with that done, your image should look something like the following:

As an exercise, draw the lips (and any other facial landmark) using the landmarks `innerLips` and `outerLips`. With that implemented, you should end up with something like this:

Before returning to our task of classifying facial expressions, let's quickly finish our detour with some practical uses for landmark detection (other than drawing or placing glasses on a face).

As highlighted earlier, our training set consists of images that are predominantly forward-facing and orientated fairly straight. With this in mind, one practical use of knowing the position of each eye is being able to qualify an image; that is, is the face sufficiently in view and orientated correctly? Another use would be to slightly realign the face so that it fits in better with your training set (keeping in mind that our images are reduced to 28 x 28, so some detriment to quality can be ignored).

For now, I'll leave the implementation of these to you but, by using the angle between the two eyes, you can apply an affine transformation to correct the orientation, that is, rotate the image.

Let's now return to our main task of classification; as we did before, we will create a VNDetectFaceRectanglesRequest request to handle identifying each face within a given image and, for each face, we will perform some preprocessing before feeding it into our model. If you recall our discussion on the model, our model is expecting a single-channel (grayscale) image of a face with the size 48 x 48 and its values normalized between 0.0 and 1.0. Let's walk through each part of the task piece by piece, starting with creating the request, as we did previously:

```
imageView.image = images[faceIdx]
let model = ExpressionRecognitionModelRaw()

if let faceDetectionResults = faceDetectionRequest.results as?
[VNFaceObservation]{
    for face in faceDetectionResults{
        if let currentImage = imageView.image{
            let bbox = face.boundingBox
            let imageSize = CGSize(width:currentImage.size.width,
                                   height: currentImage.size.height)
            let w = bbox.width * imageSize.width
            let h = bbox.height * imageSize.height
            let x = bbox.origin.x * imageSize.width
            let y = bbox.origin.y * imageSize.height
            let faceRect = CGRect(x: x,
                                  y: y,
                                  width: w,
                                  height: h)
        }
    }
}
```

The preceding code should look familiar to you now, with the only difference being the instantiation of our model (the bold statement): `let model = ExpressionRecognitionModelRaw()`. Next, we want to crop out the face from the image; in order to do this, we will need to write a utility function that will implement this. Since we want to carry this over to our application, let's write it as an extension of the `CIImage` class. Click on the `CIImageExtension.swift` file within the `Sources` folder in the left-hand panel to open up the relevant file; currently, this file is just an empty extension body, as shown in the following code:

```
extension CIImage{
}
```

Go ahead and add the following snippet of code within the body of `CIImage` to implement the functionality of cropping:

```
public func crop(rect:CGRect) -> CIImage?{
    let context = CIContext()
    guard let img = context.createCGImage(self, from: rect) else{
        return nil
    }
    return CIImage(cgImage: img)
}
```

In the preceding code, we are simply creating a new image of itself constrained to the region passed in; this method, `context.createCGImage`, returns a `CGImage`, which we then wrap in a `CIImage` before returning to the caller. With our crop method taken care of, we return to our main playground source and add the following snippet after the face rectangle declared previously to crop a face from our image:

```
let ciImage = CIImage(cgImage:images[faceIdx].cgImage!)

let cropRect = CGRect(
    x: max(x - (faceRect.width * 0.15), 0),
    y: max(y - (faceRect.height * 0.1), 0),
    width: min(w + (faceRect.width * 0.3), imageSize.width),
    height: min(h + (faceRect.height * 0.6), imageSize.height))

guard let croppedCIImage = ciImage.crop(rect: cropRect) else{
    fatalError("Failed to cropped image")
}
```

We first create an instance of `CIImage` from `CGImage` (referenced by the `UIImage` instance); we then pad out our face rectangle. The reason for doing this is to better match it with our training data; if you refer to our previous experiments, the detected bounds fit tightly around the eyes and chin while our training data encompasses a more holistic view of the face. The numbers selected were through trial and error, but I imagine there is some statistically relevant ratio between the distance between the eyes and height of the face—maybe. We finally crop our image using the `crop` method we implemented earlier.

Next, we will resize the image (to the size the model is expecting) but, once again, this functionality is not yet available. So, our next task! Jump back into the `CIImageExtension.swift` file and add the following method to handle resizing:

```
public func resize(size: CGSize) -> CIImage {
    let scale = min(size.width, size.height) / min(self.extent.size.width,
self.extent.size.height)
    let resizedImage = self.transformed(
        by: CGAffineTransform(
            scaleX: scale,
            y: scale))
    let width = resizedImage.extent.width
    let height = resizedImage.extent.height
    let xOffset = (CGFloat(width) - size.width) / 2.0
    let yOffset = (CGFloat(height) - size.height) / 2.0
    let rect = CGRect(x: xOffset,
                      y: yOffset,
                      width: size.width,
                      height: size.height)
    return resizedImage
        .clamped(to: rect)
        .cropped(to: CGRect(
            x: 0, y: 0,
            width: size.width,
            height: size.height))
}
```

 You may notice that we are not inverting the face rectangle here as we did before; the reason is that we were only required to do this to transform from the Quartz 2D coordinate system to UIKit's coordinate system, which we are not doing here.

Despite the number of lines, the majority of the code is concerned with calculating the scale and translation required to center it. Once we have calculated these, we simply pass in a `CGAffineTransform`, with our scale, to the `transformed` method and then our centrally aligned rectangle to the `clamped` method. With this now implemented, let's return to our main playground code and make use of it by resizing our cropped image, as shown in the following lines:

```
let resizedCroppedCIImage = croppedCIImage.resize(
    size: CGSize(width:48, height:48))
```

Three more steps are required before we can pass our data to our model for inference. The first is to convert it to a single channel, the second is to rescale the pixels so that they are between the values of 0.0 and 1.0, and finally we wrap it in a `MLMultiArray`, which we can then feed into our model's `predict` method. To achieve the previous, we will add another extension to our `CIImage` class. It will render out the image using a single channel, along with extracting the pixel data and returning it in an array, which we can then easily access for rescaling. Jump back into the `CIImageExtension.swift` file and add the following method:

```
public func getGrayscalePixelData() -> [UInt8]?{
    var pixelData : [UInt8]?
    let context = CIContext()
    let attributes = [
        kCVPixelBufferCGImageCompatibilityKey:kCFBooleanTrue,
        kCVPixelBufferCGBitmapContextCompatibilityKey:kCFBooleanTrue
        ] as CFDictionary
    var nullablePixelBuffer: CVPixelBuffer? = nil
    let status = CVPixelBufferCreate(
        kCFAllocatorDefault,
        Int(self.extent.size.width),
        Int(self.extent.size.height),
        kCVPixelFormatType_OneComponent8,
        attributes,
        &nullablePixelBuffer)
    guard status == kCVReturnSuccess, let pixelBuffer = nullablePixelBuffer
        else { return nil }
    CVPixelBufferLockBaseAddress(
        pixelBuffer,
        CVPixelBufferLockFlags(rawValue: 0))
    context.render(
        self,
        to: pixelBuffer,
        bounds: CGRect(x: 0,
                       y: 0,
                       width: self.extent.size.width,
```

```
                        height: self.extent.size.height),
        colorSpace:CGColorSpaceCreateDeviceGray())
    let width = CVPixelBufferGetWidth(pixelBuffer)
    let height = CVPixelBufferGetHeight(pixelBuffer);
    if let baseAddress = CVPixelBufferGetBaseAddress(pixelBuffer) {
        pixelData = Array<UInt8>(repeating: 0, count: width * height)
        let buf = baseAddress.assumingMemoryBound(to: UInt8.self)
        for i in 0..<width*height{
            pixelData![i] = buf[i]
        }
    }
    CVPixelBufferUnlockBaseAddress(
        pixelBuffer,
        CVPixelBufferLockFlags(rawValue: 0))
    return pixelData
}
```

Once again, don't be intimidated by the amount of code; there are two main tasks this method does. The first is rendering out the image to a CVPixelBuffer using a single channel, grayscale. To highlight this, the code responsible is shown in the following block:

```
public func getGrayscalePixelData() -> [UInt8]?{
    let context = CIContext()

    let attributes = [
        kCVPixelBufferCGImageCompatibilityKey:kCFBooleanTrue,
        kCVPixelBufferCGBitmapContextCompatibilityKey:kCFBooleanTrue
    ] as CFDictionary
    var nullablePixelBuffer: CVPixelBuffer? = nil
    let status = CVPixelBufferCreate(
        kCFAllocatorDefault,
        Int(self.extent.size.width),
        Int(self.extent.size.height),
        kCVPixelFormatType_OneComponent8,
        attributes,
        &nullablePixelBuffer)
    guard status == kCVReturnSuccess, let pixelBuffer = nullablePixelBuffer
        else { return nil }
    // Render the CIImage to our CVPixelBuffer and return it
    CVPixelBufferLockBaseAddress(
        pixelBuffer,
        CVPixelBufferLockFlags(rawValue: 0))
    context.render(
        self,
        to: pixelBuffer,
        bounds: CGRect(x: 0,
                       y: 0,
```

```
                        width: self.extent.size.width,
                        height: self.extent.size.height),
            colorSpace:CGColorSpaceCreateDeviceGray())
    CVPixelBufferUnlockBaseAddress(
        pixelBuffer,
        CVPixelBufferLockFlags(rawValue: 0))
    }
```

We render the image to a `CVPixelBuffer` to provide a convenient way for us to access the raw pixels that we can then use to populate our array. We then return this to the caller. The main chunk of code that is responsible for this is shown here:

```
let width = CVPixelBufferGetWidth(pixelBuffer)
let height = CVPixelBufferGetHeight(pixelBuffer);

if let baseAddress = CVPixelBufferGetBaseAddress(pixelBuffer) {
    pixelData = Array<UInt8>(repeating: 0, count: width * height)
    let buf = baseAddress.assumingMemoryBound(to: UInt8.self)
    for i in 0..<width*height{
        pixelData![i] = buf[i]
    }
}
```

Here, we first determine the dimensions by obtaining the width and height of our image, using `CVPixelBufferGetWidth` and `CVPixelBufferGetHeight` respectively. Then we use these to create an appropriately sized array to hold the pixel data. We then obtain the base address of our `CVPixelBuffer` and call its `assumingMemoryBound` method to give us a typed pointer. We can use this to access each pixel, which we do to populate our `pixelData` array before returning it.

With your `getGrayscalePixelData` method now implemented, return to the main source of the playground and resume where you left off by adding the following code:

```
guard let resizedCroppedCIImageData =
    resizedCroppedCIImage.getGrayscalePixelData() else{
        fatalError("Failed to get (grayscale) pixel data from image")
}

let scaledImageData = resizedCroppedCIImageData.map({ (pixel) -> Double in
    return Double(pixel)/255.0
})
```

In the preceding snippet, we are obtaining the raw pixels of our cropped image using our `getGrayscalePixelData` method, before rescaling them by dividing each pixel by 255.0 (the maximum value). Our final task of preparation is putting our data into a data structure that our model will accept, a `MLMultiArray`. Add the following code to do just this:

```
guard let array = try? MLMultiArray(shape: [1, 48, 48], dataType: .double)
else {
    fatalError("Unable to create MLMultiArray")
}

for (index, element) in scaledImageData.enumerated() {
    array[index] = NSNumber(value: element)
}
```

We start by creating an instance of `MLMultiArray` with the shape of our input data and then proceed to copy across our standardized pixel data.

With our model instantiated and data prepared, we can now perform inference using the following code:

```
DispatchQueue.global(qos: .background).async {
    let prediction = try? model.prediction(
        image: array)
    if let classPredictions = prediction?.classLabelProbs{
        DispatchQueue.main.sync {
            for (k, v) in classPredictions{
                print("\(k) \(v)")
            }
        }
    }
}
```

Previously, we dispatched inference on a background thread then printed out all probabilities of each class to the console. With that now complete, run your playground, and if everything is working fine, you should get something like the following:

| Angry | 0.0341557003557682 |
| Happy | 0.594196200370789 |
| Disgust | 2.19011440094619e-06 |
| Sad | 0.260873317718506 |
| Fear | 0.013140731491148 |
| Surprise | 0.000694742717314512 |
| Neutral | 0.0969370529055595 |

As a designer and builder of intelligent systems, it is your task to interpret these results and present them to the user. Some questions you'll want to ask yourself are as follows:

- What is an acceptable threshold of a probability before setting the class as true?
- Can this threshold be dependent on probabilities of other classes to remove ambiguity? That is, if **Sad** and **Happy** have a probability of 0.3, you can infer that the prediction is inaccurate, or at least not useful.
- Is there a way to accept multiple probabilities?
- Is it useful to expose the threshold to the user and have it manually set and/or tune it?

These are only a few questions you should ask. The specific questions, and their answers, will depend on your use case and users. At this point, we have everything we need to preprocess and perform inference; let's now turn our attention to the application for this chapter.

 If you find that you are not getting any output, it could be that you need to flag the playground as running indefinitely so that it doesn't exit before running the background thread. You can do this by adding the following statement in your playground:
`PlaygroundPage.current.needsIndefiniteExecution = true`
When this is set to `true`, you will need to explicitly stop the playground.

# Bringing it all together

If you haven't done already, pull down the latest code from the accompanying repository: `https://github.com/packtpublishing/machine-learning-with-core-ml`. Once downloaded, navigate to the directory `Chapter4/Start/FacialEmotionDetection` and open the project `FacialEmotionDetection.xcodeproj`. Once loaded, you will hopefully recognize the project structure as it closely resembles our first example. For this reason, we will just concentrate on the main components that are unique for this project, and I suggest reviewing previous chapters for clarification on anything that is unclear.

Let's start by reviewing our project and its main components; your project should look similar to what is shown in the following screenshot:

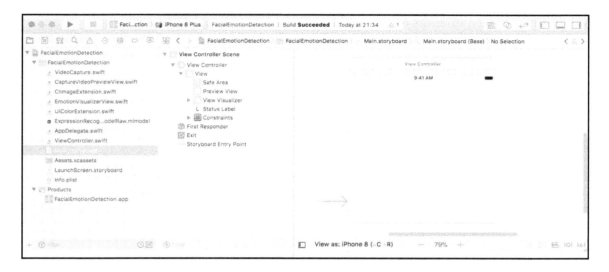

As shown in the preceding screenshot, the project looks a lot like our previous projects. I am going to make an assumption that the classes VideoCapture, CaptureVideoPreviewView, and UIColorExtension look familiar and you are comfortable with their contents. CIImageExtension is what we just implemented in the previous section, and therefore we won't be covering it here. The EmotionVisualizerView class is a custom view that visualizes the outputs from our model. And, finally, we have the bundled ExpressionRecognitionModelRaw.mlmodel. Our main focus in this section will be on wrapping the functionality we implemented in the previous section to handle preprocessing and hooking it up within the ViewController class. Before we start, let's quickly review what we are doing and consider some real-life applications for expression/emotion recognition.

In this section, we are building a simple visualization of the detected faces; we will pass in our camera feed to our preprocessor, then hand it over to our model to perform inference, and finally feed the results to our EmotionVisualizerView to render the output as an overlay on the screen. It's a simple example but sufficiently implements the mechanics required to embed in your own creations. So, what are some of its practical uses?

In a broad sense, there are three main uses: **analytical**, **reactive**, and **anticipatory**. Analytical is generally what you are likely to hear. These applications typically observe reactions by the user in relation to the content being presented; for example, you might measure arousal from content observed by the user, which is then used to drive future decisions.

While analytical experiences remain mostly passive, reactive applications proactively adjust the experience based on live feedback. One example that illustrates this well is **DragonBot**, a research project from the *Social Robotics Group* at MIT exploring intelligent tutoring systems.

DragonBot uses emotional awareness to adapt to the student; for example, one of its applications is a reading game that adapts the words based on the recognized emotion. That is, the system can adjust the difficulty of the task (words in this case) based on the user's ability, determined by the recognized emotion.

Finally, we have anticipatory applications. Anticipatory applications are semi-autonomous. They proactively try to infer the user's context and predict a likely action, therefore adjusting their state or triggering an action. An fictional example could be an email client that delays sending messages if the user had composed the message when angry.

Hopefully, this highlights some of the opportunities, but for now, let's return to our example and start building out the class that will be responsible for handling the preprocessing. Start off by creating a new swift file called `ImageProcess.swift`; and, within the file, add the following code:

```
import UIKit
import Vision

protocol ImageProcessorDelegate : class{
    func onImageProcessorCompleted(status: Int, faces:[MLMultiArray]?)
}

class ImageProcessor{
    weak var delegate : ImageProcessorDelegate?
    init(){
    }
    public func getFaces(pixelBuffer:CVPixelBuffer){
        DispatchQueue.global(qos: .background).async {

        }
    }
}
```

Here, we have defined the protocol for the delegate to handle the result once the preprocessing has completed, as well as the main class that exposes the method for initiating the task. Most of the code we will be using is what we have written in the playground; start off by declaring the request and request handler at the class level:

```
let faceDetection = VNDetectFaceRectanglesRequest()

let faceDetectionRequest = VNSequenceRequestHandler()
```

Let's now make use of the request by having our handler execute it within the body of the `getFaces` method's background queue dispatch block:

```
let ciImage = CIImage(cvPixelBuffer: pixelBuffer)
let width = ciImage.extent.width
let height = ciImage.extent.height

// Perform face detection
try? self.faceDetectionRequest.perform(
    [self.faceDetection],
    on: ciImage)

var facesData = [MLMultiArray]()

if let faceDetectionResults = self.faceDetection.results as?
[VNFaceObservation]{
    for face in faceDetectionResults{

    }
}
```

This should all look familiar to you. We pass in our request and image to the image handler. Then, we instantiate an array to hold the data for each face detected in the image. Finally, we obtain the observations and start iterating through each of them. It's within this block that we will perform the preprocessing and populate our `facesData` array as we had done in the playground. Add the following code within the loop:

```
let bbox = face.boundingBox

let imageSize = CGSize(width:width,
                       height:height)

let w = bbox.width * imageSize.width
let h = bbox.height * imageSize.height
let x = bbox.origin.x * imageSize.width
let y = bbox.origin.y * imageSize.height

let paddingTop = h * 0.2
let paddingBottom = h * 0.55
let paddingWidth = w * 0.15

let faceRect = CGRect(x: max(x - paddingWidth, 0),
                      y: max(0, y - paddingTop),
                      width: min(w + (paddingWidth * 2), imageSize.width),
                      height: min(h + paddingBottom, imageSize.height))
```

In the preceding block, we obtain the detected face's bounding box and create the cropping bounds, including padding. Our next task will be to crop the face from the image, resize it to our target size of 48 x 48, extract the raw pixel data along with normalizing the values, and finally populate an `MLMultiArray`. This is then added to our `facesData` array to be returned to the delegate; appending the following code to your script does just that:

```
if let pixelData = ciImage.crop(rect: faceRect)?
    .resize(size: CGSize(width:48, height:48))
    .getGrayscalePixelData()?.map({ (pixel) -> Double in
        return Double(pixel)/255.0
    }){
    if let array = try? MLMultiArray(shape: [1, 48, 48], dataType: .double)
{
        for (index, element) in pixelData.enumerated() {
            array[index] = NSNumber(value: element)
        }
        facesData.append(array)
    }
}
```

Nothing new has been introduced here apart from chaining the methods to make it more legible (at least for me). Our final task is to notify the delegate once we have finished; add the following just outside the observations loop block:

```
DispatchQueue.main.async {
    self.delegate?.onImageProcessorCompleted(status: 1, faces: facesData)
}
```

Now, with that complete, our `ImageProcessor` is ready to be used. Let's hook everything up. Jump into the `ViewController` class, where we will hook our `ImageProcessor`. We will pass its results to our model and finally pass the output from our model to `EmotionVisualizerView` to present the results to the user. Let's start by reviewing what currently exists:

```
import UIKit
import Vision
import AVFoundation

class ViewController: UIViewController {

    @IBOutlet weak var previewView: CapturePreviewView!
    @IBOutlet weak var viewVisualizer: EmotionVisualizerView!
    @IBOutlet weak var statusLabel: UILabel!
    let videoCapture : VideoCapture = VideoCapture()
    override func viewDidLoad() {
        super.viewDidLoad()
```

```
            videoCapture.delegate = self
            videoCapture.asyncInit { (success) in
                if success{

                    (self.previewView.layer as!
    AVCaptureVideoPreviewLayer).session = self.videoCapture.captureSession

                    (self.previewView.layer as!
    AVCaptureVideoPreviewLayer).videoGravity =
    AVLayerVideoGravity.resizeAspectFill
                        self.videoCapture.startCapturing()
                } else{
                        fatalError("Failed to init VideoCapture")
                }
            }
            imageProcessor.delegate = self
        }
    }

    extension ViewController : VideoCaptureDelegate{
        func onFrameCaptured(
            videoCapture: VideoCapture,
            pixelBuffer:CVPixelBuffer?,
            timestamp:CMTime){
            // Unwrap the parameter pixxelBuffer; exit early if nil
            guard let pixelBuffer = pixelBuffer else{
                print("WARNING: onFrameCaptured; null pixelBuffer")
                return
            }
        }
    }
```

Our `ViewController` has references to its IB counterpart, most notably the `previewView` and `viewVisualizer`. The former will render the captured camera frames and `viewVisualizer` will be responsible for visualizing the output of our model. We then have `videoCapture`, which is a utility class that encapsulates setting up, capturing, and tearing down the camera. We get access to the captured frames by assigning ourselves as the delegate and implement the appropriate protocol as we have done as an extension at the bottom.

Let's begin by declaring the model and `ImageProcessor` variables required for our task; add the following at the class level of your `ViewController`:

```
let imageProcessor : ImageProcessor = ImageProcessor()

let model = ExpressionRecognitionModelRaw()
```

Next, we need to assign ourselves as the delegate of `ImageProcessor` in order to receive the results once the processing has completed. Add the following statement to the bottom of your `viewDidLoad` method:

```
imageProcessor.delegate = self
```

We will return shortly to implement the required protocol; for now, let's make use of our `ImageProcessor` by passing in the frame we receive from the camera. Within the `onFrameCaptured` method, we add the following statement, which will pass each frame to our `ImageProcessor` instance. It's shown in bold in the following code block:

```
extension ViewController : VideoCaptureDelegate{
    func onFrameCaptured(
        videoCapture: VideoCapture,
        pixelBuffer:CVPixelBuffer?,
        timestamp:CMTime){

        guard let pixelBuffer = pixelBuffer else{
            print("WARNING: onFrameCaptured; null pixelBuffer")
            return
        }
        self.imageProcessor.getFaces(
            pixelBuffer: pixelBuffer)
    }
}
```

Our final task will be to implement the ImageProcessorDelegate protocol; this will be called when our ImageProcessor has completed identifying and extracting each face for a given camera frame along with performing the preprocessing necessary for our model. Once completed, we will pass the data to our model to perform inference, and finally pass these onto our EmotionVisualizerView. Because nothing new is being introduced here, let's go ahead and add the block in its entirety:

```
extension ViewController : ImageProcessorDelegate{
    func onImageProcessorCompleted(
        status: Int,
        faces:[MLMultiArray]?){
        guard let faces = faces else{ return }
        self.statusLabel.isHidden = faces.count > 0
        guard faces.count > 0 else{
            return
        }
        DispatchQueue.global(qos: .background).async {
            for faceData in faces{
                let prediction = try? self.model
                    .prediction(image: faceData)
                if let classPredictions =
                    prediction?.classLabelProbs{
                    DispatchQueue.main.sync {
                        self.viewVisualizer.update(
                            labelConference: classPredictions
                        )
                    }
                }
            }
        }
    }
}
```

The only notable thing to point out is that our model needs to perform inference in the background thread and our ImageProcessor calls its delegate on the main thread. For this reason, we dispatch inference to the background and then return the results on the main thread—this is necessary whenever you want to update the user interface.

With that complete, we are now in a good place to build and deploy to test; if all goes well, you should see something like the following:

Let's wrap up the chapter by reviewing what we have covered and point out some interesting areas to explore before moving on to the next chapter.

 In this chapter, we have taken a naive approach with respect to processing the captured frames; in a commercial application you would want to optimize this process such as utilizing **object tracking** from the Vision framework to replace explicit face detection, which is computationally cheaper.

# Summary

In this chapter, we applied a CNN for the task of recognizing facial expressions. Using this, we could infer the emotional state of a given face. As usual, we again spent the majority of our time understanding the required input for the model and implementing the functionality to facilitate this. But, in doing so, we uncovered some important considerations when developing intelligent applications; the first is the explicit awareness of using either an end-to-end solution or a multi-step approach, with the multi-step approach being the most common one you will use.

This essentially means you, the designer and builder of intelligent applications, will be building data pipelines consisting of many models, each transforming the data in preparation for the next. This is similar to how deep networks work but provides greater flexibility. The second consideration is highlighting the availability of complementary frameworks available on iOS, in particular the Vision framework. It was used as one of the steps in our pipeline but offers a lot of convenience for common tasks, as well as a consistent workflow.

In this example, our pipeline consisted of only two steps, face detection and then emotion recognition. But we also briefly played with a feature of the Vision framework that can be used to identify facial landmarks. So, it is plausible to consider facial landmarks to train the emotional classifier rather than the raw pixels, in which case our pipeline would consist of three steps: face detection, landmark detection, and, finally, emotion recognition.

Finally, we briefly explored some use cases showing how emotion recognition could be applied; as our computers shift away from being pure tools towards being companions, being able to detect and react to the emotional state of the user will become increasingly more important. So, it's an area well worth further exploring.

In the next chapter, we will introduce the concept of transfer learning and how we can use it to transfer styles from one image onto another.

# Locating Objects in the World 5

So far, we have limited ourselves to recognizing the single most dominant object within an image using a **convolutional neural network** (**CNN**). We have seen how a model can be trained to take in a image and extract a series of feature maps that are then fed into a **fully connected layer** to output a probability distribution of a set of classes. This is then interpreted to classify the object within the image, as shown here:

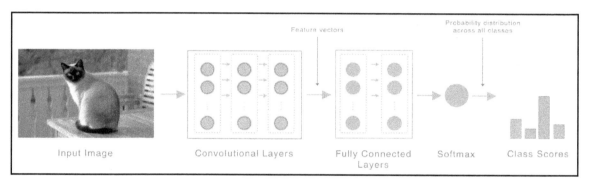

In this chapter, we will build on this and explore how we can detect and locate multiple objects within a single image. We will start by building up our understanding of how this works and then walk through implementing a image search for a photo gallery application. This application allows the user to filter and sort images not only based on what objects are present in the image, but also on their position relative to one another (object composition). Along the way, we will also get hands-on experience with Core ML Tools, the tool set Apple released to support converting models from popular **machine learning** (**ML**) frameworks to Core ML.

Let's begin by first understanding what it takes to detect multiple objects in an image.

# Object localization and object detection

As mentioned in the introduction of this chapter, we have already been introduced to the concepts behind object recognition using CNNs. For this case, we used a trained model to perform classification; it achieved this by learning a set of feature maps using convolutional layers that are fed into fully connected (or dense) layers and, finally, their output, through an activation layer which gave us the probability for each of the classes. The class was inferred by selecting the one with the largest probability.

 Let's differentiate between object recognition, object localization, and object detection. Object recognition is the task of classifying the most dominant object in a image while object localization performs classification and predicts an object's bounding box. Object detection further extends this and allows multiple classes to be detected and located, and that's the topic of this chapter.

This process is known as **object recognition** and is a classification problem, but here we don't get the full picture (pun intended). What about the location of the detected object? That would be useful for increasing the perception capabilities of robotic systems or increasing the scope for intelligent interfaces, such as intelligent cropping and image enhancements. What about detecting multiple objects and their locations? The former, detecting the location of a single object, is known as **object localization,** while the later is generally known as **object detection**, illustrated as follows:

Object Localization          Object Detection

We will start by introducing object localization and then work our way to object detection. The concepts are complementary and the former can be seen as an extension of object recognition, which you are already familiar with.

When training a model for classification, we tune the weights so that they achieve minimum loss for predicting a single class. For object localization, we essentially want to extend this to predict not only the class, but also the location of the recognized object. Let's work through a concrete example to help illustrate the concept. Imagine we are training a model to recognize and locate a cat, dog, or person. For this, our model would need to output the probabilities for each class (cat, dog, or person) as we have already seen, and also their location. This can be described using the center $x$ and $y$ position and the width and height of the object. To simplify the task of training, we also include a value indicating whether an object exists or not. The following figure illustrates two input images and their associated outputs. Let's assume here that our one-hot encoded classes are in the order of cat, dog, and person. That is, cat would be encoded as *(1,0,0)*, dog as *(0,1,0)*, and person as *(0,0,1)*:

Output (y)
[0.5, 0.5, 0.45, 0.87, 1, 1, 0, 0]

Output (y)
[?, ?, ?, ?, 0, ?, ?, ?]

The structure of the output, shown in the preceding image, consists of these elements:

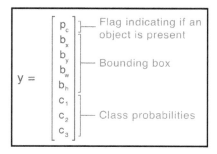

Here, we have three classes, but this can be generalized to include any arbitrary number of classes. What is of note is that if there is no object detected (the first element in our output), then we ignore the remaining elements. The other important point to highlight is that the bounding box is described in units rather than absolute values.

For example, a value of *0.5* for $b_x$ would indicate half of the width of the image, where the top left is **(0, 0)** and bottom right is **(1, 1)**, as illustrated here:

We can borrow a lot of the structure of a typical CNN used for classification. Therein, the image is fed through a series of convolutional layers and their output, a feature vector, through a series of fully connected layers, before being squeezed through a softmax activation for multi-class classification (giving us the probability distribution across all classes). Instead of just passing the feature vector from the convolutional layers to a single set of fully connected layers, we can also pass them to a layer (or layers) for binary classification (the fourth element: object present or not) and another layer (or series of layers) for predicting the bounding box using regression.

The structure of these modifications can be seen in the following figure, with the amendments in bold:

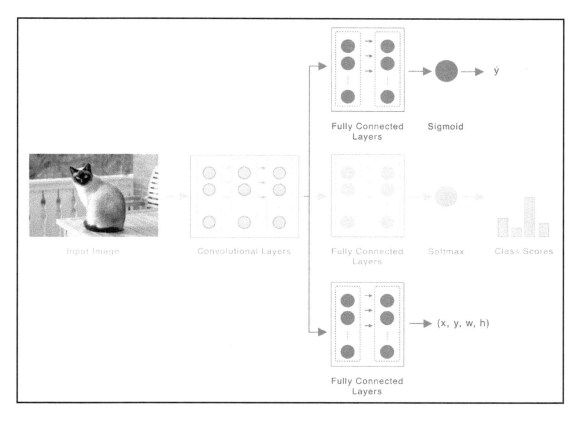

This is a good start but, more often than not, our images consist of many objects. So, let's briefly describe how we can approach this problem.

We are now moving into object detection, where we are interested in detecting and locating multiple objects (of different classes) within a single image. So far, we have seen how we can detect a single object and its location from an image, so a logical progression from this is reshaping our problem around this architecture.

By this, I mean we can use this or a similar approach, but rather than passing the full image, we can pass in cropped regions of the image; the regions are selected by sliding a window across the image, as follows (and in keeping with our cat theme):

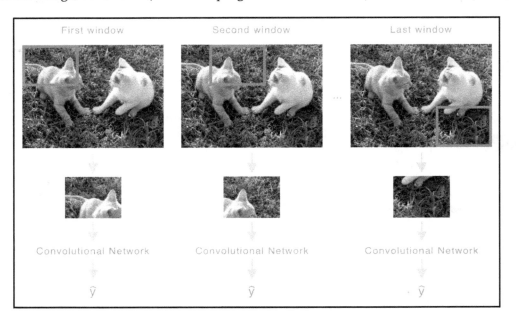

This, for obvious reasons, is called the **sliding window detection algorithm** and should be familiar to those who have experience in computer vision (used in template matching, among many others). It's important to also emphasize the difference in training; in object localization, we trained the network by passing the full image along with the associated output vector ($b_x$, $b_y$, $b_w$, $h_y$, $p_o$, $c_1$, $c_2$, $c_3$, ...), while here the network is trained on **tightly cropped images** for each of the objects, which may occupy our window size.

For the inquisitive reader wondering how this algorithm detects objects that don't fit nicely into the window size, one approach could be to simply resize your image (both decreasing and increasing) or, similarly, to use different-sized windows, that is, a set of small, medium, and large windows.

This approach has two major drawbacks; the first is that it is computationally expensive, and the second is that it doesn't allow for very accurate bounding boxes due to the dependency on window sizes and stride size. The former can be resolved by rearchitecting the CNN so that it performs the sliding window algorithm in a single pass, but we are still left with inaccurate bounding boxes.

Fortunately, for us, in 2015, J. Redmon, S. Divvala, R. Girshick, and A. Farhadi released their paper *You Only Look Once (YOLO): Unified, Real-Time Object Detection*. It describes an approach that requires just a single network capable of predicting bounding boxes and probabilities from a full image in a single pass. And because it is a unified pipeline, the whole process is efficient enough to be performed in real time, hence the network we use in this chapter.

The paper *You Only Look Once: Unified, Real-Time Object Detection* is available here: https://arxiv.org/abs/1506.02640.

Let's spend some time getting acquainted with the algorithm YOLO, where we will briefly look at the general concepts of the algorithm and interpreting the output to make use of it later in the example application for this chapter.

One of the major differences of YOLO compared to the previous approaches we have discussed in this chapter is how the model is trained. Similar to the first, when object localization was introduced, the model was trained on a image and label pair, and the elements of the label consisted of $(b_x, b_y, b_w, b_h, p_c, c_1, c_2, ...)$, so too is the case with the YOLO network. But instead of training on the whole image, the image is broken down into a grid, with each cell having an associated label, as outlined before. In the next figure, you can see this. The grid illustrated here is a 3 x 3 for legibility; these are typically more dense, as you'll soon see:

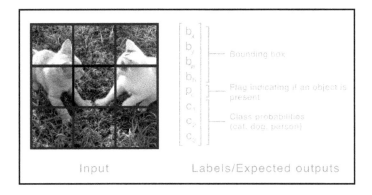

When training, we feed in the image and the network is structured so that it outputs a **vector** (as shown before) for **each grid cell**. To make this more concrete, the following figure illustrates how some of these outputs would look for the cells within this grid:

This should look familiar to you as it is, as previously mentioned, very similar to the approach we first introduced for object localization. The only major difference is that it is performed on each grid cell as opposed to the whole image.

It's worth noting that despite the object spanning across multiple cells, the training samples only label an object using a single cell (normally the cell in the center of the image), with the other encompassing cells having no object assigned to them.

Before we move on, let's unpack the bounding box variables. In the preceding figure, I have entered approximate values for each of the objects; like object localization, these values are normalized between *0.0* and *1.0* for values that fall within the cell. But, unlike object localization, these values are **local** to the cell itself rather than the image. Using the first cat as an example, we can see that the central position is *0.6* in the $x$ axis and *0.35* in the $y$ axis; this can be interpreted as being at a position 60% along the $x$ axis of the cell and 35% along the $y$ axis of the cell. Because our bounding box extends beyond the cell, there are assigned values greater than one, as we saw in the preceding figure:

Previously, we highlighted that the training sample only assigns a single cell per object but, given that we are running object detection and localization on each cell, it is likely that we will end up with multiple predictions. To manage this, YOLO uses something called **non-max suppression**, which we will introduce over the next few paragraphs, and you'll get a chance to implement it in the upcoming example.

As mentioned before, because we are performing object detection and localization on each grid cell, it is likely that we will end up with multiple bounding boxes. This is shown in the following figure. To simplify the illustration, we will just concentrate on a single object, but this of course applies to all detected objects:

In the previous figure, we can see that the network has predicted and located the cat in three cells. For each cell, I have added a fictional confidence value, located at the top-right, to each of their associated bounding boxes.

The **confidence value** is calculated by multiplying the object present probability ($p_c$) with the most likely class, that is, the class with the highest probability.

The first step in non-max suppression is simply to filter out predictions that don't meet a certain threshold; for all intents and purposes, let's set our object threshold to *0.3*. With this value, we can see that we filter out one of the predictions (with a confidence value of *0.2*), leaving us with just two, as shown in the following figure:

In the next step, we iterate over all detected boxes, from the one with the largest confidence to the least, removing any other bounding boxes that occupy the same space. In the preceding figure, we can clearly see that both bounding boxes are essentially occupying the same area, but how do we determine this programmatically?

To determine this, we calculate what is called the **intersection over union** (**IoU**) and test the returned value against a threshold. We calculate this, as the name implies, by dividing the **intersection area** of the two bounding boxes by their **union area**. A value of *1.0* tells us that the two bounding boxes occupy exactly the same space (a value you would get if you performed this calculation using a single bounding box with itself). Anything below this gives us a ratio of overlapped occupancy; a typical threshold is *0.5*. The following figure illustrates the intersection and union areas of our example:

Because these two bounding boxes would return a relatively high IoU, we would end up pruning the least probable one (the one with the lower confidence score) and end up with a single bounding box, as shown in the following figure:

We repeat this process until we have iterated over all of the model's predictions. There is just one more concept to introduce before moving on to the example project for this chapter and starting to write some code.

Up until this point, we have assumed (or have been constrained by the idea) that each cell is associated with either no object or a single object. But what about the case of objects overlapping, where two objects' center positions occupy the same grid cell? To handle circumstances like this, the YOLO algorithm implements something called **anchor boxes**. Anchor boxes allow multiple objects to occupy a single grid cell given that their bounding shape differs. Let's make this more concrete by explaining it visually. In the next figure, we have a image where the centers of two objects occupy the same grid cell. With our current output vector, we would need to label the cell as either a person or a bike, as shown in the following figure:

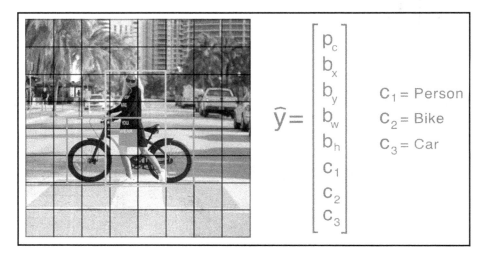

The idea with anchor boxes is that we extend our output vector to include different variations of anchor boxes (illustrated here as two, but these can be of any number). This allows each cell to encode multiple objects so long as they have different bounding shapes.

From the previous figure, we see that we can use two anchor boxes, one for the person and the other for the bike, as shown here:

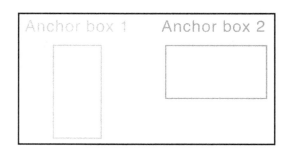

With our anchor boxes now defined, we extend our vector output such that for each grid cell we can encode the output for both anchor boxes, as illustrated in the following figure:

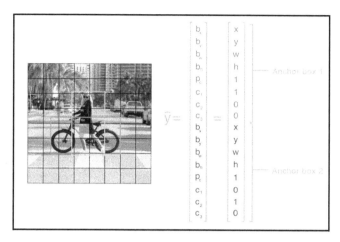

Each anchor box can be treated independently of each other output of the same cell and other cells; that is, we handle it exactly as we did previously, the only addition now being that we have more bounding boxes to process.

Just to clarify, anchor boxes are not constrained to a specific class even though some shapes are more suitable than others. They are typically generalized shapes found using some type of unsupervised learning algorithm, such as **k-means**, within an existing dataset to find the dominant shapes.

This concludes all the concepts we need to understand for this chapter's example and what we will be implementing in the coming sections but, before we do, let's walk through converting a Keras model to Core ML using the Core ML Tools Python package.

# Converting Keras Tiny YOLO to Core ML

In the previous section, we discussed the concepts of the model and algorithm we will be using in this chapter. In this section, we will be moving one step closer to realizing the example project for this chapter by converting a trained Keras model of Tiny YOLO to Core ML using Apple's Core ML Tools Python package; but, before doing so, we will quickly discuss the model and the data it was trained on.

YOLO was conceived on a neural network framework called **darknet**, which is currently not supported by the default Core ML Tools package; fortunately, the authors of YOLO and darknet have made the architecture and weights of the trained model publicly available on their website at `https://pjreddie.com/darknet/yolov2/`. There are a few variations of YOLO that have been trained on either the dataset from **Common Objects in Context** (**COCO**), which consists of 80 classes, or The PASCAL **Visual Object Classes** (**VOC**) Challenge 2007, which consists of 20 classes.

The official website can be found at `http://cocodataset.org`, and *The PASCAL VOC Challenge 2007* at `http://host.robots.ox.ac.uk/pascal/VOC/index.html`.

In this chapter, we will be using the Tiny version of YOLOv2 and the weights from the model trained on the *The PASCAL VOC Challenge 2007* dataset. The Keras model we will be using was modeled on the configuration file and weights available on the official site (link presented previously).

As usual, we will be omitting a lot of details of the model and will instead provide the model in its diagrammatic form, shown next. We'll then discuss some of the relevant parts before moving on to convert it into a Core ML model:

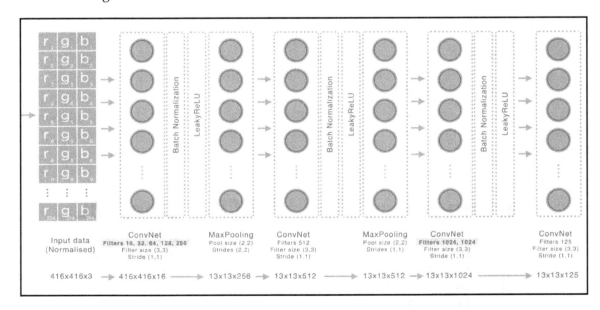

The first thing to notice is the shape of the input and output; this indicates what our model will be expecting to be fed and what it will be outputting for us to use. As shown before, the input size is 416 x 416 x 3, which, as you might suspect, is a 416 x 416 RGB image. The output shape needs a little more explanation and it will become more apparent when we arrive at coding the example for this chapter.

The output shape is 13 x 13 x 125. The 13 x 13 tells us the size of the grid being applied, that is, the 416 x 416 image is broken into a grid of 13 x 13 cells, as follows:

As discussed previously, each cell has a 125-vector encoding of the probability of an object being present and, if so, the bounding box and probabilities across all 20 classes; visually, this is explained as follows:

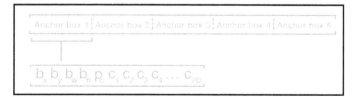

The final point about the model that I want to highlight is its simplicity; the bulk of the network is made up of convolutional blocks consisting of a convolutional layer: **Batch Normalization**, **LeakyReLU** activation, and finally a **MaxPooling** layer. This progressively increases the filter size (depth) of the network until it has reached the desired grid size and then transforms the data using only the convolutional layer, **Batch Normalization**, and **LeakyReLU** activation, dropping the **MaxPooling**.

 Now, we have introduced the terms batch normalization and leaky ReLU, which may be unfamiliar to some; here I will provide a brief description of each, starting with batch normalization. It's considered best practice to normalize the input layer before feeding it into a network. For example, we normally divide pixel values by 255 to force them into a range of 0 to 1. We do this to make it easier for the network to learn by removing any large values (or large variance in values), which may cause our network to oscillate when adjusting the weights during training. Batch normalization performs this same adjustment for the outputs of the hidden layers rather than the inputs.
ReLU is an activation function that sets anything below 0 to 0, that is, it doesn't allow non-positive values to propagate through the network. Leaky ReLU provides a less strict implementation of ReLU, allowing a small non-zero gradient to slip through when the neuron is not active.

This concludes our brief overview of the model. You can learn more about it from the official paper *YOLO9000: Better, Faster, Stronger* by J. Redmon and A. Farhadi, available at `https://arxiv.org/abs/1612.08242`. Let's now turn our attention to converting the trained Keras model of the Tiny YOLO to Core ML.

As alluded to in `Chapter 1`, *Introduction to Machine Learning*, Core ML is more of a suite of tools than a single framework. One part of this suite is the Core ML Tools Python package, which assists in converting trained models from other frameworks to Core ML for easy and rapid integration. Currently, official converters are available for Caffe, Keras, LibSVM, scikit-learn, and XGBoost, but the package is open source, with many other converters being made available for other popular ML frameworks, such as TensorFlow.

At its core, the conversion process generates a model specification that is a machine-interpretable representation of the learning models and is used by Xcode to generate the Core ML models, consisting of the following:

- **Model description**: Encodes names and type information of the inputs and outputs of the model
- **Model parameters**: The set of parameters required to represent a specific instance of the model (model weights/coefficients)

- **Additional metadata**: Information about the origin, license, and author of the model

In this chapter, we present the most simplistic of flows, but we will revisit the Core ML Tools package in `Chapter 6`, *Creating Art with Style Transfer*, to see how to deal with custom layers.

To avoid any complications when setting up the environment on your local or remote machine, we will leverage the free Jupyter cloud service provided by Microsoft. Head over to `https://notebooks.azure.com` and log in, or register if you haven't already.

Once logged in, click on the **Libraries** menu link from the navigation bar, which will take you to a page containing a list of all your libraries, similar to what is shown in the following screenshot:

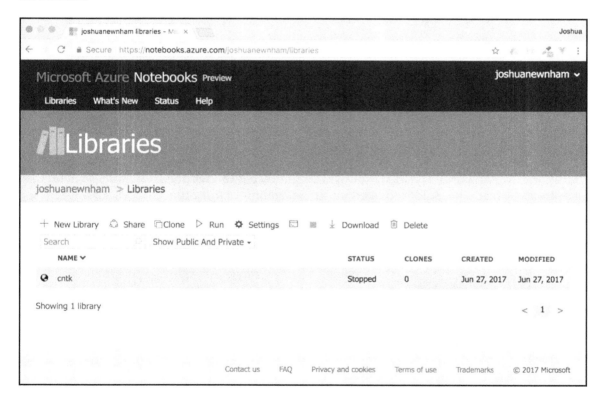

Next, click on the **+ New Library** link to bring up the **Create New Library** dialog:

Then click on the **From GitHub** tab and enter
`https://github.com/packtpublishing/machine-learning-with-core-ml` in the
**GitHub repository** field. After that, give your library a meaningful name and click on the
**Import** button to begin the process of cloning the repository and creating the library.

Once the library has been created, you will be redirected to the root; from here, click on the
`Chapter5/Notebooks` folder to open up the relevant folder for this chapter. Finally, click
on the Notebook `Tiny YOLO_Keras2CoreML.ipynb`. To help ensure that we are all on the
same page (pun intended), here is a screenshot of what you should see after clicking on the
`Chapter5/Notebooks` folder:

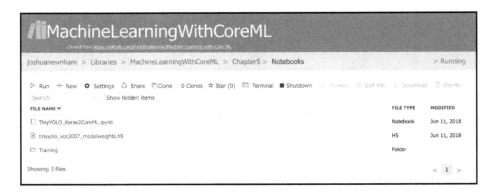

With our Notebook now loaded, it's time to walk through each of the cells to create our Core ML model; all of the required code exists and all that remains is executing each of the cells sequentially. To execute a cell, you can either use the shortcut keys *Shift + Enter* or click on the **Run** button in the toolbar (which will run the currently selected cell), as shown in the following screenshot:

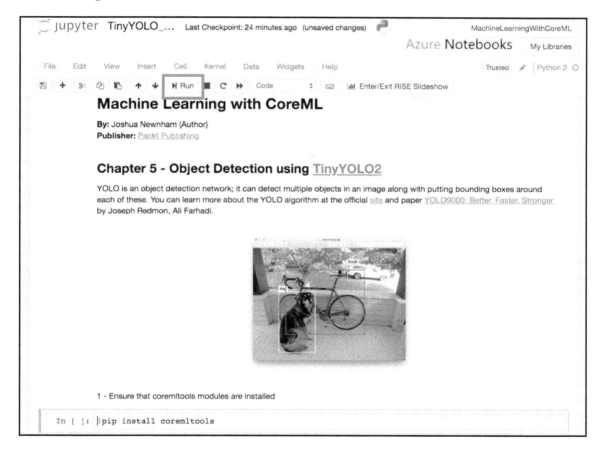

I will provide a brief explanation of what each cell does; ensure that you execute each cell as we walk through them so that we all end up with the converted model, which we will then download and use in the next section for our iOS project.

We start by ensuring that the Core ML Tools Python package is available in the environment, by running the following cell:

```
!pip install coremltools
```

Once installed, we make the package available by importing it:

```
import coremltools
```

The model architecture and weights have been serialized and saved to the file `tinyyolo_voc2007_modelweights.h5`; in the following cell, we will pass this into the convert function of the Keras converter, which will return the converted Core ML model (if no errors occur). Along with the file, we also pass in values for the parameters `input_names`, `image_input_names`, `output_names`, and `image_scale`. The `input_names` parameter takes in a single string, or a list of strings for multiple inputs, and is used to explicitly set the names that will be used in the interface of the Core ML model to refer to the inputs of the Keras model.

We also pass this input name to the `image_input_names` parameter so that the converter treats the input as an image rather than an N-dimensional array. Similar to `input_names`, values passed to `output_names` will be used in the interface of the Core ML model to refer to the outputs of the Keras model. The last parameter, `image_scale`, allows us to add a scaling factor to our input before being passed to the model. Here, we are dividing each pixel by 255, which forces each pixel to be in a range of *0.0* to *1.0*, a typical preprocessing task when working with images. There are plenty more parameters available, allowing you to tune and tweak the inputs and outputs of your model. You can learn more about these at the official documentation site here at `https://apple.github.io/coremltools/generated/ coremltools.converters.keras.convert.html`. In the next snippet, we perform the actual conversion using what we have just discussed:

```
coreml_model = coremltools.converters.keras.convert(
    'tinyyolo_voc2007_modelweights.h5',
    input_names='image',
    image_input_names='image',
    output_names='output',
    image_scale=1./255.)
```

With reference to the converted model, `coreml_model`, we add metadata, which will be made available and displayed in Xcode's ML model views:

```
coreml_model.author = 'Joshua Newnham'
coreml_model.license = 'BSD'
coreml_model.short_description = 'Keras port of YOLOTiny VOC2007 by Joseph Redmon and Ali Farhadi'
coreml_model.input_description['image'] = '416x416 RGB Image'
coreml_model.output_description['output'] = '13x13 Grid made up of: [cx, cy, w, h, confidence, 20 x classes] * 5 bounding boxes'
```

We are now ready to save our model; run the final cell to save the converted model:

```
coreml_model.save('tinyyolo_voc2007.mlmodel')
```

With our model now saved, we return to the previous tab showing the contents of the `Chapter5` directory and download the `tinyyolo_voc2007.mlmodel` file. We do so by either right-clicking on it and selecting the **Download** menu item, or by clicking on the **Download** toolbar item, as shown in the following screenshot:

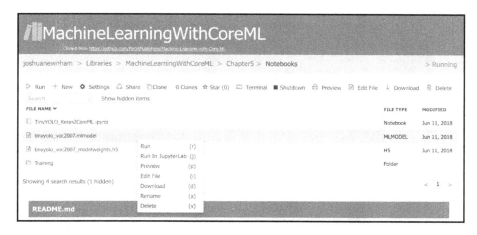

With our converted model in hand, it's now time to jump into Xcode and work through the example project for this chapter.

# Making it easier to find photos

In this section, we will put our model to work in an intelligent search application; we'll start off by quickly introducing the application, giving us a clear vision of what we intend to build. Then, we'll work through implementing the functionality related to interpreting the model's output and search heuristic for the desired functionality. We will be omitting a lot of the usual iOS functionality so that we can stay focused on the intelligent aspect of the application.

Over the past few years, we have seen a surge of intelligence being embedded in photo gallery applications, providing us with efficient ways of surfacing those cat photos hidden deep in hundreds (if not thousands) of photos we have accumulated over the years. In this section, we want to continue with this theme but push that level of intelligence a little bit further by taking advantage of the semantic information gained through object detection. Our users will be able to search for not only specific objects within a image, but also photos based on the objects and their relative positioning. For example, they can search for an image, or images, with two people standing side by side and in front of a car.

The user interface allows the user to draw the objects as they would like them positioned and their relative sizes. It will be our job in this section to implement the intelligence that returns relevant images based on this search criteria.

The next figure shows the user interface; the first two screenshots show the search screen, where the user can visually articulate what they are looking for. By using labeled bounding boxes, the user is able to describe what they are looking for, how they would like these objects arranged, and relative object sizes. The last two screenshots show the result of a search, and when expanded (last screenshot), the image will be overlaid with the detected objects and associated bounding boxes:

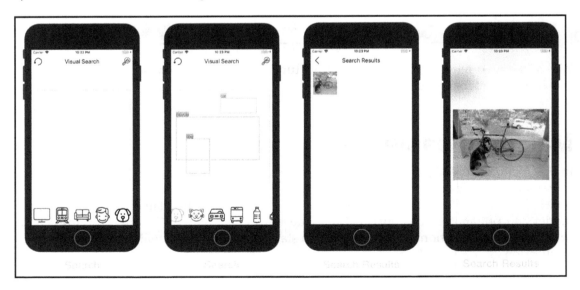

Let's start by taking a tour of the existing project before importing the model we have just converted and downloaded.

If you haven't already, pull down the latest code from the accompanying repository: `https://github.com/packtpublishing/machine-learning-with-core-ml`. Once downloaded, navigate to the directory `Chapter5/Start/` and open the project `ObjectDetection.xcodeproj`. Once loaded, you will see the project for this chapter, as shown in the following screenshot:

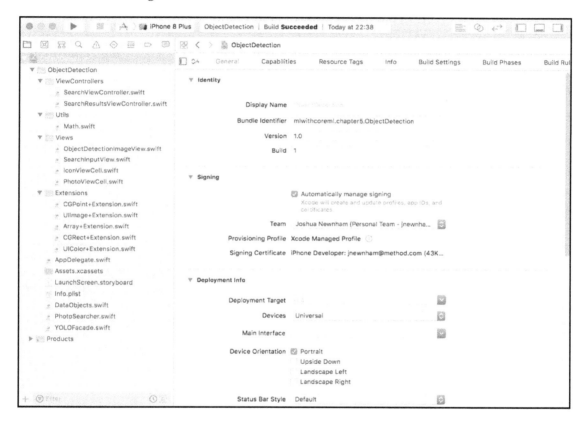

I will leave exploring the full project as an exercise for you, and I'll just concentrate on the files `PhotoSearcher.swift` and `YOLOFacade.swift` for this section. `PhotoSearcher.swift` is where we will implement the cost functions responsible for filtering and sorting the photos based on the search criteria and detected objects from `YOLOFacade.swift`, whose sole purpose is to wrap the Tiny YOLO model and implement the functionality to interpret its output. But before jumping into the code, let's quickly review the flow and data structures we will be working with.

The following diagram illustrates the general flow of the application; the user first defines the search criteria via `SearchViewController`, which is described as an array of normalized `ObjectBounds`. We'll cover more details on these later. When the user initiates the search (top-right search icon) these are passed to `SearchResultsViewController`, which delegates the task of finding suitable images to `PhotoSearcher`.

`PhotoSearcher` proceeds to iterate through all of our photos, passing each of them through to `YOLOFacade` to perform object detection using the model we converted in the previous section. The results of these are passed back to `PhotoSearcher`, which evaluates the cost of each with respect to the search criteria and then filters and orders the results, before passing them back to `SearchResultsViewController` to be displayed:

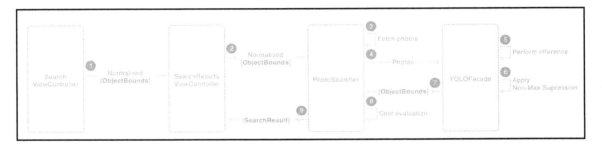

Each component communicates with the another using either the data object `ObjectBounds` or `SearchResult`. Because we will be working with them throughout the rest of this chapter, let's quickly introduce them here, all of which are defined in the `DataObjects.swift` file. Let's start with `ObjectBounds`, the structure shown in the following snippet:

```
struct ObjectBounds {
    public var object : DetectableObject
    public var origin : CGPoint
    public var size : CGSize
    var bounds : CGRect{
        return CGRect(origin: self.origin, size: self.size)
    }
}
```

As the name suggests, ObjectBounds is just that—it encapsulates the boundary of an object using the variables origin and size. The object itself is of type DetectableObject, which provides a structure to store both the class index and its associated label. It also provides a static array of objects that are available in our search, as follows:

```
struct DetectableObject{
    public var classIndex : Int
    public var label : String
    static let objects = [
        DetectableObject(classIndex:19, label:"tvmonitor"),
        DetectableObject(classIndex:18, label:"train"),
        DetectableObject(classIndex:17, label:"sofa"),
        DetectableObject(classIndex:14, label:"person"),
        DetectableObject(classIndex:11, label:"dog"),
        DetectableObject(classIndex:7, label:"cat"),
        DetectableObject(classIndex:6, label:"car"),
        DetectableObject(classIndex:5, label:"bus"),
        DetectableObject(classIndex:4, label:"bottle"),
        DetectableObject(classIndex:3, label:"boat"),
        DetectableObject(classIndex:2, label:"bird"),
        DetectableObject(classIndex:1, label:"bicycle")
    ]
}
```

ObjectBounds are used for both the search criteria defined by the user and search results returned by YOLOFacade; in the former, they describe where and which objects the user is interested in finding (search criteria), and the latter encapsulates the results from object detection.

SearchResult doesn't get any more complex; it's intended to encapsulate the result of a search with the addition of the image and cost, which is set during the cost evaluation stage (*step 8*), as shown in the previous diagram. For the complete code, the structure is as follows:

```
struct SearchResult{
    public var image : UIImage
    public var detectedObjects : [ObjectBounds]
    public var cost : Float
}
```

It's worth noting that the `ObjectBounds` messages, in the previous diagram, annotated with the word **Normalized**, refer to the values being in unit values based on the source or target size; that is, an origin of *x = 0.5* and *y = 0.5* defines the center of the source image it was defined on. The reason for this to ensure that the bounds are invariant to changes in the images they are operating on. You will soon see that, before passing images to our model, we need to resize and crop to a size of 416 x 416 (the expected input to our model), but we need to transform them back to the original for rendering the results.

Now, we have a better idea of what objects we will be consuming and generating; let's proceed with implementing the `YOLOFacade` and work our way up the stack.

Let's start by importing the model we have just converted in the previous section; locate the downloaded `.mlmodel` file and drag it onto Xcode. Once imported, select it from the left-hand panel to inspect the metadata to remind ourselves what we need to implement. It should resemble this screenshot:

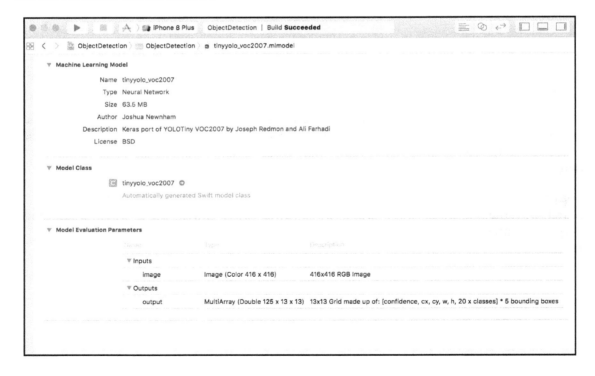

With our model now imported, let's walk through implementing the functionality YOLOFacade is responsible for; this includes preprocessing the image, passing it to our model for inference, and then parsing the model's output, including performing **non-max supression**. Select YOLOFacade.swift from the left-hand panel to bring up the code in the main window.

The class is broken into three parts, via an extension, with the first including the variables and entry point; the second including the functionality for performing inference and parsing the models outputs; and the third part including the non-max supression algorithm we discussed at the start of this chapter. Let's start at the beginning which currently looks like this:

```
class YOLOFacade{
    // TODO add input size (of image)
    // TODO add grid size
    // TODO add number of classes
    // TODO add number of anchor boxes
    // TODO add anchor shapes (describing aspect ratio)
    lazy var model : VNCoreMLModel? = {
        do{
            // TODO add model
            return nil
        } catch{
            fatalError("Failed to obtain tinyyolo_voc2007")
        }
    }()
    func asyncDetectObjects(
        photo:UIImage,
        completionHandler:@escaping (_ result:[ObjectBounds]?) -> Void){
        DispatchQueue.global(qos: .background).sync {
            self.detectObjects(photo: photo, completionHandler: { (result)
-> Void in
                DispatchQueue.main.async {
                    completionHandler(result)
                }
            })
        }
    }
}
```

The asyncDetectObjects method is the entry point of the class and is called by PhotoSearcher for each image it receives from the Photos framework; when called, this method simply delegates the task to the method detectObject in the background and waits for the results, before passing them back to the caller on the main thread. I have annotated the class with TODO to help you keep focused.

Let's start by declaring the target size required by our model; this will be used for preprocessing of the input of our model and transforming the normalized bounds to those of the source image. Add the following code:

```
// TODO add input size (of image)
var targetSize = CGSize(width: 416, height: 416)
```

Next, we define properties of our model that are used during parsing of the output; these include grid size, number of classes, number of anchor boxes, and finally, the dimensions for each of the anchor boxes (each pair describes the width and height, respectively). Make the following amendments to your YOLOFacade class:

```
// TODO add grid size
let gridSize = CGSize(width: 13, height: 13)
// TODO add number of classes
let numberOfClasses = 20
// TODO add number of anchor boxes
let numberOfAnchorBoxes = 5
// TODO add anchor shapes (describing aspect ratio)
let anchors : [Float] = [1.08, 1.19, 3.42, 4.41, 6.63, 11.38, 9.42, 5.11,
16.62, 10.52]
```

Let's now implement the model property; in this example, we will take advantage of the Vision framework for handling the preprocessing. For this, we will need to wrap our model in an instance of VNCoreMLModel so that we can pass it into a VNCoreMLRequest; make the following amendments, as shown in bold:

```
lazy var model : VNCoreMLModel = {
    do{
        // TODO add model
        let model = try VNCoreMLModel(
            for: tinyyolo_voc2007().model)
        return model
    } catch{
        fatalError("Failed to obtain tinyyolo_voc2007")
    }
}()
```

Let's now turn our attention to the detectObjects method. It will be responsible for performing inference via VNCoreMLRequest and VNImageRequestHandler, passing the model's output to the detectObjectsBounds method (which we will come to next), and finally transforming the normalized bounds to the dimensions of the original (source) image.

In this chapter, we will postpone the discussion around the Vision framework classes (VNCoreMLModel, VNCoreMLRequest, and VNImageRequestHandler) until the next chapter, where we will elaborate a little on what each does and how they work together.

Within the detectObjects method of YOLOFacade, replace the comment // TODO preprocess image and pass to model with the following code:

```
let request = VNCoreMLRequest(model: self.model)
request.imageCropAndScaleOption = .centerCrop

let handler = VNImageRequestHandler(cgImage: cgImage, options: [:])

do {
    try handler.perform([request])
} catch {
    print("Failed to perform
classification.\n\(error.localizedDescription)")
    completionHandler(nil)
    return
}
```

In the preceding snippet, we start by creating an instance of VNCoreMLRequest, passing in our model, which itself has been wrapped with an instance of VNCoreMLModel. This request performs the heavy lifting, including preprocessing (inferred by the model's metadata) and performing inference. We set its imageCropAndScaleOption property to centerCrop, which determines, as you might expect, how the image is resized to fit into the model's input. The request itself doesn't actually execute the task; this is the responsibility of VNImageRequestHandler, which we declare next by passing in our source image and then executing the request via the handler's perform method.

If all goes to plan, we should expect to have the model's output available via the request's results property. Let's move on to the last snippet for this method; replace the comment // TODO pass models results to detectObjectsBounds(::) and the following statement, completionHandler(nil), with this code:

```
guard let observations = request.results as?
[VNCoreMLFeatureValueObservation] else{
    completionHandler(nil)
    return
}

var detectedObjects = [ObjectBounds]()

for observation in observations{
```

```
guard let multiArray = observation.featureValue.multiArrayValue else{
    continue
}
if let observationDetectedObjects = self.detectObjectsBounds(array:
multiArray){
    for detectedObject in observationDetectedObjects.map(
        {$0.transformFromCenteredCropping(from: photo.size, to:
self.targetSize)}){
        detectedObjects.append(detectedObject)
    }
}
}

completionHandler(detectedObjects)
```

We begin by trying to cast the results to an array of VNCoreMLFeatureValueObservation, a type of image analysis observation that provides key-value pairs. One of them is multiArrayValue, which we then pass to the detectObjectsBounds method to parse the output and return the detected objects and their bounding boxes. Once detectObjectsBounds returns, we map each of the results with the ObjectBounds method transformFromCenteredCropping, which is responsible for transforming the normalized bounds into the space of the source image. Once each of the bounds has been transformed, we call the completion handler, passing in the detected bounds.

The next two methods encapsulate the bulk of the YOLO algorithm and the bulk of the code for this class. Let's start with the detectObjectsBounds method, making our way through it in small chunks.

This method will receive an MLMultiArray with the shape of *(125, 13, 13)*; this will hopefully look familiar to you (although reversed) where the *(13, 13)* is the size of our grid and the 125 encodes five blocks (coinciding with our five anchor boxes) each containing the bounding box, the probability of an object being present (or not), and the probability distribution across 20 classes. For your convenience, I have again added the diagram illustrating this structure:

To improve performance, we will access the MLMultiArray's raw data directly, rather than through the MLMultiArray subscript. Although having direct access gives us a performance boost, it does have a trade-off of requiring us to correctly calculate the index for each value. Let's define the constants that we will use when calculating these indexes, as well as obtaining access to the raw data buffer and some arrays to store the intermediate results; add the following code within your detectObjectsBounds method:

```
let gridStride = array.strides[0].intValue
let rowStride = array.strides[1].intValue
let colStride = array.strides[2].intValue

let arrayPointer =
UnsafeMutablePointer<Double>(OpaquePointer(array.dataPointer))

var objectsBounds = [ObjectBounds]()
var objectConfidences = [Float]()
```

As mentioned before, we start by defining constants of stride values for the grid, row, and column—each used to calculate the current value. These values are obtained through the strides property of MLMultiArray, which gives us the number of data elements in each dimension. In this case, this would be 125, 13, and 13 respectively. Next, we get a reference to the underlying buffer of the MLMultiArray and, finally, we create two arrays to store the bounds and associated confidence value.

Next, we want to iterate through the model's output and process each of the grid cells and their subsequent anchor boxes independently; we do this by using three nested loops and then calculating the relevant index. Let's do that by adding the following snippet:

```
for row in 0..<Int(gridSize.height) {
    for col in 0..<Int(gridSize.width) {
        for b in 0..<numberOfAnchorBoxes {
            let gridOffset = row * rowStride + col * colStride
            let anchorBoxOffset = b * (numberOfClasses +
numberOfAnchorBoxes)
            // TODO calculate the confidence of each class, ignoring if
under threshold
        }
    }
}
```

The important values here are `gridOffset` and `anchorBoxOffset`; `gridOffset` gives us the relevant offset for the specific grid cell (as the name implies), while `anchorBoxOffset` gives us the index of the associated anchor box. Now that we have these values, we can access each of the elements using the `[(anchorBoxOffset + INDEX_TO_VALUE) * gridStride + gridOffset` index, where `INDEX_TO_VALUE` is the relevant value within the anchor box vector we want to access, as illustrated in this diagram:

Now we know how to access each bounding box for each grid cell in our buffer, let's use it to find the most probable class and put in our first test of ignoring any prediction if it doesn't meet our threshold (defined as a method parameter with the default value of 0.3: `objectThreshold:Float = 0.3`). Add the following code, replacing the comment `// TODO calculate the confidence of each class, ignoring if under threshold`, as seen previously:

```
let confidence = sigmoid(x: Float(arrayPointer[(anchorBoxOffset + 4) *
gridStride + gridOffset]))

var classes = Array<Float>(repeating: 0.0, count: numberOfClasses)
for c in 0..<numberOfClasses{
    classes[c] = Float(arrayPointer[(anchorBoxOffset + 5 + c) * gridStride
+ gridOffset])
}
classes = softmax(z: classes)

let classIdx = classes.argmax
let classScore = classes[classIdx]
let classConfidence = classScore * confidence
```

```
if classConfidence < objectThreshold{
    continue
}
```

**// TODO obtain bounding box and transform to image dimensions**

In the preceding code snippet, we first obtain the probability of an object being present and store it in the constant `confidence`. Then, we populate an array with the probabilities of all the classes, before applying a softmax across them all. This will squash the values so that the accumulated value of them equals *1.0*, essentially providing us with our probability distribution across all classes.

We then find the class index with the largest probability and multiply it with our `confidence` constant, which gives us the class confidence we will threshold against and use during non-max suppression, ignoring the prediction if it doesn't meet our threshold.

Before continuing with the procedure, I want to take a quick detour to highlight and explain a couple of the methods used in the preceding snippet, namely the `softmax` method and `argmax` property of the classes array. Softmax is a logistic function that essentially squashes a vector of numbers so that all values in the vector add up to 1; it's an activation function commonly used when dealing with multi-class classification problems where the result is interpreted as the likelihood of each class, typically taking the class with the largest value as the predicted class (within a threshold). The implementation can be found in the `Math.swift` file, which makes use of the Accelerate framework to improve performance. The equation and implementation are shown here for completeness, but the details are omitted and left for you to explore:

$$softmax(y)_i = \frac{exp(y_i)}{\sum_j exp(y_j)}$$

Here, we use a slightly modified version of the equation shown previously; in practice, calculating the softmax values can be problematic if any of the values are very large. Applying an exponential operation on it will make it explode, and dividing any value by a huge value can cause arithmetic computation problems. To avoid this, it is often best practice to subtract the maximum value from all elements.

Because there are quite a few functions for this operation, let's build it up piece by piece, from the inside out. The following is the function that performs element-wise subtraction:

```
/**
 Subtract a scalar c from a vector x
 @param x Vector x.
 @param c Scalar c.
```

```
@return A vector containing the difference of the scalar and the vector
*/
public func sub(x: [Float], c: Float) -> [Float] {
    var result = (1...x.count).map{_ in c}
    catlas_saxpby(Int32(x.count), 1.0, x, 1, -1.0, &amp;result, 1)
    return result
}
```

Next, the function that computes the element-wise exponential for an array:

```
/**
 Perform an elementwise exponentiation on a vector
 @param x Vector x.
 @returns A vector containing x exponentiated elementwise.
 */
func exp(x: [Float]) -> [Float] {
    var results = [Float](repeating: 0.0, count: x.count)
    vvexpf(&amp;results, x, [Int32(x.count)])
    return results
}
```

Now, the function to perform summation on an array, as follows:

```
/**
 Compute the vector sum of a vector
 @param x Vector.
 @returns A single precision vector sum.
 */
public func sum(x: [Float]) -> Float {
    return cblas_sasum(Int32(x.count), x, 1)
}
```

This is the last function used by the softmax function! This will be responsible for performing element-wise division for a given scalar, as follows:

```
/**
 Divide a vector x by a scalar y
 @param x Vector x.
 @parame c Scalar c.
 @return A vector containing x dvidided elementwise by vector c.
 */
public func div(x: [Float], c: Float) -> [Float] {
    let divisor = [Float](repeating: c, count: x.count)
    var result = [Float](repeating: 0.0, count: x.count)
    vvdivf(&amp;result, x, divisor, [Int32(x.count)])
    return result
}
```

Finally, we the softmax function (using the max trick as described previously):

```
/**
 Softmax function
 @param z A vector z.
 @return A vector y = (e^z / sum(e^z))
 */
func softmax(z: [Float]) -> [Float] {
    let x = exp(x:sub(x:z, c: z.maxValue))
    return div(x:x, c: sum(x:x))
}
```

In addition to the preceding functions, it uses an extension property, maxValue, of Swift's
array class; this extension also includes the argmax property alluded to previously. So, we
will present both together in the following snippet, found in the Array+Extension.swift
file. Before presenting the code, just a reminder about the function of the argmax
property—its purpose is to return the index of the largest value within the array, a common
method available in the Python package NumPy:

```
extension Array where Element == Float{
    /**
     @return index of the largest element in the array
     **/
    var argmax : Int {
        get{
            precondition(self.count > 0)
            let maxValue = self.maxValue
            for i in 0..<self.count{
                if self[i] == maxValue{
                    return i
                }
            }
            return -1
        }
    }
    /**
     Find the maximum value in array
     */
    var maxValue : Float{
        get{
            let len = vDSP_Length(self.count)
            var max: Float = 0
            vDSP_maxv(self, 1, &max, len)
            return max
        }
    }
}
```

Let's now turn our attention back to the parsing of the model's output and extracting the detected objects and associated bounding boxes. Within the loop, we now have a prediction we are somewhat confident with, having passed our threshold filter. The next task is to extract and transform the bounding box of the predicted object. Add the following code, replacing the line `// TODO obtain bounding box and transform to image dimensions`:

```
let tx = CGFloat(arrayPointer[anchorBoxOffset * gridStride + gridOffset])
let ty = CGFloat(arrayPointer[(anchorBoxOffset + 1) * gridStride +
gridOffset])
let tw = CGFloat(arrayPointer[(anchorBoxOffset + 2) * gridStride +
gridOffset])
let th = CGFloat(arrayPointer[(anchorBoxOffset + 3) * gridStride +
gridOffset])

let cx = (sigmoid(x: tx) + CGFloat(col)) / gridSize.width
let cy = (sigmoid(x: ty) + CGFloat(row)) / gridSize.height
let w = CGFloat(anchors[2 * b + 0]) * exp(tw) / gridSize.width
let h = CGFloat(anchors[2 * b + 1]) * exp(th) / gridSize.height

// TODO create a ObjectBounds instance and store it in our array of
candidates
```

We start by getting the first four values of from the grid cell's anchor box segment; this returns the center position and size relative to the grid. The next block is responsible for transforming these values from the grid coordinate system to the image coordinate system. For the center position, we pass the returned value through a `sigmoid` function, keeping it between *0.0 - 1.0*, and offset based on the relevant column (or row). Finally we divide it by the grid size (13). Similarly with the dimensions, we first get the associated anchor box, multiplying it by the exponential of the predicted dimension and then dividing it by the grid size.

As we have done previously, I now present the implementations for the function `sigmoid` for reference, which can found in the `Math.swift` file. The equation is shown as follows:

$$sigmoid(y) = \frac{1}{exp(-y)}$$

```
/**
 A sigmoid function
 @param x Scalar
 @return 1 / (1 + exp(-x))
 */
public func sigmoid(x: CGFloat) -> CGFloat {
    return 1 / (1 + exp(-x))
}
```

The final chunk of code simply creates an instance `ObjectBounds`, passing in the transformed bounding box and the associated `DetectableObject` class (filtering on the class index). Add the following code, replacing the comment `// TODO create a ObjectBounds instance and store it in our array of candidates`:

```
guard let detectableObject = DetectableObject.objects.filter(
    {$0.classIndex == classIdx}).first else{
    continue
}

let objectBounds = ObjectBounds(
    object: detectableObject,
    origin: CGPoint(x: cx - w/2, y: cy - h/2),
    size: CGSize(width: w, height: h))

objectsBounds.append(objectBounds)
objectConfidences.append(classConfidence)
```

In addition to storing the `ObjectBounds`, we also store `confidence`, which will be used when we get to implementing non-max suppression.

This completes the functionality required within the nested loops; by the end of this process, we have an array populated with our candidate detected objects. Our next task will be to filter them. Near the end of the `detectObjectsBounds` method, add the following statement (outside any loops):

```
return self.filterDetectedObjects(
    objectsBounds: objectsBounds,
    objectsConfidence: objectConfidences)
```

Here, we are simply returning the results from the `filterDetectedObjects` method, which we will now turn our attention to. The method has been blocked out but is vacant of functionality, as follows:

```
func filterDetectedObjects(
    objectsBounds:[ObjectBounds],
    objectsConfidence:[Float],
    nmsThreshold : Float = 0.3) -> [ObjectBounds]?{
    // If there are no bounding boxes do nothing
    guard objectsBounds.count > 0 else{
        return []
    }
    // TODO implement Non-Max Supression
    return nil
}
```

Our job will be to implement the non-max suppression algorithm; just to recap, the algorithm can be described as follows:

1. Order the detected boxes from most confident to least
2. While valid boxes remain, do the following:
    1. Pick the box with the highest confidence value (the top of our ordered array)
    2. Iterate through all the remaining boxes, discarding any with an IoU value greater than a predefined threshold

Let's start by creating a clone of the confidence array passed into the method; we will use this to obtain an array of sorted indices, as well as to flag any boxes that are sufficiently overlapped by the preceding box. This is done by simply setting its confidence value to 0. Add the following statement to do just this, along with creating the sorted array of indices, replacing the comment `// TODO implement Non-Max Suppression`:

```
var detectionConfidence = objectsConfidence.map{
    (confidence) -> Float in
    return confidence
}

let sortedIndices = detectionConfidence.indices.sorted {
    detectionConfidence[$0] > detectionConfidence[$1]
}

var bestObjectsBounds = [ObjectBounds]()

// TODO iterate through each box
```

As mentioned previously, we start by cloning the confidence array, assigning it to the variable detectionConfidence. Then, we sort the indices in descending order and, finally, create an array to store the boxes we want to keep and return.

Next, we will create the loops that embody the bulk of the algorithm, including picking the next box with the highest confidence and storing it in our bestObjectsBounds array. Add the following code, replacing the comment // TODO iterate through each box:

```
for i in 0..<sortedIndices.count{
    let objectBounds = objectsBounds[sortedIndices[i]]
    guard detectionConfidence[sortedIndices[i]] > 0 else{
        continue
    }

    bestObjectsBounds.append(objectBounds)
    for j in (i+1)..<sortedIndices.count{
        guard detectionConfidence[sortedIndices[j]] > 0 else {
            continue
        }
        let otherObjectBounds = objectsBounds[sortedIndices[j]]
        // TODO calculate IoU and compare against our threshold
    }
}
```

Most of the code should be self-explanatory; what's worth noting is that within each loop, we test that the associated boxes confidence is greater than 0. As mentioned before, we use this to indicate that an object has been discarded due to being sufficiently overlapped by a box with higher confidence.

What remains is calculating the IoU between objectBounds and otherObjectBounds, and invaliding otherObjectBounds if it doesn't meet our IoU threshold, nmsThreshold. Replace the comment // TODO calculate IoU and compare against our threshold, with this:

```
if Float(objectBounds.bounds.computeIOU(
    other: otherObjectBounds.bounds)) > nmsThreshold{
    detectionConfidence[sortedIndices[j]] = 0.0
}
```

Here, we are using a CGRect extension method, computeIOU, to handle the calculation. Let's have a peek at this, implemented in the file CGRect+Extension.swift:

```
extension CGRect{
    ...
    var area : CGFloat{
```

```
        get{
            return self.size.width * self.size.height
        }
    }
    func computeIOU(other:CGRect) -> CGFloat{
        return self.intersection(other).area / self.union(other).area
    }
}
```

Thanks to the existing `intersection` and `union` of the `CGRect` structure, this method is nice and concise.

One final thing to do before we finish with the `YOLOFacade` class as well as the YOLO algorithm is to return the results. At the bottom of the `filterDetectedObjects` method, return the array `bestObjectsBounds`; with that done, we can now turn our attention to the last piece of functionality before implementing our intelligent search photo application.

This chapter does a good job highlighting that most of the effort integrating ML into your applications surrounds the **preprocessing** of the data before feeding it into the model and **interpreting** the output of the model. The **Vision framework** does a good job alleviating the preprocessing tasks, but there is still significant effort handling the output. Fortunately, no doubt because object detection is compelling for many applications, Apple has added a new observation type explicitly for object detection called **VNRecognizedObjectObservation**. Although we don't cover it here; I encourage you to review the official documentation `https://developer.apple.com/documentation/vision/vnrecognizedobjectobservation`.

The next piece of functionality is concerned with evaluating a cost on each of the returned detected objects with respect to the user's search criteria; by this, I mean filtering and sorting the photos so that the results are relevant to what the user sought. As a reminder, the search criteria is defined by an array of `ObjectBounds`, collectively describing the objects the user wants within a image, their relative positions, as well as the sizes relative to each other and to the image itself. The following figure shows how the user defines their search within our application:

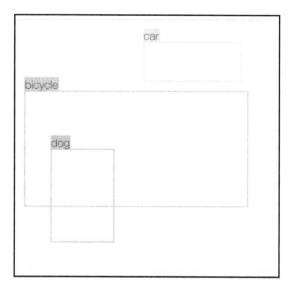

Here, we will implement only two of the four evaluations, but it should provide a sufficient base for you to implement the remaining two yourself.

The cost evaluation is performed within the PhotoSearcher class once the YOLOFacade has returned the detected objects for all of the images. This code resides in the asyncSearch method (within the PhotoSearcher.swift file), highlighted in the following code snippet:

```swift
public func asyncSearch(
    searchCriteria : [ObjectBounds]?,
    costThreshold : Float = 5){
    DispatchQueue.global(qos: .background).async {
        let photos = self.getPhotosFromPhotosLibrary()
        let unscoredSearchResults = self.detectObjects(photos: photos)
        var sortedSearchResults : [SearchResult]?
        if let unscoredSearchResults = unscoredSearchResults{
            sortedSearchResults = self.calculateCostForObjects(
                detectedObjects:unscoredSearchResults,
                searchCriteria: searchCriteria).filter({
                    (searchResult) -> Bool in
                    return searchResult.cost < costThreshold
                }).sorted(by: { (a, b) -> Bool in
                    return a.cost < b.cost
                })
        }
        DispatchQueue.main.sync {
            self.delegate?.onPhotoSearcherCompleted(
```

```
                        status: 1,
                        result: sortedSearchResults)
            }
        }
    }
```

`calculateCostForObjects` takes in the search criteria and results from the `YOLOFacade` and returns an array of `SearchResults` from the `detectObjects` with their cost properties set, after which they are filtered and sorted before being returned to the delegate.

Let's jump into the `calculateCostForObjects` method and discuss what we mean by cost; the code of the method `calculateCostForObjects` is as follows:

```
    private func calculateCostForObjects(
        detectedObjects:[SearchResult],
        searchCriteria:[ObjectBounds]?) -> [SearchResult]{
        guard let searchCriteria = searchCriteria else{
            return detectedObjects
        }
        var result = [SearchResult]()
        for searchResult in detectedObjects{
            let cost = self.costForObjectPresences(
                detectedObject: searchResult,
                searchCriteria: searchCriteria) +
                self.costForObjectRelativePositioning(
                    detectedObject: searchResult,
                    searchCriteria: searchCriteria) +
                self.costForObjectSizeRelativeToImageSize(
                    detectedObject: searchResult,
                    searchCriteria: searchCriteria) +
                self.costForObjectSizeRelativeToOtherObjects(
                    detectedObject: searchResult,
                    searchCriteria: searchCriteria)
            let searchResult = SearchResult(
                image: searchResult.image,
                detectedObjects:searchResult.detectedObjects,
                cost: cost)
            result.append(searchResult)
        }
        return result
    }
```

A `SearchResult` incurs a cost each time it differs from the user's search criteria, meaning that the results with the least cost are those that better match the search criteria. We perform cost evaluation on four different heuristics; each method will be responsible for adding the calculated cost to each result. Here we will only implement `costForObjectPresences` and `costForObjectRelativePositioning`, leaving the remaining two as an exercise for your.

Let's jump straight in and start implementing the `costForObjectPresences` method; at the moment, it's nothing more than a stub, as follows:

```
private func costForObjectPresences(
    detectedObject:SearchResult,
    searchCriteria:[ObjectBounds],
    weight:Float=2.0) -> Float{
    var cost : Float = 0.0
    // TODO implement cost function for object presence
    return cost * weight
}
```

Before writing the code, let's quickly discuss what we are evaluating for. Maybe, a better name for this function would have been `costForDifference` as we not only want to assess that the image has objects declared in the search criteria, but also we equally want to increase the cost for additional objects. That is, if the user searches for just two dogs but a photo has three dogs or two dogs and a cat, we want to increase the cost for these additional objects such that we are favoring the one that is most similar to the search criteria (just two dogs).

To calculate this, we simply need to find the absolute difference between the two arrays; to do this, we first create a dictionary of counts for all classes in both `detectedObject` and `searchCriteria`. The directory's key will be the object's label and the corresponding value will be the count of objects within the array. The following figure illustrates these arrays and formula used to calculate:

Let's now implement it; add the following code to do this, replacing the comment `// TODO implement cost function for object presence`:

```
var searchObjectCounts = searchCriteria.map {
    (detectedObject) -> String in
    return detectedObject.object.label
}.reduce([:]) {
    (counter:[String:Float], label) -> [String:Float] in
    var counter = counter
    counter[label] = counter[label]?.advanced(by: 1) ?? 1
    return counter
}

var detectedObjectCounts = detectedObject.detectedObjects.map {
    (detectedObject) -> String in
    return detectedObject.object.label
}.reduce([:]) {
    (counter:[String:Float], label) -> [String:Float] in
    var counter = counter
    counter[label] = counter[label]?.advanced(by: 1) ?? 1
    return counter
}

// TODO accumulate cost based on the difference
```

Now, with our count dictionaries created and populated, it's simply a matter of iterating over all available classes (using the items in `DetectableObject.objects`) and calculating the cost based on the absolute difference between the two. Add the following code, which does this, by replacing the comment `// TODO accumulate cost based on the difference`:

```
for detectableObject in DetectableObject.objects{
    let label = detectableObject.label
    let searchCount = searchObjectCounts[label] ?? 0
    let detectedCount = detectedObjectCounts[label] ?? 0
    cost += abs(searchCount - detectedCount)
}
```

The result of this is a cost that is larger for images that differ the most from the search criteria; the last thing worth noting is that the cost is multiplied by a weight before being returned (function parameter). Each evaluation method has a weight parameter which allows for easy tuning (during either design time or runtime) of the search, giving preference to one evaluation over another.

The next, and last, cost evaluation function we are going to implement is the method `costForObjectRelativePositioning`; the stub of this method is as follows:

```
private func costForObjectRelativePositioning(
    detectedObject:SearchResult,
    searchCriteria:[ObjectBounds],
    weight:Float=1.5) -> Float{
    var cost : Float = 0.0
    // TODO implement cost function for relative positioning
    return cost * weight
}
```

As we did before, let's quickly discuss the motivation behind this evaluation and how we plan to implement it. This method is used to favor items that match the composition of the user's search; this allows our search to surface images that closely resemble the arrangement the user is searching for. For example, the user may be looking for an image or images where two dogs are sitting next to each other, side by side, or they may want an image with two dogs sitting next to each other on a sofa.

There are no doubt many approaches you could take for this, and it's perhaps a use case for a neural network, but the approach taken here is the simplest I could think of to avoid having to explain complicated code; the algorithm used is described as follows:

1. For each object (a) of type `ObjectBounds` within `searchCriteria`
    1. Find the closest object (b) in proximity (still within `searchCriteria`)
    2. Create a normalized direction vector from a to b
    3. Find the matching object a' (the same class) within the `detectedObject`
        1. Search all other objects (b') in `detectedObject` that have the same class as b
            1. Create a normalized direction vector from a' to b'
            2. Calculate the dot product between the two vectors (angle); in this case, our vectors are a->b and a'->b'
    4. Using a' and b', which have the lowest dot product, increment the cost by how much the angle differs from the search criteria and images

Essentially, what we are doing is finding two matching pairs from the `searchCriteria` and `detectedObject` arrays, and calculating the cost based on the difference in the angles.

A direction vector of two objects is calculated by subtracting one's position from the other and then normalizing it. The dot product can then be used on two (normalized) vectors to find their angle, where *1.0* would be returned if the vectors are pointing in the same direction, *0.0* if they are perpendicular, and *-1.0* if pointing in opposite directions.

The following figure presents part of this process; we first find an object pair in close proximity within the search criteria. After calculating the dot product, we iterate over all the objects detected in the image and find the most suitable pair; "suitable" here means the same object type and the closest angle to the search criteria within the possible matching pairs:

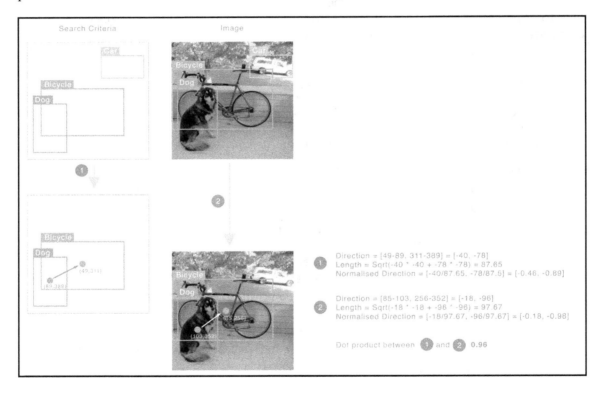

Once comparable pairs are found, we calculate the cost based on the difference in angle, as we will soon see. But we are getting a little ahead of ourselves; we first need a way to find the closest object. Let's do this using a nested function we can call within our costForObjectRelativePositioning method. Add the following code, replacing the comment // TODO implement cost function for relative positioning:

```
func indexOfClosestObject(
    objects:[ObjectBounds],
    forObjectAtIndex i:Int) -> Int{
    let searchACenter = objects[i].bounds.center
    var closestDistance = Float.greatestFiniteMagnitude
    var closestObjectIndex : Int = -1
    for j in 0..<objects.count{
        guard i != j else{
            continue
        }
        let searchBCenter = objects[j].bounds.center
        let distance = Float(searchACenter.distance(other: searchBCenter))
        if distance < closestDistance{
            closestObjectIndex = j
            closestDistance = distance
        }
    }
    return closestObjectIndex
}

// TODO Iterate over all items in the searchCriteria array
```

The preceding function will be used to find the closest object, given an array of ObjectBounds and index of the object we are searching against. From there, it simply iterates over all of the items in the array, returning the one that is, well, closest.

With our helper function now implemented, let's create the loop that will inspect the search item pair from the user's search criteria. Append the following code to the costForObjectRelativePositioning method, replacing the comment // TODO Iterate over all items in the searchCriteria array:

```
for si in 0..<searchCriteria.count{
    let closestObjectIndex = indexOfClosestObject(
        objects: searchCriteria,
        forObjectAtIndex: si)
    if closestObjectIndex < 0{
        continue
    }
    // Get object types
    let searchAClassIndex = searchCriteria[si].object.classIndex
```

```
        let searchBClassIndex =
searchCriteria[closestObjectIndex].object.classIndex
        // Get centers of objects
        let searchACenter = searchCriteria[si].bounds.center
        let searchBCenter = searchCriteria[closestObjectIndex].bounds.center
        // Calcualte the normalised vector from A -> B
        let searchDirection = (searchACenter - searchBCenter).normalised
        // TODO Find matching pair
}
```

We start by searching for the closest object to the current object, jumping to the next item if nothing is found. Once we have our search pair, we proceed to calculate the direction by subtracting the first bound's center from its pair and normalizing the result.

We now need to find all objects of both classes, whereby we will proceed to evaluate each of them to find the best match. Before that, let's get all the classes with the index of searchAClassIndex and searchBClassIndex; add the following code, replacing the comment // TODO Find matching pair:

```
// Find comparable objects in detected objects
let detectedA = detectedObject.detectedObjects.filter {
    (objectBounds) -> Bool in
    objectBounds.object.classIndex == searchAClassIndex
}

let detectedB = detectedObject.detectedObjects.filter {
    (objectBounds) -> Bool in
    objectBounds.object.classIndex == searchBClassIndex
}

// Check that we have matching pairs
guard detectedA.count > 0, detectedB.count > 0 else{
    continue
}

// TODO Search for the most suitable pair
```

If we are unable to find a matching pair, we continue to the next item, knowing that a cost has already been added for the mismatch in objects of both arrays. Next, we iterate over all pairs. For each pair, we calculate the normalized direction vector and then the dot product against our `searchDirection` vector, taking the one that has the closest dot product (closest in angle). Add the following code in place of the comment `// TODO Search for the most suitable pair`:

```
var closestDotProduct : Float = Float.greatestFiniteMagnitude
for i in 0..<detectedA.count{
    for j in 0..<detectedB.count{
        if detectedA[i] == detectedB[j]{
            continue
        }
        let detectedDirection = (detectedA[i].bounds.center -
detectedB[j].bounds.center).normalised
        let dotProduct = Float(searchDirection.dot(other:
detectedDirection))
        if closestDotProduct > 10 ||
            (dotProduct < closestDotProduct &amp;&amp;
                dotProduct >= 0) {
            closestDotProduct = dotProduct
        }
    }
}
```

**// TODO Add cost**

Similar to what we did with our search pair, we calculate the direction vector by subtracting the pair's center positions and then normalize the result. Then, with the two vectors `searchDirection` and `detectedDirection`, we calculate the dot product, keeping reference to it if it is the first or lowest dot product so far.

There is just one last thing we need to do for this method, and this project. But before doing so, let's take a little detour and look at a couple of extensions made to `CGPoint`, specifically the `dot` and `normalize` used previously. You can find these extensions in the `CGPoint+Extension.swift` file. As I did previously, I will list the code for reference rather than describing the details, most of which we have already touched upon:

```
extension CGPoint{
    var length : CGFloat{
        get{
            return sqrt(
                self.x * self.x + self.y * self.y
            )
        }
```

```
    }
    var normalised : CGPoint{
        get{
            return CGPoint(
                x: self.x/self.length,
                y: self.y/self.length)
        }
    }
    func distance(other:CGPoint) -> CGFloat{
        let dx = (self.x - other.x)
        let dy = (self.y - other.y)
        return sqrt(dx*dx + dy*dy)
    }
    func dot(other:CGPoint) -> CGFloat{
        return (self.x * other.x) + (self.y * other.y)
    }
    static func -(left: CGPoint, right: CGPoint) -> CGPoint{
        return CGPoint(
            x: left.x - right.x,
            y: left.y - right.y)
    }
}
```

Now, back to the `costForObjectRelativePositioning` method to finish our method and project. Our final task is to add to the cost; this is done simply by subtracting the stored `closestDotProduct` from `1.0` (remembering that we want to increase the cost for larger differences where the dot product of two normalized vectors pointing in the same direction is `1.0`) and ensuring that the value is positive by wrapping it in an `abs` function. Let's do that now; add the following code, replacing the comment `// TODO add cost`:

```
cost += abs((1.0-closestDotProduct))
```

With that done, we have finished this method, and the coding for this chapter. Well done! It's time to test it out; build and run the project to see your hard work in action. Shown here are a few searches and their results:

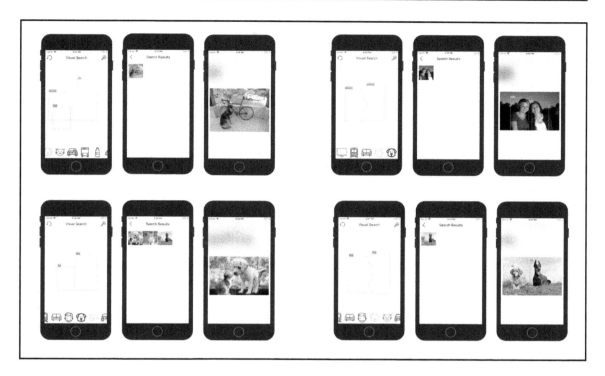

Although the YOLO algorithm is performant and feasible for near real-time use, our example is far from optimized and unlikely to perform well on large sets of photos. With the release of Core ML 2, Apple provides one avenue we can use to make our process more efficient. This will be the topic of the next section before wrapping up.

# Optimizing with batches

At the moment, our process involves iterating over each photo and performing inference on each one individually. With the release of Core ML 2, we now have the option to create a batch and pass this batch to our model for inference. As with efficiencies gained with economies of scale, here, we also gain significant improvements; so let's walk through adapting our project to process our photos in a single batch rather than individually.

Let's work our way up the stack, starting in our YOLOFacade class and moving up to the PhotoSearcher. For this we will be using our model directly rather than proxying through Vision, so our first task is to replace the model property of our YOLOFacade class with the following declaration:

```
let model = tinyyolo_voc2007().model
```

Now, let's rewrite the detectObjects method to handle an array of photos rather than a single instance; because this is where most of the changes reside, we will start from scratch. So, go ahead and delete the method from your YOLOFacade class and replace it with the following stub:

```
func detectObjects(photos:[UIImage], completionHandler:(_
result:[[ObjectBounds]]?) -> Void){
    // TODO batch items (array of MLFeatureProvider)

    // TODO Wrap our items in an instance of MLArrayBatchProvider

    // TODO Perform inference on the batch
    // TODO (As we did before) Process the outputs of the model

    // TODO Return results via the callback handler
}
```

I have made the changes to the signature of the method bold and listed our remaining tasks. The first is to create an array of MLFeatureProvider. If you recall from Chapter 3, *Recognizing Objects in the World*, when we import a Core ML model into Xcode, it generates interfaces for the model, its input and output. The input and output are subclasses of MLFeatureProvider, so here we want to create an array of tinyyolo_voc2007Input, which can be instantiated with instances of CVPixelBuffer.

To create this, we will transform the array of photos passed into the method, including the required preprocessing steps (resizing to 416 x 416). Replace the comment // TODO batch items (array of MLFeatureProvider) with the following code:

```
let X = photos.map({ (photo) -> tinyyolo_voc2007Input in
    guard let ciImage = CIImage(image: photo) else{
        fatalError("\(#function) Failed to create CIImage from UIImage")
    }
    let cropSize = CGSize(
        width:min(ciImage.extent.width, ciImage.extent.height),
        height:min(ciImage.extent.width, ciImage.extent.height))
    let targetSize = CGSize(width:416, height:416)
    guard let pixelBuffer = ciImage
        .centerCrop(size:cropSize)?
```

```
        .resize(size:targetSize)
        .toPixelBuffer() else{
        fatalError("\(#function) Failed to create CIImage from UIImage")
    }
    return tinyyolo_voc2007Input(image:pixelBuffer)
})
```

```
// TODO Wrap our items in an instance of MLArrayBatchProvider
```

```
// TODO Perform inference on the batch
// TODO (As we did before) Process the outputs of the model
```

```
// TODO Return results via the callback handler
```

 For reasons of simplicity and readability, we are omitting any kind of error handling; obviously, in production you want to handle exceptions appropriately.

To perform inference on a batch, we need to have our input conform to the `MLBatchProvider` interface. Fortunately, Core ML provides a concrete implementation that conveniently wraps array. Let's do this now; replace the comment `// TODO Wrap our items in an instance of MLArrayBatchProvider` with the following code:

```
let batch = MLArrayBatchProvider(array:X)
```

```
// TODO Perform inference on the batch
// TODO (As we did before) Process the outputs of the model
```

```
// TODO Return results via the callback handler
```

To perform inference, it's simply a matter of calling the `predictions` method on our model; as usual, replace the comment `// TODO Perform inference on the batch` with the following code:

```
guard let batchResults = try? self.model.predictions(
    from: batch,
    options: MLPredictionOptions()) else{
        completionHandler(nil)
        return
}
```

```
// TODO (As we did before) Process the outputs of the model
```

```
// TODO Return results via the callback handler
```

What we get back is an instance of MLBatchProvider (if successful); this is more or less a collection of results for each of our samples (inputs). We can access an specific result via the batch providers features(at: Int) method, which returns an instance of MLFeatureProvider (in our case, an in tinyyolo_voc2007Output).

Here we simply process each result as we had done before to obtain the most salient; replace the comment // TODO (As we did before) Process the outputs of the model with the following code:

```
var results = [[ObjectBounds]]()

for i in 0..<batchResults.count{
    var iResults = [ObjectBounds]()
    if let features = batchResults.features(at: i)
        as? tinyyolo_voc2007Output{
        if let observationDetectObjects = self.detectObjectsBounds(
            array: features.output){
            for detectedObject in observationDetectObjects.map(
                {$0.transformFromCenteredCropping(
                    from: photos[i].size,
                    to: self.targetSize)}){
                iResults.append(detectedObject)
            }
        }
    }
    results.append(iResults)
}

// TODO Return results via the callback handler
```

The only difference here, than before, is that we are iterating over a batch of outputs rather than a single one. The last thing we need to do is call the handler; replace the comment // TODO Return results via the callback handler with the following statement:

```
completionHandler(results)
```

This now completes the changes required to our YOLOFacade class; let's jump into the PhotoSearcher and make the necessary, and final, changes.

The big change here is that we now need to pass in all photos at once rather than passing each one individually. Locate the `detectObjects` method and replace its body with the following code:

```
var results = [SearchResult]()

yolo.detectObjects(photos: photos) { (photosObjectBounds) in
    if let photosObjectBounds = photosObjectBounds,
        photos.count == photosObjectBounds.count{
        for i in 0..<photos.count{
            results.append(SearchResult(
                image: photos[i],
                detectedObjects: photosObjectBounds[i],
                cost: 0.0))
        }
    }
}

return results
```

Same code but organised a little differently to handle batch inputs and output from and to the `YOLOFacade` class. Now is a good time to build, deploy and run the application; paying particular attention to efficiencies gained from adapting batch inference. When you return; we will conclude this chapter with a quick summary.

# Summary

In this chapter, we introduced the concept of object detection, comparing it with object recognition and object localization. While the other two are limited to a single dominant object, object detection allows multi-object classification, including predicting their bounding boxes. We then spent some time introducing one particular algorithm, YOLO, before getting acquainted with Apple's Core ML Tools Python package, walking through converting a trained Keras model to Core ML. Once we had the model in hand, we moved on to implementing YOLO in Swift with the goal of creating an intelligent search application.

Despite this being a fairly lengthy chapter, I hope you found it valuable and gained deeper intuition into how deep neural networks learn and understand images and how they can be applied in novel ways to create new experiences. It's helpful to remind ourselves that using the same architecture, we can create devise new applications by simply swapping the data we train it on. For example, you could train this model on a dataset of hands and their corresponding bounding boxes to create a more immersive **augmented reality (AR)** experience by allowing the user to interact with digital content through touch.

But for now, let's continue our journey of understanding Core ML and explore how else we can apply it. In the next chapter, you will see how the popular Prisma creates those stunning photos with style transform.

# 6
# Creating Art with Style Transfer

In this chapter, we will explore what was one of the most popular mainstream applications of deep learning in 2017—style transfer. We begin by introducing the concepts of style transfer and then its faster alternative, appropriately named fast neural style transfer. Similar to other chapters, we will provide the intuition behind the models (rather than granular details) and, in doing so, you will gain a deeper understanding and appreciation for the potential of deep learning algorithms. Unlike previous chapters, this chapter will focus more on the steps involved in getting the model working on iOS rather than building up the application, in order to keep it concise.

By the end of this chapter you will have achieved the following:

- Gained an intuitive understanding of how style transfer works
- Gained hands-on experience of working with the Core ML Tools Python package and custom layers to get Keras models working in Core ML

Let's get started by introducing style transfer and building our understanding of how it works.

# Transferring style from one image to another

Imagine being able to have one of the greatest painters in history, such as Vincent van Gogh or Pablo Picasso, recreate a photo of your liking using their own unique style. In a nutshell, this is what style transfer allows us to do. Quite simply, it's the process of generating a photo using the style of one with the content of another, as shown here:

In this section, we will describe, albeit at a high level, how this works and then move on to an alternative that allows us to perform a similar process in significantly less time.

 I encourage you to read the original paper, *A Neural Algorithm of Artistic Style*, by Leon A. Gatys, Alexander S. Ecker, and Matthias Bethge, for a more comprehensive overview. This paper is available at `https://arxiv.org/abs/1508.06576`.

At this stage, we have learned that neural networks learn by iteratively reducing a loss, calculated using some specified cost function that is to indicate how well the neural network did with respect to the expected output. The difference between the **predicted output** and **expected output** is then used to adjust the model's weights, through a process known as **backpropagation**, such to minimize this loss.

 The preceding description (intentionally) skips the details of this process as our goal here is to provide an intuitive understanding, rather than the granular details. I recommend reading Andrew Trask's *Grokking Deep Learning* for a gentle introduction to the underlying details of neural networks.

Unlike the classification models we have worked with thus far, where the output is a probability distribution across some set of labels, we are instead interested in the model's generative abilities. That is, instead of adjusting the model's weights, we want to adjust the generated image's pixel values so as to reduce some defined cost function.

So if we were to define a cost function that could measure the loss between the generated image and content image, and another to measure the loss between the generated image and style image, we could then simply combine them. Thus we obtain the overall loss and use this to adjust the generated image pixels values, to create something that has the targets content in the style of our targets style as illustrated in the following image:

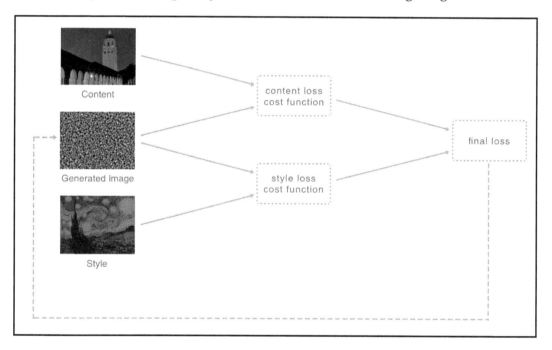

At this point, we have a general idea of the required process; what is left is building some intuition behind these cost functions. That is, how do you determine how well your generated image is, with respect to some content of the content image and with respect to a style of the style image? For this, we will backtrack a little and review what other layers of a CNN learn by inspecting each of their activations.

The details and images demonstrating what **convolutional neural networks** (**CNNs**) learn have been taken from the paper *Visualizing and Understanding Convolutional Networks*, by Matthew D. Zeiler and Rob Fergus, which is available at https://arxiv.org/abs/1311.2901.

A typical architecture of a CNN consists of a series of convolutional and pooling layers, which is then fed into a fully connected network (for case of classification), as illustrated in this image:

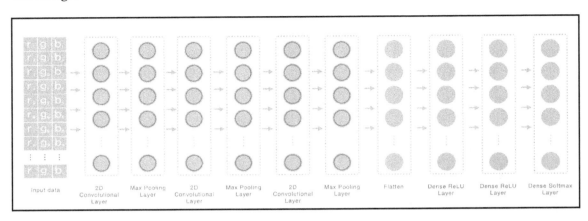

This flat representation misses an important property of a CNN, which is how, after each subsequent pair of convolution and pooling layers, the input's width and height reduce in size. The consequence of this is that the receptive field increases depth into the network; that is, deeper layers have a larger receptive field and thus capture higher level features than shallower layers.

To better illustrate what each layer learns, we will reference the paper *Visualizing and Understanding Convolutional Networks*, by Matthew D. Zeiler and Rob Fergus. In their paper (previously referenced), they pass through images from their training set to identify the image patches that maximize each layer's activations; by visualizing these patches, we get a sense of what each neuron (hidden unit) at each of the layers learns. Here is an screenshot showing some of these patches across a CNN:

Source: Visualizing and Understanding Convolutional Networks; Matthew D Zeiler, Rob Fergus

What you can see in the preceding figure are nine image patches that maximize an individual hidden unit at each of the layers of this particular network. What has been omitted from the preceding figure is the variance in size; that is, the deeper you go, the larger the image patch will be.

What is hopefully obvious from the preceding image is that the shallower layers extract simple features. For example, we can see that a single hidden unit at **Layer 1** is activated by a diagonal edge and a single hidden unit at **Layer 2** is activated with a vertically striped patch. While the deeper layers extract higher-level features, or more complex features, again, in the preceding figure, we can see that a single hidden unit at **Layer 4** is activated by patches of dog faces.

We return to our task of defining a cost function for content and style, starting with the cost function for content. Given a content image and a generated image, we want to measure how close we are so as to minimize this difference, so that we retain the content. We can achieve this by selecting one of the deeper layers from our CNN, which we saw before have a large receptive field, and capture complex features. We pass through both the content images and the generated image and measure the distance between outputted activations (on this layer). This will hopefully seem logical given that the deeper layers learn complex features, such as a dog's face or a car, but decouple them from lower-level features such as edges, color, and textures. The following figure depicts this process:

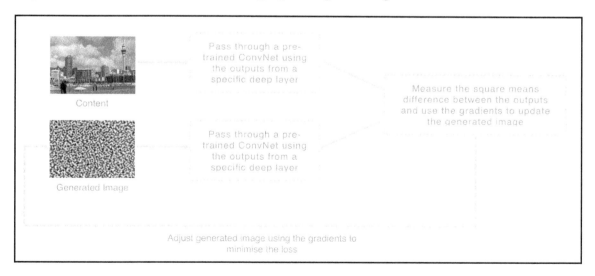

This takes care of our cost function for the content which can be easily tested by running a network that implements this. If implemented correctly, it should result in a generated image that looks similar to that of the input (content image). Let's now turn our attention to measuring style.

We saw in the preceding figure that shallower layers of a network learn simple features such as edges, textures, and color combinations. This gives us a clue as to which layers would be useful when trying to measure style, but we still need a way of extracting and measuring style. However, before we start, what exactly is style?

A quick search on `http://www.dictionary.com/` reveals style being defined as *a distinctive appearance, typically determined by the principles according to which something is designed*. Let's take Katsushika Hokusai's *The Great Wave off Kanagawa* as an example:

*The Great Wave off Kanagawa* is an output of a process known as **woodblock printing**; this is where an artist's sketch is broken down into layers (carved wooden blocks), with each layer (usually one for each color) used to reproduce the art piece. It's similar to a manual printing press; this process produces a distinctive flat and simplistic style. Another dominate style (and possibly side-effect) that can be seen in the preceding image is that a limited range of colors is being used; for example, the water consists of no more than four colors.

The way we can capture style is as defined in the paper *A Neural Algorithm of Artistic Style*, by L. Gatys, A. Ecker, and M. Bethge. This way is to use a style matrix (also known as **gram matrix**) to find the correlation between the activations across different channels for a given layer. It is these correlations that define the style and something we can then use to measure the difference between our style image and generated image to influence the style of the generated image.

To make this more concrete, borrowing from an example used by Andrew Ng in his Coursera course on deep learning, let's take **Layer 2** from the earlier example. What the style matrix calculates is the correlation across all channels for a given layer. If we use the following illustration, showing nine activations from two channels, we can see that a correlation exists between vertical textures from the first channel with orange patches from the second channel. That is, when we see a vertical texture in the first channel, we would expect the image patches that maximize the second channel's activations to have an orange tint:

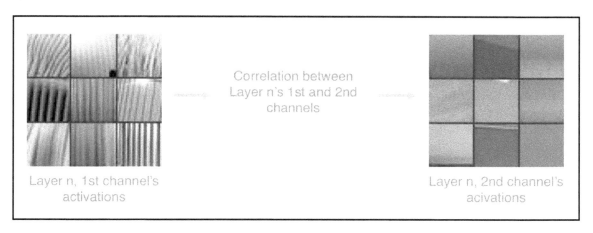

Correlation between Layer n's 1st and 2nd channels

Layer n, 1st channel's activations

Layer n, 2nd channel's acivations

This style matrix is calculated for both the style image and generated image, with our optimization forcing our generated image to adopt these correlations. With both style matrices calculated, we can then calculate the loss by simply finding the sum of the square difference between the two matrices. The following figure illustrates this process, as we have previously done when describing the content loss function:

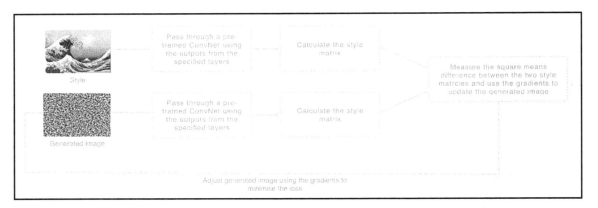

With that, we have now concluded our introduction to style transfer, and hopefully given you some intuition of how we can use the network's perceptual understanding of images to extract content and style. This approach works well, but there is one drawback that we will address in the next section.

# A faster way to transfer style

As you may have inferred from the title of this section, the big drawback of the approach introduced in the previous section is that the process requires iterative optimization, as summarized in the following figure:

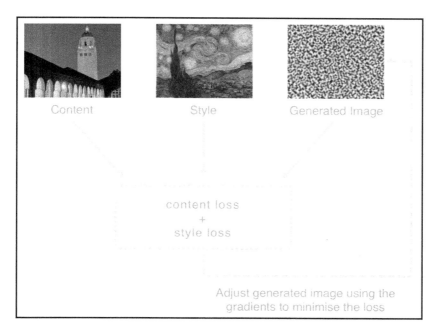

This optimization is akin to training, in terms of performing many iterations to minimize the loss. Therefore, it typically takes a considerable amount of time, even when using a modest computer. As implied at the start of this book, we ideally want to restrict ourselves to performing inference on the edge as it requires significantly less compute power and can be run in near-real time, allowing us to adopt it for interactive applications. Luckily for us, in their paper *Perceptual Losses for Real-Time Style Transfer and Super-Resolution*, J. Johnson, A. Alahi, and L. Fei-Fei describe a technique that decouples training (optimization) and inference for style transfer.

Previously, we described a network that took as its input a generated image, a style image, and a content image. The network minimized loss by iteratively adjusting the generated image using the loss functions for content and style; this provided the flexibility of allowing us to plug in any style and content image, but came at the cost of being computationally expensive, that is, slow. What if we sacrifice this flexibility for performance by restraining ourselves to a single style and, instead of performing the optimization to generate the image, train a CNN? The CNN would learn the style and, once trained, could generate a stylized image given a content image with a single pass through the network (inference). This is, in essence, what the paper *Perceptual Losses for Real-Time Style Transfer and Super-Resolution*, describes, and it is the network we will use in this chapter.

To better elucidate the difference between the previous approach and this approach, take a moment to review and compare the preceding figure with the following one:

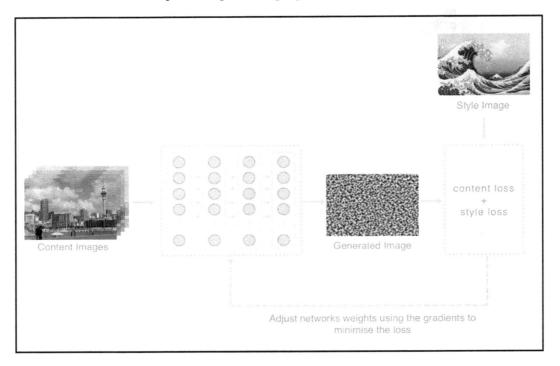

Unlike the previous approach, where we optimized for a given set of content, style, and generated images and adjusted the generated image to minimize loss, we now feed a CNN with a set of content images and have the network generate the image. We then perform the same loss functions as described earlier for a single style. But, instead of adjusting the generated image, we adjust the weights of the networks using the gradients from the loss function. And we repeat until we have sufficiently minimized the mean loss across all of our content images.

Now, with our model trained, we can have our network stylize an image with a single pass, as shown here:

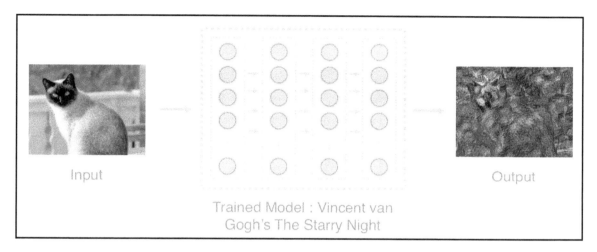

Over the last two sections we have described, at a high-level, how these networks work. Now, it's time to build an application that takes advantage of all this. In the next section, we will quickly walk through converting the trained Keras model to Core ML before moving on to the main topic of this chapter—implementing custom layers for Core ML.

# Converting a Keras model to Core ML

Similar to what we did in the previous chapter, in this section we will be converting a trained Keras model into a Core ML model using the **Core ML Tools** package. To avoid any complications of setting up the environment on your local or remote machine, we will leverage the free Jupyter cloud service provided by Microsoft. Head over to `https://notebooks.azure.com` and log in (or register if you haven't already).

Once logged in, click on the **Libraries** menu link from the navigation bar, which will take you to a page containing a list of all of your libraries, similar to what is shown in the following screenshot:

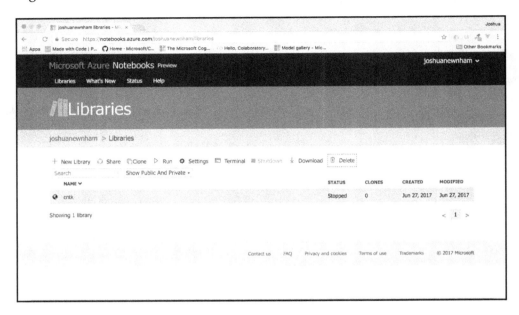

Next, click on the **+ New Library** link to bring up the **Create New Library** dialog:

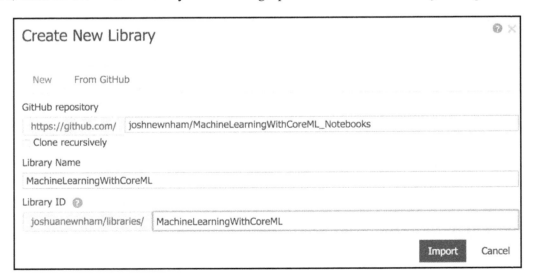

Then, click on the **From GitHub** tab and enter `https://github.com/packtpublishing/machine-learning-with-core-ml` in the **GitHub repository** field. After that, give your library a meaningful name and click on the **Import** button to begin the process of cloning the repository and creating the library.

Once the library has been created, you will be redirected to the root. From there, click on the `Chapter6/Notebooks` folder to open up the relevant folder for this chapter, and finally click on the Notebook `FastNeuralStyleTransfer_Keras2CoreML.ipynb`. Here is a screenshot of what you should see after clicking on the `Chapter6` folder:

It's beyond the scope of this book to walk you through the details of the Notebook, including the details of the network and training. For the curious reader, I have included the original Notebooks for each of the models used throughout this book in the accompanying `chapters` folder within the `training` folder.

With our Notebook now loaded, it's time to walk through each of the cells to create our Core ML model; all of the required code exists and all that remains is executing each of the cells sequentially. To execute a cell, you can either use the shortcut keys *Shift + Enter* or click on the **Run** button in the toolbar (which will run the currently selected cell), as shown in the following screenshot:

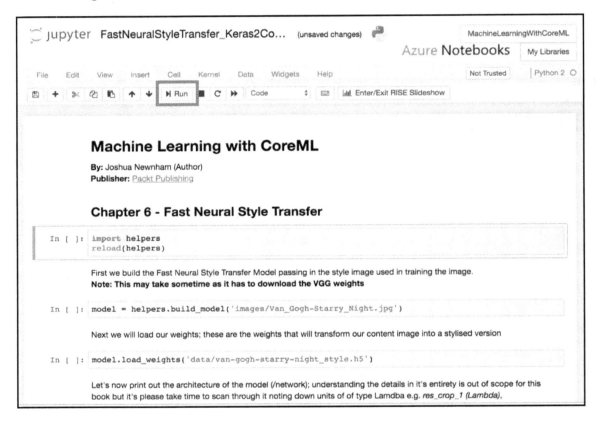

I will provide a brief explanation of what each cell does. Ensure that you execute each cell as we walk through them so that we all end up with the converted model, which we can then download and import into our iOS project:

```
import helpers
reload(helpers)
```

We first import a module that includes the a function that will create and return the Keras model we want to convert:

```
model = helpers.build_model('images/Van_Gogh-Starry_Night.jpg')
```

We then use our `helpers` method `build_model` to create the model, passing in the style image that the model was trained on. Remember that we are using a feedforward network that has been trained on a single style; while the network can be reused for different styles, the weights are unique per style.

 Calling `build_model` will take some time to return; this is because the model uses a trained model (VGG16) that is downloaded before returning.

Talking of weights (previously trained model), let's now load them by running the following cell:

```
model.load_weights('data/van-gogh-starry-night_style.h5')
```

Similar to the aforementioned code, we are passing in the weights for the model that was trained on Vincent van Gogh's *Starry Night* painting for its style.

Next, let's inspect the architecture of the model by calling the `summary` method on the model itself:

```
model.summary()
```

Calling this will return, as the name suggests, a summary of our model. Here is an extract of the summary produced:

```
Layer (type) Output Shape Param # Connected to
=================================================================
input_1 (InputLayer) (None, 320, 320, 3) 0

zero_padding2d_1 (ZeroPadding2D) (None, 400, 400, 3) 0 input_1[0][0]

conv2d_1 (Conv2D) (None, 400, 400, 64) 15616 zero_padding2d_1[0][0]

batch_normalization_1 (BatchNorm (None, 400, 400, 64) 256 conv2d_1[0][0]

activation_1 (Activation) (None, 400, 400, 64) 0
batch_normalization_1[0][0]

...
...

res_crop_1 (Lambda) (None, 92, 92, 64) 0 add_1[0][0]

...
```

. . .

```
rescale_output (Lambda)  (None, 320, 320, 3)  0 conv2d_16[0][0]
===================================================================
Total params: 552,003
Trainable params: 550,083
Non-trainable params: 1,920
```

As previously mentioned, it's out of scope to go into the details of Python, Keras, or the specifics of this model. Instead I present an extract here to highlight the custom layers embedded in the model (the bold lines). In the context of Core ML Tools, custom layers are layers that have not been defined and, therefore, are not handled during the conversion process, so it is our responsibility to handle these. You can think of the conversion process as a process of mapping layers from a machine learning framework, such as Keras, to Core ML. If no mapping exists, then it is left up to us to fill in the details, as illustrated in the following figure:

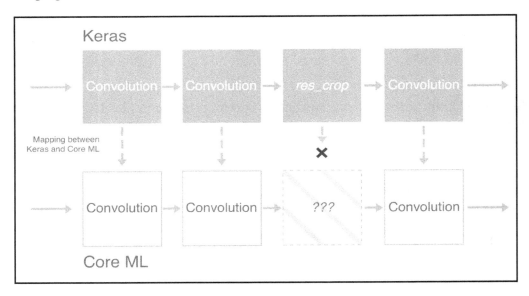

The two custom layers shown previously are both Lambda layers; a Lambda layer is a special Keras class that conveniently allows writing quick-and-dirty layers using just a function or a Lambda expression (similar to a closure in Swift). Lambda is useful for layers that don't have a state and are commonly seen in Keras models for doing basic computations. Here, we see two being used, `res_crop` and `rescale_output`.

`res_crop` is part of the ResNet block that crops (as implied by the name) the output; the function is simple enough, with its definition shown in the following code:

```
def res_crop(x):
    return x[:, 2:-2, 2:-2]
```

 I refer you to the paper *Deep Residual Learning for Image Recognition*, by K. He, X. Zhang, S. Ren, and J. Sun to learn more about ResNet and residual blocks, available here at `https://arxiv.org/pdf/1512.03385.pdf`.

Essentially, all that this is doing is cropping the outputs with a padding of 2 for the width and height axis. We can further interrogate this by inspecting the input and output shapes of this layer, by running the following cell:

```
res_crop_3_layer = [layer for layer in model.layers if layer.name ==
'res_crop_3'][0]

print("res_crop_3_layer input shape {}, output shape {}".format(
    res_crop_3_layer.input_shape, res_crop_3_layer.output_shape))
```

This cell prints the input and output shape of the layer `res_crop_3_layer`; the layer receives a tensor of shape `(None, 88, 88, 64)` and outputs a tensor of shape `(None, 84, 84, 64)`. Here the tuple is broken down into: (batch size, height, width, channels). The batch size is set to `None`, indicating that it is dynamically set during training.

Our next Lambda layer is `rescale_output`; this is used at the end of the network to rescale the outputs from the Convolution 2D layer, which passes its data through a tanh activation. This forces our data to be constrained between -1.0 and 1.0, where as we want it in a range of 0 and 255 so that we can convert it into an image. As we did before, let's look at its definition to get a better idea of what this layer does, as shown in the following code:

```
def rescale_output(x):
    return (x+1)*127.5
```

This method performs an element-wise operation that maps the values -1.0 and 1.0 to 0 and 255. Similar to the preceding method (`res_crop`), we can inspect the input and output shapes of this layer by running the following cell:

```
rescale_output_layer = [layer for layer in model.layers if layer.name ==
'rescale_output'][0]

print("rescale_output_layer input shape {}, output shape {}".format(
    rescale_output_layer.input_shape,
    rescale_output_layer.output_shape))
```

Once run, this cell prints the layer's input shape of (None, 320, 320, 3) and output shape of (None, 320, 320, 3). This tells us that this layer doesn't change the shape of the tensor, as well as shows us the output dimensions of our image as 320 x 320 with three channels (RGB).

We have now reviewed the custom layers and seen what they actually do; the next step is to perform the actual conversion. Run the following cell to ensure that the environment has the Core ML Tools modules installed:

```
!pip install coremltools
```

Once installed, we can load the required modules by running the following cell:

```
import coremltools
from coremltools.proto import NeuralNetwork_pb2, FeatureTypes_pb2
```

In this instance, I have prewarned you that our model contains custom layers; in some (if not most) instances, you may discover this only when the conversion process fails. Let's see exactly what this looks like by running the following cell and examining its output:

```
coreml_model = coremltools.converters.keras.convert(
    model,
    input_names=['image'],
    image_input_names=['image'],
    output_names="output")
```

In the preceding snippet, we are passing our model to the method coremltools.converters.keras.convert, which is responsible for converting our Keras model to Core ML. Along with the model, we pass in the input and output names for our model, as well as setting image_input_names to inform the method that we want the input image to be treated as an image rather than a multidimensional array.

As expected, after running this cell, you will receive an error. If you scroll to the bottom of the output, you will see the line ValueError: Keras layer '<class 'keras.layers.core.Lambda'>' not supported. At this stage, you will need to review the architecture of your model to identify the layer that caused the error and proceed with what you are about to do.

By enabling the parameter add_custom_layers in the conversion call, we prevent the method from failing when the converter encounters a layer it doesn't recognize. A placeholder layer named custom will be inserted as part of the conversion process. In addition to recognizing custom layers, we can pass in a delegate function to the parameter custom_conversion_functions, which allows us to add metadata to the model's specification stating how the custom layer will be handled.

Let's create this `delegate` method now; run the cell with the following code:

```
def convert_lambda(layer):
    if layer.function.__name__ == 'rescale_output':
        params = NeuralNetwork_pb2.CustomLayerParams()
        params.className = "RescaleOutputLambda"
        params.description = "Rescale output using ((x+1)*127.5)"
        return params
    elif layer.function.__name__ == 'res_crop':
        params = NeuralNetwork_pb2.CustomLayerParams()
        params.className = "ResCropBlockLambda"
        params.description = "return x[:, 2:-2, 2:-2]"
        return params
    else:
        raise Exception('Unknown layer')
    return None
```

This `delegate` is passed each custom layer the converter comes across. Because we are dealing with two different layers, we first check which layer we are dealing with and then proceed to create and return an instance of `CustomLayerParams`. This class allows us to add some metadata used when creating the model's specification for the Core ML conversion. Here we are setting its `className`, which is the name of the Swift (or Objective-C) class in our iOS project that implements this layer, and `description`, which is the text shown in Xcode 's ML model viewer.

With our `delegate` method now implemented, let's rerun the converter, passing in the appropriate parameters, as shown in the following code:

```
coreml_model = coremltools.converters.keras.convert(
    model,
    input_names=['image'],
    image_input_names=['image'],
    output_names="output",
    add_custom_layers=True,
    custom_conversion_functions={ "Lambda": convert_lambda })
```

If all goes well, you should see the converter output each layer it visits, with no error messages, and finally returning a Core ML model instance. We can now add metadata to our model, which is what is displayed in Xcode 's ML model views:

```
coreml_model.author = 'Joshua Newnham'
coreml_model.license = 'BSD'
coreml_model.short_description = 'Fast Style Transfer based on the style of
Van Gogh Starry Night'
coreml_model.input_description['image'] = 'Preprocessed content image'
coreml_model.output_description['output'] = 'Stylized content image'
```

At this stage, we could save the model and import into Xcode , but there is just one more thing I would like to do to make our life a little easier. At its core (excuse the pun), the Core ML model is a specification of the network (including the model description, model parameters, and metadata) used by Xcode to build the model when imported. We can get a reference to this specification by calling the following statement:

```
spec = coreml_model.get_spec()
```

With reference to the specification of the models, we next search for the output layer, as shown in the following snippet:

```
output = [output for output in spec.description.output if output.name ==
'output'][0]
```

We can inspect the output simply by printing it out; run the cell with the following code to do just that:

```
output
```

You should see something similar to this:

```
name: "output"
shortDescription: "Stylized content image"
type {
  multiArrayType {
    shape: 3
    shape: 320
    shape: 320
    dataType: DOUBLE
  }
}
```

Take note of the type, which is currently `multiArrayType` (its iOS equivalent is `MLMultiArray`). This is fine but would require us to explicitly convert it to an image; it would be more convenient to just have our model output an image instead of a multidimensional array. We can do this by simply modifying the specification. Specifically, in this instance, this means populating the type's `imageType` properties to hint to Xcode that we are expecting an image. Let's do that now by running the cell with this code:

```
output.type.imageType.colorSpace =
FeatureTypes_pb2.ImageFeatureType.ColorSpace.Value('RGB')
output.type.imageType.width = width
output.type.imageType.height = height
coreml_model = coremltools.models.MLModel(spec)
```

We first set the color space to RGB, then we set the expected width and height of the image. Finally, we create a new model by passing in the updated specification with the statement `coremltools.models.MLModel(spec)`. Now, if you interrogate the output, you should see something like the following output:

```
name: "output"
shortDescription: "Stylized content image"
type {
  imageType {
    width: 320
    height: 320
    colorSpace: RGB
  }
}
```

We have now saved ourselves a whole lot of code to perform this conversion; our final step is to save the model before importing it into Xcode . Run the last cell, which does just that:

```
coreml_model.save('output/FastStyleTransferVanGoghStarryNight.mlmodel')
```

Before closing the browser, let's download the model. You can do this by returning the `Chapter6/Notebooks` directory and drilling down into the `output` folder. Here you should see the file `FastStyleTransferVanGoghStarryNight.mlmodel`; simply right-click on it and select the **Download** menu item (or do it by left-clicking and selecting the **Download** toolbar item):

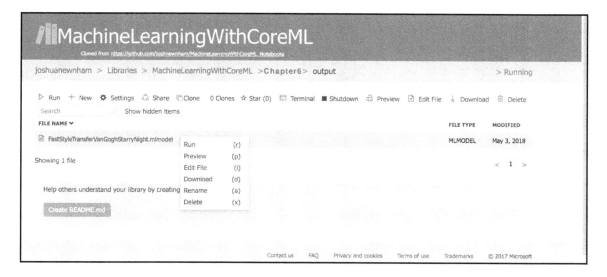

With our model in hand, it's now time to jump into Xcode and implement those custom layers.

# Building custom layers in Swift

In this section, we will be mainly focusing on implementing the custom layers that our model is dependent on, and we'll omit a lot of the application's details by working with an existing template—a structure you have no doubt become quite familiar with.

If you haven't done so already, pull down the latest code from the accompanying repository: `https://github.com/packtpublishing/machine-learning-with-core-ml`. Once downloaded, navigate to the directory `Chapter6/Start/StyleTransfer/` and open the project `StyleTransfer.xcodeproj`. Once loaded, you will see the project for this chapter:

The application consists of two view controllers. The first, `CameraViewController`, provides the user with a live stream of the camera and the ability to take a photo. When a photo is taken, the controller presents the other view controller, `StyleTransferViewController`, passing along with the captured photo. `StyleTransferViewController` then presents the image, along with a horizontal `CollectionView` at the bottom containing a set of styles that the user can select by tapping on them.

Each time the user selects a style, the controller updates the `ImageProcessors` style property and then calls its method, `processImage`, passing in the assigned image. It is here that we will implement the functionality responsible for passing the image to the model and returning the result via the assigned delegates `onImageProcessorCompleted` method, which is then presented to the user.

Now, with our project loaded, let's import the model we have just created; locate the downloaded `.mlmodel` file and drag it onto Xcode . Once imported, we select it from the left-hand \ panel to inspect the metadata, to remind ourselves what we need to implement:

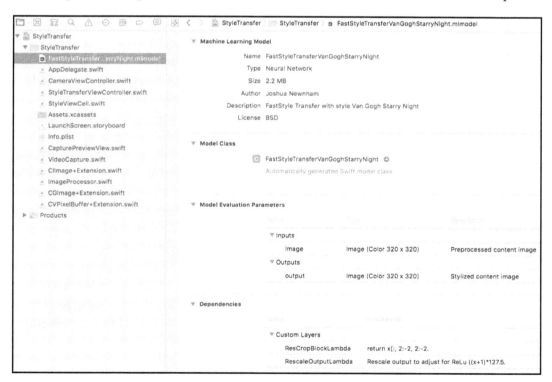

By inspecting the model, we can see that it is expecting an input RGB image of size 320 x 320, and it will output an image with the same dimensions. We can also see that the model is expecting two custom layers named ResCropBlockLambda and RescaleOutputLambda. Before implementing these classes, let's hook the model up and, just for fun, see what happens when we try to run it without the custom layers implemented.

Select ImageProcessor.swift from the left-hand-side panel; in this project, we will get the Vision framework to do all the preprocessing. Start by adding the following properties within the body of the ImageProcessor class, somewhere such as underneath the style property:

```
lazy var vanCoghModel : VNCoreMLModel = {
    do{
        let model = try VNCoreMLModel(for:
FastStyleTransferVanGoghStarryNight().model)
        return model
    } catch{
        fatalError("Failed to obtain VanCoghModel")
    }
}()
```

The first property returns an instance of VNCoreMLModel, wrapping our FastStyleTransferVanGoghStarryNight model. Wrapping our model is necessary to make it compatible with the Vision framework's requests classes.

Just underneath, add the following snippet, which will be responsible for returning the appropriate VNCoreMLModel, based on the selected style:

```
var model : VNCoreMLModel{
    get{
        if self.style == .VanCogh{
            return self.vanCoghModel
        }
        // default
        return self.vanCoghModel
    }
}
```

Finally, we create the method that will be responsible for returning an instance of VNCoreMLRequest, based on the currently selected model (determined by the current style):

```
func getRequest() -> VNCoreMLRequest{
    let request = VNCoreMLRequest(
```

```
        model: self.model,
        completionHandler: { [weak self] request, error in
            self?.processRequest(for: request, error: error)
        })
    request.imageCropAndScaleOption = .centerCrop
    return request
}
```

VNCoreMLRequest is responsible for performing the necessary preprocessing on the input image before passing it to the assigned Core ML model. We instantiate VNCoreMLRequest, passing in a completion handler that will simply pass its results to the processRequest method, of the ImageProcessor class, when called. We also set the imageCropAndScaleOption to .centerCrop so that our image is resized to 320 x 320 whilst maintaining its aspect ratio (cropping the centered image on its longest side, if necessary).

With our properties now defined, it's time to jump into the processImage method to initiate the actual work; add the following code (shown in bold, and replacing the // TODO comments):

```
public func processImage(ciImage:CIImage){
    DispatchQueue.global(qos: .userInitiated).async {
        let handler = VNImageRequestHandler(ciImage: ciImage)
        do {
            try handler.perform([self.getRequest()])
        } catch {
            print("Failed to perform
classification.\n\(error.localizedDescription)")
        }
    }
}
```

The preceding method is our entry point to stylizing an image; we start by instantiating an instance of VNImageRequestHandler, passing in the image, and initiating the process by calling the perform method. Once the analysis has finished, the request will call the delegate we assigned to it, processRequest, passing in a reference of the associated request and the results (or errors if any). Let's flesh out this method now:

```
func processRequest(for request:VNRequest, error: Error?){
    guard let results = request.results else {
        print("ImageProcess", #function, "ERROR:",
            String(describing: error?.localizedDescription))
        self.delegate?.onImageProcessorCompleted(
            status: -1,
            stylizedImage: nil)
```

```
        return
    }
    let stylizedPixelBufferObservations =
        results as! [VNPixelBufferObservation]
    guard stylizedPixelBufferObservations.count > 0 else {
        print("ImageProcess", #function,"ERROR:",
            "No Results")
        self.delegate?.onImageProcessorCompleted(
            status: -1,
            stylizedImage: nil)
        return
    }
    guard let cgImage = stylizedPixelBufferObservations[0]
        .pixelBuffer.toCGImage() else{
        print("ImageProcess", #function, "ERROR:",
            "Failed to convert CVPixelBuffer to CGImage")
        self.delegate?.onImageProcessorCompleted(
            status: -1,
            stylizedImage: nil)
        return
    }
    DispatchQueue.main.sync {
        self.delegate?.onImageProcessorCompleted(
            status: 1,
            stylizedImage:cgImage)
    }
}
```

 While `VNCoreMLRequest` is responsible for the image analysis, `VNImageRequestHandler` is responsible for executing the request (or requests).

If no errors occurred during the analysis, we should be returned the instance of our request with its results property set. As we are only expecting one request and result type, we cast the results to an array of `VNPixelBufferObservation`, a type of observation suitable for image analysis with a Core ML model whose role is image-to-image processing, such as our style transfer model.

We can get a reference to our stylized image via the property `pixelBuffer`, from the observation obtained from the results. And then we can call the extension method `toCGImage` (found in `CVPixelBuffer+Extension.swift`) to conveniently obtain the output in a format we can easily use, in this case, updating the image view.

As previously discussed, let's see what happens when we try to run an image through our model without implementing the custom layers. Build and deploy to a device and proceed to take a photo, then select the Van Cogh style from the styles displayed. In doing so, you will observe the build failing and reporting the error: `Error creating Core ML custom layer implementation from factory for layer "RescaleOutputLambda"` (as we were expecting).

Let's address this now by implementing each of our custom layers, starting with the `RescaleOutputLambda` class. Create a new Swift file named `RescaleOutputLamdba.class` and replace the template code with the following:

```
import Foundation
import CoreML
import Accelerate

@objc(RescaleOutputLambda) class RescaleOutputLambda: NSObject,
MLCustomLayer {
    required init(parameters: [String : Any]) throws {
        super.init()
    }
    func setWeightData(_ weights: [Data]) throws {
    }
    func outputShapes(forInputShapes inputShapes: [[NSNumber]]) throws
        -> [[NSNumber]] {
    }
    func evaluate(inputs: [MLMultiArray], outputs: [MLMultiArray]) throws {
    }
}
```

Here, we have created a concrete class of the protocol `MLCustomLayer`, a protocol that defines the behavior of a custom layer in our neural network model. The protocol consists of four required methods and one optional method, which are as follows:

- `init(parameters)`: Initializes the custom layer implementation that is passed the dictionary `parameters` that includes any additional configuration options for the layer. As you may recall, we created an instance of `NeuralNetwork_pb2.CustomLayerParams` for each of our custom layers when converting our Keras model. Here we can add more entries, which will be passed into this dictionary. This provides some flexibility, such as allowing you to adjust your layer based on the set parameters.
- `setWeightData()`: Assigns the weights for the connections within the layer (for layers with trainable weights).

- `outputShapes(forInputShapes)`: This determines how the layer modifies the size of the input data. Our `RescaleOutputLambda` layer doesn't change the size of the layer, so we simply need to return the input shape, but we will make use of this when implementing the next custom layer.
- `evaluate(inputs, outputs)`: This performs the actual computation; this method is required and gets called when the model is run on the CPU.
- `encode(commandBuffer, inputs, outputs)`: This method is optional and acts as an alternative to the method `evaluate`, which uses the GPU rather than the CPU.

Because we are not passing in any custom parameters or setting any trainable weights, we can skip the constructor and `setWeightData` methods; let's walk through the remaining methods, starting with `outputShapes(forInputShapes)`.

As previously mentioned, this layer doesn't change the shape of the input, therefore, we can simply return the input shape, as shown in the following code:

```
func outputShapes(forInputShapes inputShapes: [[NSNumber]]) throws
    -> [[NSNumber]] {
        return inputShapes
}
```

With our `outputShapes(forInputShapes)` method now implemented, let's turn our attention to the workhorse of the layer responsible for performing the actual computation, the `evaluate` method. The `evaluate` method receives an array of `MLMultiArray` objects as inputs, along with another array of `MLMultiArray` objects, where it is expected to store the results. Having the `evaluate` method accept arrays for its input and outputs allows for greater flexibility in supporting different architectures, but, in this example, we are expecting only one input and one output.

As a reminder, this layer is for scaling each element from a range of -1.0 - 1.0 to a range of 0 - 255 (that's what a typical image would be expecting). The simplest approach is to iterate through each element and scale it using the equation we saw in Python: `((x+1)*127.5`. This is exactly what we'll do; add the following code (in bold) to the body of your `evaluate` method:

```
func evaluate(inputs: [MLMultiArray],outputs: [MLMultiArray]) throws {
    let rescaleAddition = 1.0
    let rescaleMulitplier = 127.5
    for (i, input) in inputs.enumerated(){
        // expecting [1, 1, Channels, Kernel Width, Kernel Height]
        let shape = input.shape
        for c in 0..<shape[2].intValue{
```

```
            for w in 0..<shape[3].intValue{
                for h in 0..<shape[4].intValue{
                    let index = [
                        NSNumber(value: 0),
                        NSNumber(value: 0),
                        NSNumber(value: c),
                        NSNumber(value: w),
                        NSNumber(value: h)]
                    let outputValue = NSNumber(
                        value:(input[index].floatValue + rescaleAddition)
                            * rescaleMulitplier)
                    outputs[i][index] = outputValue
                }
            }
        }
    }
}
```

The bulk of this method is made up of code used to create the index for obtaining the appropriate value from the input and pointing to its output counterpart. Once an index has been created, the Python formula is ported across to Swift: input[index].doubleValue + rescaleAddition) * rescaleMulitplier. This concludes our first custom layer; let's now implement our second customer layer, ResCropBlockLambda.

Create a new file called ResCropBlockLambda.swift and add the following code, overwriting any existing code:

```
import Foundation
import CoreML
import Accelerate

@objc(ResCropBlockLambda) class ResCropBlockLambda: NSObject, MLCustomLayer
{
    required init(parameters: [String : Any]) throws {
        super.init()
    }
    func setWeightData(_ weights: [Data]) throws {
    }
    func outputShapes(forInputShapes inputShapes: [[NSNumber]]) throws
        -> [[NSNumber]] {
    }
    func evaluate(inputs: [MLMultiArray], outputs: [MLMultiArray]) throws {
    }
}
```

As we have done with the previous custom layer, we have stubbed out all the required methods as determined by the `MLCustomLayer` protocol. Once again, we can ignore the constructor and `setWeightData` method as neither are used in this layer.

If you recall, and as the name suggests, the function of this layer is to crop the width and height of one of the inputs of the residual block. We need to reflect this within the `outputShapes(forInputShapes)` method, so that the network knows the input dimensions for subsequent layers. Update the `outputShapes(forInputShapes)` method with the following code:

```
func outputShapes(forInputShapes inputShapes: [[NSNumber]]) throws
    -> [[NSNumber]] {
        return [[NSNumber(value:inputShapes[0][0].intValue),
                NSNumber(value:inputShapes[0][1].intValue),
                NSNumber(value:inputShapes[0][2].intValue),
                NSNumber(value:inputShapes[0][3].intValue - 4),
                NSNumber(value:inputShapes[0][4].intValue - 4)]];
}
```

Here, we are removing a constant of 4 from the width and height, essentially padding 2 from the width and height. Next, we implement the `evaluate` method, which performs this cropping. Replace the `evaluate` method with the following code:

```
func evaluate(inputs: [MLMultiArray], outputs: [MLMultiArray]) throws {
    for (i, input) in inputs.enumerated(){
        // expecting [1, 1, Channels, Kernel Width, Kernel Height]
        let shape = input.shape
        for c in 0..<shape[2].intValue{
            for w in 2...(shape[3].intValue-4){
                for h in 2...(shape[4].intValue-4){
                    let inputIndex = [
                        NSNumber(value: 0),
                        NSNumber(value: 0),
                        NSNumber(value: c),
                        NSNumber(value: w),
                        NSNumber(value: h)]
                    let outputIndex = [
                        NSNumber(value: 0),
                        NSNumber(value: 0),
                        NSNumber(value: c),
                        NSNumber(value: w-2),
                        NSNumber(value: h-2)]
                    outputs[i][outputIndex] = input[inputIndex]
                }
            }
        }
```

```
        }
    }
```

Similar to the `evaluate` method of our `RescaleOutputLambda` layer, the bulk of this method has to do with creating the indices for the input and output arrays. We simply pad it by restraining the ranges of our loops to the desired width and height.

Now, if you build and run the project, you will be able to run an image through the Van Gogh network getting a stylized version of it back, similar to what is shown in the following image:

When running on the simulator, the whole process took approximately **22.4 seconds**. In the following two sections, we will spend some time looking at how we can reduce this.

# Accelerating our layers

Let's return to the layer `RescaleOutputLambda` and see where we might be able to shed a second or two off the processing time. As a reminder, the function of this layer is to rescale each element in the output, where our output can be thought of as a large vector. Luckily for us, Apple provides an efficient framework and API for just this. Instead of operating on each element within a loop, we will take advantage of the `Accelerate` framework and its vDSPAPI to perform this operation in a single step. This process is called **vectorization** and is made possible by exploiting the CPU's **Single Instruction, Multiple Data (SIMD)** instruction set. Return to the `RescaleOutputLambda` class and update the `evaluate` method with the following code:

```
func evaluate(inputs: [MLMultiArray], outputs: [MLMultiArray]) throws {
    var rescaleAddition : Float = 1.0
    var rescaleMulitplier : Float = 127.5
    for (i, _) in inputs.enumerated() {
        let input = inputs[i]
        let output = outputs[i]
        let count = input.count
        let inputPointer = UnsafeMutablePointer<Float>(
            OpaquePointer(input.dataPointer)
        )
        let outputPointer = UnsafeMutablePointer<Float>(
            OpaquePointer(output.dataPointer)
        )
        vDSP_vsadd(inputPointer, 1,
                    &rescaleAddition,
                    outputPointer, 1,
                    vDSP_Length(count))
        vDSP_vsmul(outputPointer, 1,
                    &rescaleMulitplier,
                    outputPointer, 1,
                    vDSP_Length(count))
    }
}
```

In the preceding code, we first get a reference to the pointers to each of the input and output buffers, wrapping them in `UnsafeMutablePointer`, as required by the vDSP functions. Then, it's simply a matter of applying each of our scaling operations using the equivalent vDSP functions, which we will walk through.

First, we add our constant of 1 to the input and save the results in the output buffer, as shown in the following snippet:

```
vDSP_vsadd(inputPointer, 1,
        &rescaleAddition,
        outputPointer, 1,
        vDSP_Length(count))
```

Where the function vDSP_vsadd takes in a pointer to our vector (inputPointer) and adds rescaleAddition to each of its elements before storing it into the output.

Next, we apply our multiplier to each of the elements of the output (which currently has each of its values set to the input with 1 added to it); the code for this is shown in the following snippet:

```
vDSP_vsmul(outputPointer, 1,
        &rescaleMulitplier,
        outputPointer, 1,
        vDSP_Length(count))
```

Similar to vDSP_vsadd, vDSP_vsmul takes in the input (in this case, our output); the scalar we want to multiply each element by; the output; the stride for persisting the result; and finally, the number of elements we want to operate on.

If you rerun the application, you will see that we have managed to shed a few seconds off the total execution time—not bad considering this layer is run only once at the end of our network. Can we do better?

# Taking advantage of the GPU

You may recall that when we introduced the MLCustomLayer protocol, there was an optional method, encode(commandBuffer, inputs, outputs), reserved for performing the evaluation on the GPU if the hosting device supported it. This flexibility is one of the advantages Core ML has over other machine learning frameworks; it allows mixing layers, which run on the CPU and GPU, and allows them to work coherently together.

To use the GPU, we will be using Apple's `Metal` framework, a graphics framework equivalent to OpenGL and DirectX (and now Vulkan), for those who are familiar with 3D graphics. Unlike our previous solutions, which included all code in a single method, we need to write the code that performs the computation in an external file called a **Metal shader** file. Within this file we will define a kernel, which will be complied and stored on the GPU (when loaded), allowing it to fan out the data in parallel across the GPU. Let's create this kernel now; create a new `metal` file called `rescale.metal` and add the following code:

```
#include <metal_stdlib>
using namespace metal;

kernel void rescale(
    texture2d_array<half, access::read> inTexture [[texture(0)]],
    texture2d_array<half, access::write> outTexture [[texture(1)]],
    ushort3 gid [[thread_position_in_grid]])
{
    if (gid.x >= outTexture.get_width() || gid.y >=
outTexture.get_height())
    {
        return;
    }
    const float4 x = float4(inTexture.read(gid.xy, gid.z));
    const float4 y = (1.0f + x) * 127.5f;
    outTexture.write(half4(y), gid.xy, gid.z);
}
```

It is out of scope to discuss the details of `metal`, so instead, we'll just highlight some of the key differences and commonalities between this and the previous approaches. First, it's worth recognizing why GPUs have been a major catalyst for the resurgence of neural networks. The GPU architecture allows a kernel (seen earlier) to be spawned for each element in our array—mass parallelism!

Because GPU frameworks were traditionally built with graphics manipulation in mind, there are some nuances with how we operate on data and what we operate on. The most notable of them is that we have swapped `MLMultiArray` for `texture2d_array` (textures) and we access them through sampling, using `thread_position_in_grid`. Nonetheless, the actual computation should look familiar from the original Python code, `const float4 y = (1.0f + x) * 127.5f`. Once calculated, we cast it to float 16 (half) and write it to the output texture.

Our next step is to configure our RescaleOutputLambda class to use Metal and the GPU, rather than the CPU. Return to the RescaleOutputLambda.swift file and make the following amendments.

Start by importing the Metal framework by adding the following statement at the top of your file:

```
import Metal
```

Next, we define a class variable of the type MTLComputePipelineState as a handler to the kernel we have just created, along with setting this up within the constructor of the RescaleOutputLambda class. Make the following amendments to the class and constructor, as shown in bold in the snippet:

```
@objc(RescaleOutputLambda) class RescaleOutputLambda: NSObject,
MLCustomLayer {
    let computePipeline: MTLComputePipelineState
    required init(parameters: [String : Any]) throws {
        let device = MTLCreateSystemDefaultDevice()!
        let library = device.makeDefaultLibrary()!
        let rescaleFunction = library.makeFunction(name: "rescale")!
        self.computePipeline = try!
device.makeComputePipelineState(function: rescaleFunction)
        super.init()
    }
    ...
}
```

If no errors are thrown, we will have reference to a complied version of our rescale kernel; the final step is making use of it. Within the RescaleOutputLambda class, add the following method:

```
func encode(commandBuffer: MTLCommandBuffer,
            inputs: [MTLTexture],
            outputs: [MTLTexture]) throws {
    guard let encoder = commandBuffer.makeComputeCommandEncoder() else{
        return
    }
    let w = computePipeline.threadExecutionWidth
    let h = computePipeline.maxTotalThreadsPerThreadgroup / w
    let threadGroupSize = MTLSizeMake(w, h, 1)
    for i in 0..<inputs.count {
        let threadGroups = MTLSizeMake(
            (inputs[i].width + threadGroupSize.width - 1) /
                threadGroupSize.width,
            (inputs[i].height+ threadGroupSize.height - 1) /
```

```
            threadGroupSize.height,
        (inputs[i].arrayLength + threadGroupSize.depth - 1) /
            threadGroupSize.depth)
    encoder.setTexture(inputs[i], index: 0)
    encoder.setTexture(outputs[i], index: 1)
    encoder.setComputePipelineState(computePipeline)
    encoder.dispatchThreadgroups(
        threadGroups,
        threadsPerThreadgroup:
        threadGroupSize)
    encoder.endEncoding()
}
```

As mentioned before, we will omit the details here and only highlight some key differences and commonalities between this approach and the previous approaches.

In short, the bulk of this method is responsible for passing data through to the compute kernel via the encoder and then dispatching it across the GPU. We first pass the input and output textures, as shown in the following snippet:

```
encoder.setTexture(inputs[i], index: 0)
encoder.setTexture(outputs[i], index: 1)
```

And then we're setting the handler, which points to the rescale kernel we created in the preceding snippet:

```
encoder.setComputePipelineState(computePipeline)
```

Finally, dispatch the job to the GPU; in this instance, our compute kernel is invoked for every pixel in every channel of the input texture:

```
encoder.dispatchThreadgroups(
    threadGroups,
    threadsPerThreadgroup:
    threadGroupSize)
encoder.endEncoding()
```

If you build and run again, you will hopefully get the same result but in less time. We have now seen two approaches to optimizing our network; I leave optimizing `ResCropBlockLambda` as an exercise for you. For now, let's shift our focus to talking about your model's weight before we wrap up this chapter.

# Reducing your model's weight

We have spent considerable time discussing layers of a network; we have learned that layers are made up of weights, configured in such a way that they can transform an input into a desirable output. These weights come at a cost, though; each one (by default) is a 32-bit floating-point number with a typical model, especially in computer vision, having millions resulting in networks that are hundreds of megabytes in size. On top of that; it's plausible that your application will have multiple models (with this chapter being a good example, requiring a model for each style).

Fortunately, our model in this chapter has a moderate number of weights and weighs in at a mere 2.2 MB; but this is possibly an exception. So we'll use this chapter as an excuse to explore some ways we can reduce our model's weights. But before doing so, let's quickly discuss why, even though it's probably obvious. The three main reasons why you should be conscious of your model's size include:

- Download time
- Application footprint
- Demands on memory

These could all hinder the user experience and are reasons for a user to either uninstall the application quickly or not even download it in the first place. So how do you reduce your model's size to avoid deterring the user. There are three broad approaches:

- Reduce the number of layers your network uses
- Reduce the number of units in each of those layers
- Reduce the size of the weights

The first two require that you have access to the original network and tools to re-architect and train the model; the last is the most accessible and it's the one we will discuss now.

In iOS 11.2, Apple allowed your networks to use half-precision floating-point numbers (16-bit). Now, with the release of iOS 12, Apple has taken this even further and introduced quantization, which allows us to use eight or less bits to encode our model's weights. In the following figure, we can see how these options compare with one another:

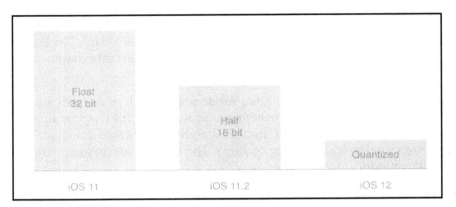

Let's discuss each in turn, starting with reducing our weights precision by converting it's floating points from 32-bits to 16-bits.

For both of these techniques (half-precision and quantization), we will be using the Core ML Tools Python package; so, begin by opening up your browser and heading over to https://notebooks.azure.com. Once the page is loaded navigate to the folder Chapter6/Notebooks/ and open the Jupyter Notebook FastNeuralStyleTransfer_OptimizeCoreML.ipynb. As we did before, we'll walk through each of the Notebook's cells here with the assumption that you will be executing each one as we cover it (if you are working along).

We begin by importing the Core ML Tools package; execute the cell with the following code:

```
try:
    import coremltools
except:
    !pip install coremltools
    import coremltools
```

For convenience, we have wrapped the import in an exception block, so that it automatically installs the package if it doesn't exist.

At the time of writing, Core ML 2 was still in beta and only recently publicly announced. If you're using a version of Core ML Tools that is less than 2.0 then replace `!pip install coremltools` with `!pip install coremltools>=2.0b1` to install the latest beta version to have access to the necessary modules for this section.

Next, we will load our `mlmodel` file that we had previously saved, using the following statement:

```
coreml_model =
coremltools.models.MLModel('output/FastStyleTransferVanGoghStarryNight.mlmo
del')
```

Next, we perform the conversion by simply calling `coremltools.utils.convert_neural_network_weights_to_fp16` and passing in your model. If successful, this method will return an equivalent model (that you passed in), using half precision weights instead of 32-bits for storing its weights. Run the cell with the following code to do just that:

```
fp16_coreml_model =
coremltools.utils.convert_neural_network_weights_to_fp16(coreml_model)
```

Finally, we save it so we can later download it and import into our project; run the next cell with the code:

```
fp16_coreml_model.save('output/fp16_FastStyleTransferVanGoghStarryNight.mlm
odel')
```

And with that executed (essentially three lines of code), we have managed to have our models size, going from 2.2 MB to 1.1 MB - so, what's the catch?

As you might suspect, there is a trade-off here; reducing the precision of your models weights will affect its accuracy, but possibly not enough to be concerned with. The only way you will know is by comparing the optimized model with the original and re-evaluating it on your test data, ensuring that it satisfies your required accuracy/results. For this, Core ML Tools provides a collection of utilities that makes this fairly seamless, which you can learn at the official website `https://apple.github.io/coremltools/index.html`.

Quantization is no more complicated (with respect to using it via Core ML Tools rather than concept); it's a clever technique, so let's quickly discuss how it achieves 8-bit compression before running through the code.

At a high-level, quantization is a technique that maps a continuous range of values to a discrete set; you can think of it as a process of clustering your values into a discrete set of groups and then creating a lookup table which maps your values to the closest group. The size is then dependent on the number of clusters used (index) rather than value, which allows you to encode your weights using anything from 8-bits to 2-bits.

To make this concept more concrete, the following figure illustrates the results of color quantization; where a 24-bit image is mapped to 16 discrete colors:

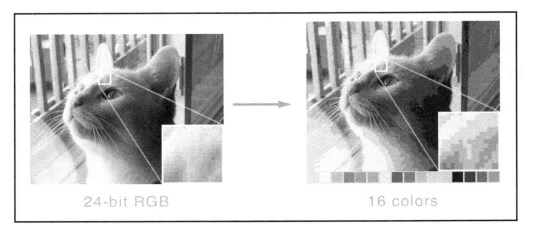

Instead of each pixel representing its color (using 24-bits/8-bits per channel), they now are indexes to the 16 color palette, that is, from 24-bits to 4-bits.

Before moving onto how we optimize our models using quantization with the Core ML Tools package, you maybe wondering how this palette (or discrete set of values) is derived. The short answer is that there are many ways, from linearly separating the values into groups, to using an unsupervised learning technique such as k-means, or even using a custom, domain-specific technique. Core ML Tools allows for all variations and the choice will be dependent on your data distribution and that results achieved during testing. Let's jump into it; first, we will start by importing the module:

```
from coremltools.models.neural_network import quantization_utils as
quant_utils
```

With this statement, we have imported the module and assigned it the alias `quant_utils`; the next cell, we optimize our model using a variation of sizes and methods:

```
lq8_coreml_model = quant_utils.quantize_weights(coreml_model, 8, 'linear')
lq4_coreml_model = quant_utils.quantize_weights(coreml_model, 4, 'linear')
km8_coreml_model = quant_utils.quantize_weights(coreml_model, 8, 'kmeans')
km4_coreml_model = quant_utils.quantize_weights(coreml_model, 4, 'kmeans')
```

Once this is completed, let's save each of our optimized models to the output directory before downloading them to our local disk to import them into Xcode (this may take some time):

```
coremltools.models.MLModel(lq8_coreml_model) \
    .save('output/lq8_FastStyleTransferVanGoghStarryNight.mlmodel')
coremltools.models.MLModel(lq4_coreml_model) \
    .save('output/lq4_FastStyleTransferVanGoghStarryNight.mlmodel')
coremltools.models.MLModel(km8_coreml_model) \
    .save('output/km8_FastStyleTransferVanGoghStarryNight.mlmodel')
coremltools.models.MLModel(km4_coreml_model) \
    .save('output/km8_FastStyleTransferVanGoghStarryNight.mlmodel')
```

I will omit the details of downloading and importing the model into your project as we have already gone through these steps previously in this chapter, but I do encourage that you to inspect the results from each model to get a feel for how each optimization affects the results - of course, these effects are highly dependent on the model, data, and domain. The following figure shows the results of each of the optimizations along with the model's size:

Admittedly, it's difficult to see the differences due to the low-resolution of the image (and possibly because you're reading this in black and white) but generally, the quality appears minimal between the original and k-means 8-bit version.

With the release of Core ML 2, Apple offers another powerful feature to optimize you Core ML models; specifically around consolidating multiple models into a single package. This not only reduces the size of your application but also convenient for you, the developer, when interfacing with your model. For example, flexible shapes and sizes allows for variable input and output dimensions, that is, instead of a single fixed input and output dimension, you have the flexibility of having multiple variants or a variable range within a limit. You can learn more about this feature on their official website at `https://developer.apple.com/machine-learning`; but for now, we will wrap up this chapter with a quick summary before moving on to the next chapter.

# Summary

In this chapter, we introduced the concept of style transfer; a technique that aims to separate the content of an image from its style. We discussed how it achieves this by leveraging a trained CNN, where we saw how deeper layers of a network extract features that distill information about the content of an image, while discarding any extraneous information.

Similarly, we saw that shallower layers extracted the finer details, such as texture and color, which we could use to isolate the style of a given image by looking for the correlations between the feature maps (also known as **convolutional kernels** or **filters**) in each layer. These correlations are what we use to measure style and how we steer our network. Having isolated the content and style, we generated a new image by combining the two.

We then highlighted the limitations of performing style transfer in real time (with current technologies) and introduced a slight variation. Instead of optimizing the style and content each time, we could train a model to learn a particular style. This would allow us to generate a stylized image for a given image with a single pass through the network, as we have done with many other examples we have worked through in this book.

Having introduced the concepts, we then walked through converting the Keras model to Core ML and used this as an opportunity to implement custom layers, a Swift-centric way of implementing layers that have no direct mapping between the machine learning framework and Core ML. Having implemented custom layers, we then spent some time looking at how we can optimize them using the `Accelerate` (SIMD) and `Metal` frameworks (GPU).

The theme of optimization continued into the next section, where we discussed some of the tools available for reducing a model's size; there, we looked at two approaches and how we could make use of them using the Core ML Tools package along with a cautionary warning of the trade-off between size and accuracy.

In the next chapter, we look at how we can apply what we have learned to recognizing user sketches.

# Assisted Drawing with CNNs

## 7

So far, we have seen how we can leverage Core ML and, in general, **machine learning** (**ML**) to better understand the physical world we live in (perceptual tasks). From the perspective of designing user interfaces, this allows us to reduce the friction between the user and the system. For example, if you are able to identify the user from a picture of their face, you can remove the steps required for authentication, as demonstrated with Apple's Face ID feature which is available on iPhone X. With Core ML, we have the potential to have devices better serve us rather than us serving them. This adheres to a rule stated by developer Eric Raymond that *a computer should never ask the user for any information that it can auto detect, copy, or deduce.*

We can take this idea even further; given sufficient amounts of data, we can anticipate what the user is trying to do and assist them in achieving their tasks. This is the premise of this chapter. Largely inspired and influenced by Google's AutoDraw AI experiment, we will implement an application that will attempt to guess what the user is trying to draw and provide pre-drawn drawings that the user can subtitute with (image search).

In this chapter, we'll explore this idea by looking at how we can try to predict what the user is trying to draw, and find suggestions for them to substitute it with. We will be exploring two techniques. The first is using a **convolutional neural network** (**CNN**), which we are becoming familiar with, to make the prediction, and then look at how we can apply a context-based similarity sorting strategy to better align the suggestions with what the user is trying to sketch. In the next chapter, we will continue our exploration by looking at how we can use a **recurrent neural network** (**RNN**) for the same task.

By the end of this chapter, you will have:

- Applied CNNs to the task of sketch recognition
- Gained further experience preparing input for a model
- Learned how feature maps can be extracted from CNNs and used to measure how similar two images are

There is a lot to cover, so let's get started by building a simple drawing application.

# Towards intelligent interfaces

Before jumping into how, let's quickly discuss the why in order to motivate us as well as encourage creative exploration of this concept. As alluded to in the introduction, the first motivator is to reduce friction. Consider the soft keyboard (keyboard with no physical buttons) on your phone; due to the constraints of the medium, such as lack of space and feedback, inputting text without predictive text would be cumbersome to the point of rendering it unusable. Similarly, despite the convenience of drawing with our fingers, our fingers are not that accurate, which makes things difficult to draw.

The other reason why this concept (augmentation) is advantageous is its ability to democratize the technical skill of drawing. It's common for people to not even attempt to draw because they have convinced themselves that it is beyond their abilities, or possibly that we can enhance one's ability to draw. This was the motivation behind the research project *ShadowDraw* presented at SIGGRAPH in 2011 by Yong Jae Lee, Larry Zitnick, and Michael Cohen. Their project had shown that guiding the user with a shadow image underlying the user's stroke significantly improved the quality of the output.

Finally, the last reason I want to highlight as to why this concept is interesting is providing a way for users to work at a higher level of abstraction. For example, imagine you were tasked with sketching out the storyboard for a new animation. As you sketch out your scene, the system would substitute your sketches with their associated characters and props as they were being worked on, allowing you to design at a higher level of fidelity without sacrificing speed.

Hopefully, by now, I have convinced you of the potential opportunity of integrating artificial intelligence into the user interface. Let's shift our focus to the how, which we will begin to do in the next section.

# Drawing

In this section, we will start off by inspecting an existing starter application and implement the drawing functionality. Then, in the next section, we will look at how we can augment the user by predicting what they are trying to draw and providing substitutes they can swap with.

If you haven't done so, pull down the latest code from the accompanying repository at `https://github.com/packtpublishing/machine-learning-with-core-ml`. Once downloaded, navigate to the `Chapter7/Start/QuickDraw/` directory and open the project `QuickDraw.xcodeproj`. Once loaded, you will see the starter project for this chapter, as shown in the following screenshot:

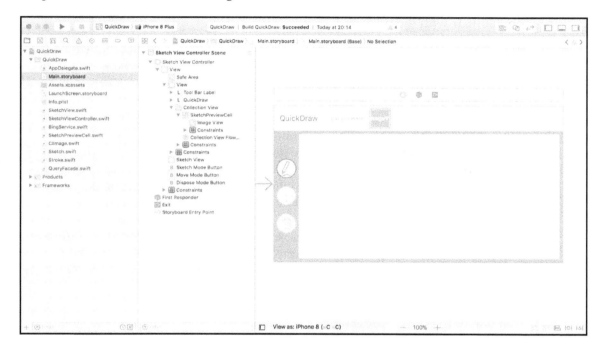

In the previous screenshot, you can see the application in its entirety; the interface consists of a single view, which contains a simple toolbar down on the left, allowing the user to toggle between sketch and move. There is a button for clearing everything. The area to the right of the toolbar is the canvas, which will be responsible for rendering what the user has drawn and any substituted images. Finally, the top area consists of a label and collection view. The collection view will make the suggested images that the user can substitute with available, while the label is simply something that is made visible to make the user aware of the purpose of the images presented to them via the collection view.

Our first task, as previously mentioned, will be to implement the functionality of drawing. Some of the plumbing has already been done but a majority is left out, giving us the opportunity to walk through the code to better understand the architecture of the application and how ML has been integrated. Before jumping into the code, let's briefly discuss the purpose of each relevant source file within the project. Like a contents page of a book, this will give you a better sense of how things are stitched together and help you become more familiar with the project:

- SketchView: This is a custom UIControl that will be responsible for capturing the user's touches and converting them to drawings. It will also be responsible for rendering these drawings and substituted drawings, that is, sketches that have been replaced. As seen earlier, this control has already been added to the view. In this section, we will be implementing the functionality of touch events.

- SketchViewController: The controller behind the main view, and it is responsible for listening for when the user finishes editing (lifts their finder) and passing the current sketch to the QueryFacade for processing. This controller is also responsible for handling mode switches (sketching, moving, or clearing everything) and dragging the sketches around the screen when in the move mode.

- BingService: We will be using Microsoft's Bing Image Search API to find our suggested images. Bing provides a simple RESTful service to allow for image searches, along with relevant parameters for fine-tuning of your search. Note: we won't be editing this.

- SketchPreviewCell: A simple extension of the UICollectionViewCell class that makes the UIImageView nested within the cell available. Note: we won't be editing this.

- CIImage: This should look familiar to you—something we implemented back in Chapter 3, *Recognizing Objects in the World*. We'll use it extensively in this chapter for resizing and getting access to raw data of the images (including the sketch).

- Sketch: This is our model of a sketch; we will implement two versions of this. One is for rendering sketches from the user, created by strokes, and the other is for encapsulating a UIImage, which has substituted a sketch (of strokes).

- Stroke: A data object that describes part of a sketch, essentially encoding the path the user draws so that we can render it.

- QueryFacade: This is the class that will do all the heavy lifting. Once the user has finished editing, the view controller will export the sketch and pass it to QueryFacade, which will be responsible for three things: guessing what the user is trying to draw, fetching and downloading relevant suggestions, and sorting them before passing back to the view controller to present to the user via the collection view. An illustration of this process can be seen here:

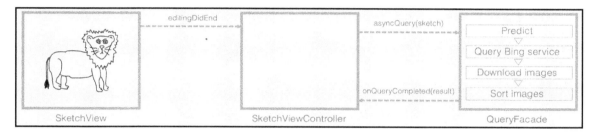

Hopefully, you now have a better sense of how everything fits together; let's bring it to life, starting at the bottom and working our way up. Click on the Stroke.swift file to focus the file in the main area; once open, you will be greeted by an unassuming amount of code, as shown in this snippet:

```
import UIKit
    class Stroke{
}
```

Just to recap, the purpose of a Stroke is to encapsulate a single path the user has drawn such as to be able to recreate it when rendering it back onto the screen. A path is nothing more than a list of points that are captured as the user moves their finger along the screen. Along with the path, we will also store a color and width of the stroke; these determine the visual aesthetics of the stroke. Add the following properties to the Stroke class along with the class's constructor:

```
var points : [CGPoint] = [CGPoint]()
var color : UIColor!
var width : CGFloat!

init(startingPoint:CGPoint,
     color:UIColor=UIColor.black,
     width:CGFloat=10.0) {
    self.points.append(startingPoint)
    self.color = color
    self.width = width
}
```

Next, we will add some computed properties to our `Stroke` class that we will make use of when rendering and exporting the sketch. Starting with the property to assist with rendering, we'll be using the Core Graphics framework to render the path of each stroke associated with a sketch. Rendering is done using a Core Graphics context (`CGContext`), which conveniently exposes methods for rendering a path using the methods `addPath` and `drawPath`, as we'll see soon. The `addPath` method expects a type of `CGPath`, which is nothing more than a series of drawing instructions describing how to draw the path, something we can easily derive from our stroke's points. Let's do that now; add the `path` property to the `Stroke` class:

```
var path : CGPath{
    get{
        let path = CGMutablePath.init()
        if points.count > 0{
            for (idx, point) in self.points.enumerated(){
                if idx == 0{
                    path.move(to: point)
                } else{
                    path.addLine(to: point)
                }
            }
        }
        return path
    }
}
```

As mentioned previously, a `CGPath` is made up of a series of drawing instructions. In the preceding snippet, we are creating a path using the points associated with `Stroke`. All except the first connects each point by a line while the first simply moves it into position.

The Core Graphics framework is a lightweight and low-level 2D drawing engine. It includes drawing functionality, such as path-based drawing, transformations, color management, off-screen rendering, patterns and shadings, image creation, and image masking.

Our next two properties are used to obtain the bounding box of the sketch, that is, the bounds that would encompass the minimum and maximum x and y positions of all strokes. Implementing these within the stroke itself will make our task easier later on. Add the properties `minPoint` and `maxPoint` to your `Stroke` class, as shown in the following code block:

```
var minPoint : CGPoint{
    get{
        guard points.count > 0 else{
```

```
            return CGPoint(x: 0, y: 0)
        }
        let minX : CGFloat = points.map { (cp) -> CGFloat in
            return cp.x
            }.min() ?? 0
        let minY : CGFloat = points.map { (cp) -> CGFloat in
            return cp.y
            }.min() ?? 0
        return CGPoint(x: minX, y: minY)
    }
}

var maxPoint : CGPoint{
    get{
        guard points.count > 0 else{
            return CGPoint(x: 0, y: 0)
        }
        let maxX : CGFloat = points.map { (cp) -> CGFloat in
            return cp.x
            }.max() ?? 0
        let maxY : CGFloat = points.map { (cp) -> CGFloat in
            return cp.y
            }.max() ?? 0
        return CGPoint(x: maxX, y: maxY)
    }
}
```

For each property, we simply map each axis (*x* and *y*) into its own array and then find either the minimum or maximum with respect to their method. This now completes our Stroke class. Let's move our way up the layers and implement the functionality of the Sketch class. Select Sketch.swift from the left-hand-side panel to open in the editing window. Before making amendments, let's inspect what is already there and what's left to do:

```
protocol Sketch : class{
    var boundingBox : CGRect{ get }
    var center : CGPoint{ get set }
    func draw(context:CGContext)
    func exportSketch(size:CGSize?) -> CIImage?
}
```

Currently, no concrete class exists and this will be our task for this part of this section. Before we start coding, let's review the responsibility of the Sketch. As implied earlier, our Sketch will be responsible for rendering either the collection of strokes associated with the user's drawing or an image that the user has selected to substitute their own drawing with. For this reason, we will be using two implementations of the Stroke class, one specifically for dealing with strokes and the other for images; we'll start with the one responsible for managing and rendering strokes.

Each implementation is expected to expose a draw and exportSketch method and the properties boundingBox and center. Let's now briefly describe each of these methods, starting with the most obvious: draw. We are expecting Sketch to be responsible for rendering itself, either drawing each stroke or rendering the assigned image depending on the type of sketch. The exportSketch method will be used to obtain a rasterized version of the sketch and is dependent on the boundingBox property, using it to determine what area of the canvas contains information (that is, drawings). Then, it proceeds to rasterize the sketch to a CIImage, which can then be used to feed the model. The last property, center, returns and sets the center and is used when the user drags it around the screen while in move mode, as described earlier.

Let's now proceed to implement a concrete version of a Sketch for dealing with strokes. Add the following code in the Sketch class, still within the Sketch.swift file:

```
class StrokeSketch : Sketch{
    var label : String?
    var strokes = [Stroke]()
    var currentStroke : Stroke?{
        get{
            return strokes.count > 0 ? strokes.last : nil
        }
    }
    func addStroke(stroke:Stroke){
        self.strokes.append(stroke)
    }
}
```

Here, we have defined a new class, StrokeSketch, adhering to the Sketch protocol. We have defined two properties: a list for holding all the strokes and a string we can use to annotate the sketch. We have also exposed two helper methods. One is for returning the current stroke, which will be used while the user is drawing, and another is a convenient method for adding a new stroke.

Let's now implement the functionality that will be responsible for rendering the sketch; add the following code to the `StrokeSketch` class:

```
func draw(context:CGContext){
    self.drawStrokes(context:context)
}

func drawStrokes(context:CGContext){
    for stroke in self.strokes{
        self.drawStroke(context: context, stroke: stroke)
    }
}

private func drawStroke(context:CGContext, stroke:Stroke){
    context.setStrokeColor(stroke.color.cgColor)
    context.setLineWidth(stroke.width)
    context.addPath(stroke.path)
    context.drawPath(using: .stroke)
}
```

We will implement the protocol's `draw` method but delegate the task of drawing to the methods `drawStrokes` and `drawStroke`. The `drawStrokes` method simply iterates over all strokes currently held by our sketch class and passes them to the `drawStoke` method, passing a reference of the Core Graphics context and current `Stroke`. Within the `drawStroke` method, we first update the context's stroke color and line width, and then we proceed to add and draw the associated path. With this now implemented, we have enough functionality for the user to draw. But for completeness, let's implement the functionality for obtaining the bounding box, obtaining and updating the sketches, center, and rasterizing the sketch to a `CIImage`. We start with the `boundingBox` property and associated methods. Add the following code to the `StrokeSketch` class:

```
var minPoint : CGPoint{
    get{
        guard strokes.count > 0 else{
            return CGPoint(x: 0, y: 0)
        }
        let minPoints = strokes.map { (stroke) -> CGPoint in
            return stroke.minPoint
        }
        let minX : CGFloat = minPoints.map { (cp) -> CGFloat in
            return cp.x
        }.min() ?? 0
        let minY : CGFloat = minPoints.map { (cp) -> CGFloat in
            return cp.y
        }.min() ?? 0
        return CGPoint(x: minX, y: minY)
```

```
        }
    }

    var maxPoint : CGPoint{
        get{
            guard strokes.count > 0 else{
                return CGPoint(x: 0, y: 0)
            }
            let maxPoints = strokes.map { (stroke) -> CGPoint in
                return stroke.maxPoint
            }
            let maxX : CGFloat = maxPoints.map { (cp) -> CGFloat in
                return cp.x
            }.max() ?? 0
            let maxY : CGFloat = maxPoints.map { (cp) -> CGFloat in
                return cp.y
            }.max() ?? 0
            return CGPoint(x: maxX, y: maxY)
        }
    }

    var boundingBox : CGRect{
        get{
            let minPoint = self.minPoint
            let maxPoint = self.maxPoint
            let size = CGSize(width: maxPoint.x - minPoint.x, height:
maxPoint.y - minPoint.y)
            let paddingSize = CGSize(width: 5,
                                     height: 5)
            return CGRect(x: minPoint.x - paddingSize.width,
                          y: minPoint.y - paddingSize.height,
                          width: size.width + (paddingSize.width * 2),
                          height: size.height + (paddingSize.height * 2))
        }
    }
```

We first implement the properties minPoint and maxPoint; they resemble our minPoint and maxPoint in our Stroke class. But instead of operating on a collection of points, they operate on a collection of strokes and utilize their counterparts (the minPoint and maxPoint properties of the Stroke class). Next, we implement the boundingBox property, which creates a CGRect that encapsulates these minimum and maximum points with the addition of some padding to avoid cropping the stroke itself.

Now, we will implement the `center` property declared within the `Stroke` protocol. The protocol of this is expecting both `get` and `set` blocks to be implemented. The getter will simply return the center of the bounding box, which we have just implemented, while the setter will iterate over all strokes and translate each point using the difference of the previous center and new center value. Let's implement this now. Add the following code to your `StrokeSketch` class; here, the `boundingBox` property is a good place:

```
var center : CGPoint{
    get{
        let bbox = self.boundingBox
        return CGPoint(x:bbox.origin.x + bbox.size.width/2,
                       y:bbox.origin.y + bbox.size.height/2)
    }
    set{
        let previousCenter = self.center
        let newCenter = newValue
        let translation = CGPoint(x:newCenter.x - previousCenter.x,
                                  y:newCenter.y - previousCenter.y)
        for stroke in self.strokes{
            for i in 0..<stroke.points.count{
                stroke.points[i] = CGPoint(
                    x:stroke.points[i].x + translation.x,
                    y:stroke.points[i].y + translation.y)
            }
        }
    }
}
```

Here, we first obtain the current center and then calculate the difference between this and the new center assigned to the property. After that, we iterate over all strokes and their corresponding points, adding this offset.

The final method we need to implement to adhere to the Sketch protocol is `exportSketch`. The purpose of this method is to rasterize the sketch into an image (`CIImage`) along with scaling it in accordance to the `size` argument, if available; otherwise it defaults to the actual size of the sketch itself. The method itself is fairly long but does nothing overly complicated. We have already implemented the functionality to render the sketch (via the `draw` method). But rather than rendering to a Core Graphic context that has been passed in by the view, we want to create a new context, adjust the scale with respect to the size argument and the actual sketch size, and finally create a `CIImage` instance from it.

To make it more readable, let's break the method down into these parts, starting with calculating the scale. Then we'll look at creating and rendering to a `context`, and finally wrap it in a `CIImage`; add the following code to your `StrokeSketch` class:

```
func exportSketch(size:CGSize?=nil) -> CIImage?{
    let boundingBox = self.boundingBox
    let targetSize = size ?? CGSize(
        width: max(boundingBox.width, boundingBox.height),
        height: max(boundingBox.width, boundingBox.height))
    var scale : CGFloat = 1.0
    if boundingBox.width > boundingBox.height{
        scale = targetSize.width / (boundingBox.width)
    } else{
        scale = targetSize.height / (boundingBox.height)
    }
    guard boundingBox.width > 0, boundingBox.height > 0 else{
        return nil
    }
}
```

In this code block, we declare our method and implement the functionality that determines the export size and scale. If no size is passed in, we simply fall back to the size of the sketch's bounding box property. Finally, we ensure that we have something to export.

Now our task is to create the `context` and render out our sketch with respect to the derived scale; append the following code to the `exportSketch` method:

```
UIGraphicsBeginImageContextWithOptions(targetSize, true, 1.0)

guard let context = UIGraphicsGetCurrentContext() else{
    return nil
}

UIGraphicsPushContext(context)

UIColor.white.setFill()
context.fill(CGRect(x: 0, y: 0,
                width: targetSize.width, height: targetSize.height))

context.scaleBy(x: scale, y: scale)

let scaledSize = CGSize(width: boundingBox.width * scale, height:
boundingBox.height * scale)

context.translateBy(x: -boundingBox.origin.x + (targetSize.width -
scaledSize.width)/2,
                y: -boundingBox.origin.y + (targetSize.height -
```

```
    scaledSize.height)/2)

    self.drawStrokes(context: context)

    UIGraphicsPopContext()
```

We use `UIGraphicsBeginImageContextWithOptions` from Core Graphics to create a new `context` and obtain reference to this `context` using the `UIGraphicsGetCurrentContext` method. `UIGraphicsBeginImageContextWithOptions` creates a temporary rendering context, where the first argument is the target size for this context, the second determines whether we are using an opaque or transparent background, and the final argument determines the display scale factor. We then fill the `context` with white and update the context's `CGAffineTransform` property using the `scaleBy` method. Subsequent draw methods, such as moving and drawing, will be transformed by this, which nicely takes care of scaling for us. We then pass in this `context` to our sketch's `draw` method, which takes care of rendering the sketch to the context. Our final task is obtaining the image from the `context` and wrapping it in an instance of `CIImage`. Let's do that now; append the following code to your `exportSketch` method:

```
    guard let image = UIGraphicsGetImageFromCurrentImageContext() else{
        UIGraphicsEndImageContext()
        return nil
    }
    UIGraphicsEndImageContext()

    return image.ciImage != nil ? image.ciImage : CIImage(cgImage:
    image.cgImage!)
```

Thanks to the Core Graphics method `UIGraphicsGetImageFromCurrentImageContext`, the task is painless. `UIGraphicsGetImageFromCurrentImageContext` returns an instance of `CGImage` with a rasterized version of the context. To create an instance of `CIImage`, we simply pass in our image to the constructor and return it.

We have finished the `Sketch` class—for now—and slowly we're making our way up the layers. Next, we will flesh our the `SketchView` class, which will be responsible for facilitating the creation and drawing of the sketches. Select the `SketchView.swift` file from the left-hand panel to bring it up in the editing window, and let's quickly review the existing code. `SketchView` has been broken down into chunks using extensions; to make the code more legible, we will present each of the chunks along with its core functionality:

```swift
class SketchView: UIControl {
    var clearColor : UIColor = UIColor.white
    var strokeColor : UIColor = UIColor.black
    var strokeWidth : CGFloat = 1.0
    var sketches = [Sketch]()
    var currentSketch : Sketch?{
        get{
            return self.sketches.count > 0 ? self.sketches.last : nil
        }
        set{
            if let newValue = newValue{
                if self.sketches.count > 0{
                    self.sketches[self.sketches.count-1] = newValue
                } else{
                    self.sketches.append(newValue)
                }
            } else if self.sketches.count > 0{
                self.sketches.removeLast()
            }
            self.setNeedsDisplay()
        }
    }
    override init(frame: CGRect) {
        super.init(frame: frame)
    }
    required init?(coder aDecoder: NSCoder) {
        super.init(coder: aDecoder)
    }
    func removeAllSketches(){
        self.sketches.removeAll()
        self.setNeedsDisplay()
    }
}
```

The majority of the previous code should be self-explanatory, but I do want to quickly draw your attention to the `currentSketch` property; we will use this getter to provide a convenient way for us to get access to the last sketch, which we will consider the currently active sketch. The setter is a little more ambiguous; it provides us with an easy way of replacing the currently active (last) sketch, which we will use when we come to handling the replacement of a user's sketch with an image suggested to them. The next chunk implements the drawing functionality, which should look familiar to you; here, we simply clear the `context` and iterate over all sketches, delegating the drawing to them:

```
extension SketchView{
    override func draw(_ rect: CGRect) {
        guard let context = UIGraphicsGetCurrentContext() else{ return }
        self.clearColor.setFill()
        UIRectFill(self.bounds)
        // them draw themselves
        for sketch in self.sketches{
            sketch.draw(context: context)
        }
    }
}
```

Our final chunk will be responsible for implementing the drawing functionality; currently, we have just stubbed out the methods to intercept the touch events. Fleshing these methods out will be our next task:

```
extension SketchView{
    override func beginTracking(_ touch: UITouch,
                               with event: UIEvent?) -> Bool{
        return true
    }
    override func continueTracking(_ touch: UITouch?,
                                   with event: UIEvent?) -> Bool {
        return true
    }
    override func endTracking(_ touch: UITouch?,
                              with event: UIEvent?) {
    }
    override func cancelTracking(with event: UIEvent?) {
    }
}
```

Before we proceed with writing the code, let's briefly review what we are trying to achieve here. As mentioned previously, SketchView will be responsible for the functionality, allowing the user to sketch using their finger. We have spent the past few pages building the data objects (Stroke and Sketch) to support this functionality and it is here that we will make use of them.

A touch begins when the user first touches the view (beginTracking). When we detect this, we want to first check whether we have a currently active and appropriate sketch; if not, then we will create one and set it as the current sketch. Next, we will create a stroke that will be used to track the user's finger as they drag it around the screen. It is considered complete once the user has either lifted their finger or their finger is dragged outside the bounds of the view. We will then request the view to redraw itself and finally notify any listening parties by broadcasting the event UIControlEvents.editingDidBegin action. Let's put this into code; append the following code to beginTracking within the SketchView class:

```
let point = touch.location(in: self)
if sketches.count == 0 || !(sketches.last is StrokeSketch){
    sketches.append(StrokeSketch())
}
guard let sketch = self.sketches.last as? StrokeSketch else {
    return false
}
sketch.addStroke(stroke:Stroke(startingPoint: point,
                               color:self.strokeColor,
                               width:self.strokeWidth))
self.setNeedsDisplay()
self.sendActions(for: UIControlEvents.editingDidBegin)
return true
```

 As described in the iOS documentation, here, we are adhering to the target-action mechanism, common in controls, by which we broadcast interesting events to simplify how other classes can integrate with this control.

Next, we will implement the body of the `continueTracking` method; here, we simply append a new point to the current sketches current stroke. As we did before, we request that the view to redraw itself and broadcast the `UIControlEvents.editingChanged` action. Append the following code to the body of the `continueTracking` method:

```
guard let sketch = self.sketches.last as? StrokeSketch, let touch = touch
else{
    return false
}
let point = touch.location(in: self)
sketch.currentStroke?.points.append(point)
self.setNeedsDisplay()
self.sendActions(for: UIControlEvents.editingChanged)
return true
```

The previous code resembles much of what we need when the user lifts their finger, with the exception of returning true (which tells the platform that this view wishes to continue consuming events) and replacing the `UIControlEvents.editingChanged` event with `UIControlEvents.editingDidEnd`. Add the following code to the body of your `endTracking` method:

```
guard let sketch = self.sketches.last as? StrokeSketch, let touch = touch
else{
    return
}
let point = touch.location(in: self)
sketch.currentStroke?.points.append(point)
self.setNeedsDisplay()
self.sendActions(for: UIControlEvents.editingDidEnd)
```

The final piece of code we need to add to the `SketchView` class is for dealing with when the current finger tracking is canceled (triggered when the finger moves off the current view or out of the device's tracking range, that is, off the screen). Here, we are simply treating it as if the tracking has finished, with the exception of not adding the last point. Append the following code to the body of your `cancelTracking` method:

```
guard let _ = self.sketches.last as? StrokeSketch else{
    return
}
self.setNeedsDisplay()
self.sendActions(for: UIControlEvents.editingDidEnd)
```

With our `SketchView` finished, our application now supports the functionality of sketching. Now would be a good time to build and run the application on either the simulator or device and check that everything is working correctly. If it is, then you should be able to draw onto the screen, as shown in the following image:

The functionality of moving and clearing the canvas has already been implemented; tap on the Move button to drag your sketch around, and tap on the Trash button to clear the canvas. Our next task will be to import a trained Core ML model and implement the functionality of classifying and suggesting images to the user.

# Recognizing the user's sketch

In this section, we will first review the dataset and model we will use to guess what the user is drawing. We will then proceed to integrate it into the workflow of the user who is sketching, and implement the functionality to support swapping out the user's sketch with a selected image.

# Reviewing the training data and model

For this chapter, a CNN was trained on the dataset that was used and made available from the research paper *How Do Humans Sketch Objects?* by Mathias Eitz, James Hays, and Marc Alexa. The paper, presented at SIGGRAPH in 2012, compares the performance of humans classifying sketches to that of a machine. The dataset consists of 20,000 sketches evenly distributed across 250 object categories, ranging from airplanes to zebras; a few examples are shown here:

From a perceptual study, they found that humans correctly identified the object category (such as snowman, grapes, and many more) of a sketch 73% of the time. The competitor, their ML model, got it right 56% of the time. Not bad! You can find out more about the research and download the accompanying dataset here at the official web page: `http://cybertron.cg.tu-berlin.de/eitz/projects/classifysketch/`.

In this project, we will be using a slightly smaller set, with 205 out of the 250 categories; the exact categories can be found in the CSV file `/Chapter7/Training/sketch_classes.csv`, along with the Jupyter Notebooks used to prepare the data and train the model. The original sketches are available in SVG and PNG formats. Because we're using a CNN, rasterized images (PNG) were used but rescaled from 1111 x 1111 to 256 x 256; this is the expected input of our model. The data was then split into a training and a validation set, using 80% (64 samples from each category) for training and 20% (17 samples from each category) for validation.

The architecture of the network was not too dissimilar to what has been used in previous chapters, with the exception of a larger kernel window used in the first layer to extract the spare features of the sketch, as presented here:

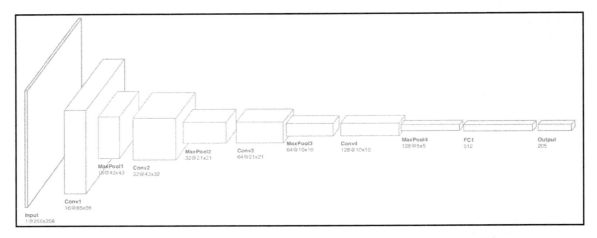

Recall that stacking convolution layers on top of each other allows the model to build up a shared set of high-level patterns that can then be used to perform classification, as opposed to using the raw pixels. The last convolution layer is flattened and then fed into a fully connected layer, where the prediction is finally made. You can think of these fully connected nodes as switches that turn on when certain (high-level) patterns are present in the input, as illustrated in the following diagram. We will return to this concept later on in this chapter when we implement sorting:

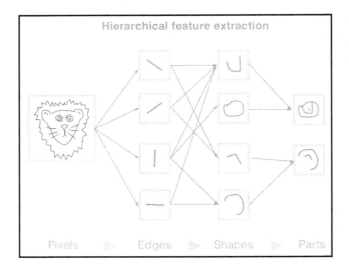

After 68 iterations (epochs), the model was able to achieve an accuracy of approximately 65% on the validation data. Not exceptional, but if we consider the top two or three predictions, then this accuracy increases to nearly 90%. The following diagram shows the plots comparing training and validation accuracy, and loss during training:

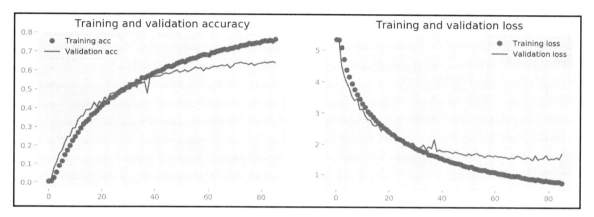

With our model trained, our next step is to export it using the Core ML Tools made available by Apple (as discussed in previous chapters) and imported into our project.

# Classifying sketches

In this section, we will walk though importing the Core ML model into our project and hooking it up, including using the model to perform inference on the user's sketch and also searching and suggesting substitute images for the user to swap their sketch with. Let's get started with importing the Core ML model into our project.

Locate the model in the project repositories folder
`/CoreMLModels/Chapter7/cnnsketchclassifier.mlmodel`; with the model selected,
drag it into your Xcode project, leaving the defaults for the **Import** options. Once imported,
select the model to inspect the details, which should look similar to the following
screenshot:

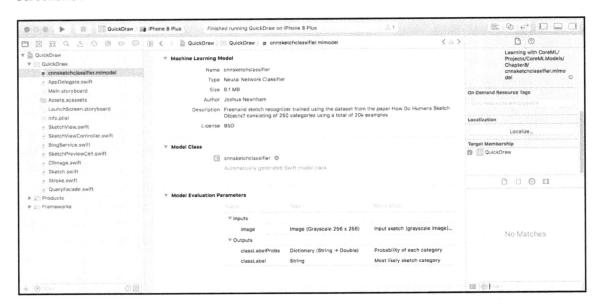

As with all our models, we verify that the model is included in the target by verifying that
the appropriate **Target Membership** is checked, and then we turn our attention to the
inputs and outputs, which should be familiar by now. We can see that our model is
expecting a single-channel (grayscale) 256 x 256 image and it returns the dominate class via
the **classLabel** property of the output, along with a dictionary of probabilities of all classes
via the **classLabelProbs** property.

With our model now imported, let's discuss the details of how we will be integrating it into
our project. Recall that our `SketchView` emits the events
`UIControlEvents.editingDidStart`, `UIControlEvents.editingChanged`, and
`UIControlEvents.editingDidEnd` as the user draws. If you inspect the
`SketchViewController`, you will see that we have already registered to listen for the
`UIControlEvents.editingDidEnd` event, as shown in the following code snippet:

```
override func viewDidLoad() {
    super.viewDidLoad()
    ...
```

```
...
self.sketchView.addTarget(self, action:
    #selector(SketchViewController.onSketchViewEditingDidEnd),
                            for: .editingDidEnd)
queryFacade.delegate = self
}
```

Each time the user ends a stroke, we will start the process of trying to guess what the user is sketching and search for suitable substitutes. This functionality is triggered via the .editingDidEnd action method onSketchViewEditingDidEnd, but will be delegated to the class QueryFacade, which will be responsible for implementing this functionality. This is where we will spend the majority of our time in this section and the next section. It's also probably worth highlighting the statement queryFacade.delegate = self in the previous code snippet. QueryFacade will be performing most of its work off the main thread and will notify this delegate of the status and results once finished, which we will get to in a short while.

Let's start by implementing the functionality of the onSketchViewEditingDidEnd method, before turning our attention to the QueryFacade class. Within the SketchViewController class, navigate to the onSketchViewEditingDidEnd method and append the following code:

```
guard self.sketchView.currentSketch != nil,
    let sketch = self.sketchView.currentSketch as? StrokeSketch else{
    return
}

queryFacade.asyncQuery(sketch: sketch)
```

Here, we are getting the current sketch, and returning it if no sketch is available or if it's not a StrokeSketch; we hand it over to our queryFacade (an instance of the QueryFacade class). Let's now turn our attention to the QueryFacade class; select the QueryFacade.swift file from the left-hand panel within Xcode to bring it up in the editor area. A lot of plumbing has already been implemented to allow us to focus our attention on the core functionality of predicting, searching, and sorting. Let's quickly discuss some of the details, starting with the properties:

```
let context = CIContext()
let queryQueue = DispatchQueue(label: "query_queue")
var targetSize = CGSize(width: 256, height: 256)
weak var delegate : QueryDelegate?
var currentSketch : Sketch?{
    didSet{
        self.newQueryWaiting = true
```

```
            self.queryCanceled = false
        }
    }

    fileprivate var queryCanceled : Bool = false
    fileprivate var newQueryWaiting : Bool = false
    fileprivate var processingQuery : Bool = false
    var isProcessingQuery : Bool{
        get{
            return self.processingQuery
        }
    }

    var isInterrupted : Bool{
        get{
            return self.queryCanceled || self.newQueryWaiting
        }
    }
```

`QueryFacade` is only concerned with the most current sketch. Therefore, each time a new sketch is assigned using the `currentSketch` property, `queryCanceled` is set to `true`. During each task (such as performing prediction, search, and downloading), we check the `isInterrupted` property, and if `true`, we will exit early and proceed to process the latest sketch.

When you pass the sketch to the `asyncQuery` method, the sketch is assigned to the `currentSketch` property and then proceeds to call `queryCurrentSketch` to do the bulk of the work, unless there is one currently being processed:

```
    func asyncQuery(sketch:Sketch){
        self.currentSketch = sketch
        if !self.processingQuery{
            self.queryCurrentSketch()
        }
    }

    fileprivate func processNextQuery(){
        self.queryCanceled = false
        if self.newQueryWaiting && !self.processingQuery{
            self.queryCurrentSketch()
        }
    }

    fileprivate func queryCurrentSketch(){
        guard let sketch = self.currentSketch else{
            self.processingQuery = false
```

```
        self.newQueryWaiting = false
        return
    }
    self.processingQuery = true
    self.newQueryWaiting = false
    queryQueue.async {
        DispatchQueue.main.async{
            self.processingQuery = false
            self.delegate?.onQueryCompleted(
                status:self.isInterrupted ? -1 : -1,
                result:nil)
            self.processNextQuery()
        }
    }
}
```

Eventually, we end up in the `queryCurrentSketch` method, where we will now turn our attention and implement the required functionality. But before doing so, let's quickly discuss what we'll be doing.

Recall that our goal is to assist the user in quickly sketching out a scene; we plan on achieving this by anticipating what the user is trying to draw and suggesting images, which the user can swap with their sketch. Prediction is a major component of this system and is made using the trained model we have just imported, but recall that we achieved approximately 65% accuracy on the validation dataset. This leaves a lot of room for errors, potentially inhibiting the user rather than augmenting them. To mitigate this and provide more utility, we will take the top 3-4 predictions and pull down the relevant images rather than relying on a single classification.

We pass these predicted classes to Microsoft's Bing Image Search API to find relevant images and then proceed to download each of them (admittedly not the most optimized approach, but sufficient for realizing this prototype). Once we have downloaded the images, we will perform some further processing by sorting the images based on how similar each image is to what the user has sketched; we will return to this in the next section, but for now we will concentrate on the steps preceding this. Let's move on to guessing what the user is trying to do.

As we have done previously, let's work bottom-up by implementing all the supporting methods before we tie everything together within the `queryCurrentSketch` method. Let's start by declaring an instance of our model; add the following variable within the `QueryFacade` class near the top:

```
let sketchClassifier = cnnsketchclassifier()
```

Now, with our model instantiated and ready, we will navigate to the `classifySketch` method of the `QueryFacade` class; it is here that we will make use of our imported model to perform inference, but let's first review what already exists:

```
func classifySketch(sketch:Sketch) -> [(key:String,value:Double)]?{
    if let img = sketch.exportSketch(size: nil)?
        .resize(size: self.targetSize).rescalePixels(){
        return self.classifySketch(image: img)
    }
    return nil
}
func classifySketch(image:CIImage) -> [(key:String,value:Double)]?{
    return nil
}
```

Here, we see that the `classifySketch` is overloaded, with one method accepting a `Sketch` and the other a `CIImage`. The former, when called, will obtain the rasterize version of the sketch using the `exportSketch` method. If successful, it will resize the rasterized image using the `targetSize` property. Then, it will rescale the pixels before passing the prepared `CIImage` along to the alternative `classifySketch` method.

 Pixel values are in the range of 0-255 (per channel; in this case, it's just a single channel). Typically, you try to avoid having large numbers in your network. The reason is that they make it more difficult for your model to learn (converge)—somewhat analogous to trying to drive a car whose steering wheel can only be turned hard left or hard right. These extremes would cause a lot of over-steering and make navigating anywhere extremely difficult.

The second `classifySketch` method will be responsible for performing the actual inference; we have already seen how we can do this in Chapter 3, *Recognizing Objects in the world*. Add the following code within the `classifySketch(image:CIImage)` method:

```
if let pixelBuffer = image.toPixelBuffer(context: self.context, gray:
true){
    let prediction = try? self.sketchClassifier.prediction(image:
pixelBuffer)
```

```
    if let classPredictions = prediction?.classLabelProbs{
        let sortedClassPredictions = classPredictions.sorted(by: { (kvp1,
kvp2) -> Bool in
            kvp1.value > kvp2.value
        })
        return sortedClassPredictions
    }
}

return nil
```

Here, we use the images, `toPixelBuffer` method, an extension we added to the `CIImage` class back in Chapter 3, *Recognizing Objects in the World*, to obtain a grayscale `CVPixelBuffer` representation of itself. Now, with reference to its buffer, we pass it onto the `prediction` method of our model instance, `sketchClassifier`, to obtain the probabilities for each label. We finally sort these probabilities from the most likely to the least likely before returning the sorted results to the caller.

Now, with some inkling as to what the user is trying to sketch, we will proceed to search and download the ones we are most confident about. The task of searching and downloading will be the responsibility of the `downloadImages` method within the `QueryFacade` class. This method will make use of an existing `BingService` that exposes methods for searching and downloading images. Let's hook this up now; jump into the `downloadImages` method and append the following highlighted code to its body:

```
func downloadImages(searchTerms:[String],
                    searchTermsCount:Int=4,
                    searchResultsCount:Int=2) -> [CIImage]?{
    var bingResults = [BingServiceResult]()

    for i in 0..<min(searchTermsCount, searchTerms.count){
        let results = BingService.sharedInstance.syncSearch(
            searchTerm: searchTerms[i], count:searchResultsCount)
        for bingResult in results{
            bingResults.append(bingResult)
        }
        if self.isInterrupted{
            return nil
        }
    }
}
```

The `downloadImages` method takes the arguments `searchTerms`, `searchTermsCount`, and `searchResultsCount`. The `searchTerms` is a sorted list of labels returned by our `classifySketch` method, from which the `searchTermsCount` determines how many of these search terms we use (defaulting to 4). Finally, `searchResultsCount` limits the results returned for each search term.

The preceding code performs a sequential search using the search terms passed into the method. And as mentioned previously, here we are using Microsoft's Bing Image Search API, which requires registration, something we will return to shortly. After each search, we check the property `isInterrupted` to see whether we need to exit early; otherwise, we continue on to the next search.

The result returned by the search includes a URL referencing an image; we will use this next to download the image with each of the results, before returning an array of `CIImage` to the caller. Let's add this now. Append the following code to the `downloadImages` method:

```
var images = [CIImage]()

for bingResult in bingResults{
    if let image = BingService.sharedInstance.syncDownloadImage(
        bingResult: bingResult){
        images.append(image)
    }
    if self.isInterrupted{
        return nil
    }
}

return images
```

As before, the process is synchronous and after each download, we check the `isInterrupted` property to see if we need to exit early, otherwise returning the list of downloaded images to the caller.

So far, we have implemented the functionality to support prediction, searching, and downloading; our next task is to hook all of this up. Head back to the `queryCurrentSketch` method and add the following code within the `queryQueue.async` block. Ensure that you replace the `DispatchQueue.main.async` block:

```
queryQueue.async {
    guard let predictions = self.classifySketch(
        sketch: sketch) else{
            DispatchQueue.main.async{
```

```
                    self.processingQuery = false
                    self.delegate?.onQueryCompleted(
                        status:-1, result:nil)
                    self.processNextQuery()
                }
                return
        }
        let searchTerms = predictions.map({ (key, value) -> String in
            return key
        })
        guard let images = self.downloadImages(
            searchTerms: searchTerms,
            searchTermsCount: 4) else{
                DispatchQueue.main.async{
                    self.processingQuery = false
                    self.delegate?.onQueryCompleted(
                        status:-1, result:nil)
                    self.processNextQuery()
                }
                return
        }
        guard let sortedImage = self.sortByVisualSimilarity(
            images: images,
            sketch: sketch) else{
                DispatchQueue.main.async{
                    self.processingQuery = false
                    self.delegate?.onQueryCompleted(
                        status:-1, result:nil)
                    self.processNextQuery()
                }
                return
        }
        DispatchQueue.main.async{
            self.processingQuery = false
            self.delegate?.onQueryCompleted(
                status:self.isInterrupted ? -1 : 1,
                result:QueryResult(
                    predictions: predictions,
                    images: sortedImage))
            self.processNextQuery()
        }
    }
}
```

It's a large block of code but nothing complicated; let's quickly walk our way through it. We start by calling the `classifySketch` method we just implemented. As you may recall, this method returns a sorted list of label and probability peers unless interrupted, in which case `nil` will be returned. We should handle this by notifying the delegate before exiting the method early (a check we apply to all of our tasks).

Once we've obtained the list of sorted labels, we pass them to the `downloadImages` method to receive the associated images, which we then pass to the `sortByVisualSimilarity` method. This method currently returns just the list of images, but it's something we will get back to in the next section. Finally, the method passes the status and sorted images wrapped in a `QueryResult` instance to the delegate via the main thread, before checking whether it needs to process a new sketch (by calling the `processNextQuery` method).

At this stage, we have implemented all the functionality required to download our substitute images based on our guess as to what the user is currently sketching. Now, we just need to jump into the `SketchViewController` class to hook this up, but before doing so, we need to obtain a subscription key to use Bing's Image Search.

Within your browser, head to `https://azure.microsoft.com/en-gb/services/cognitive-services/bing-image-search-api/` and click on the **Try Bing Image Search API**, as shown in the following screenshot:

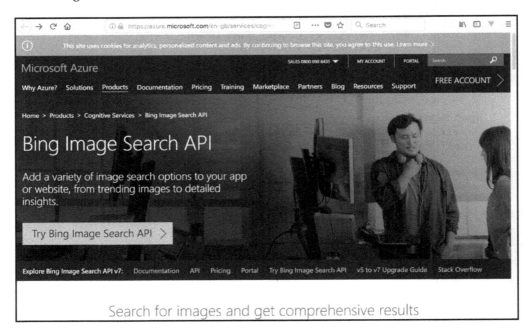

After clicking on **Try Bing Image Search API**, you will be presented with a series of dialogs; read, and once (if) agreed, sign in or register. Continue following the screens until you reach a page informing you that the Bing Search API has been successfully added to your subscription, as shown in the following screenshot:

On this page, scroll down until you come across the entry **Bing Search APIs v7**. If you inspect this block, you should see a list of **Endpoints** and **Keys**. Copy and paste one of these keys within the `BingService.swift` file, replacing the value of the constant `subscriptionKey`; the following screenshot shows the web page containing the service key:

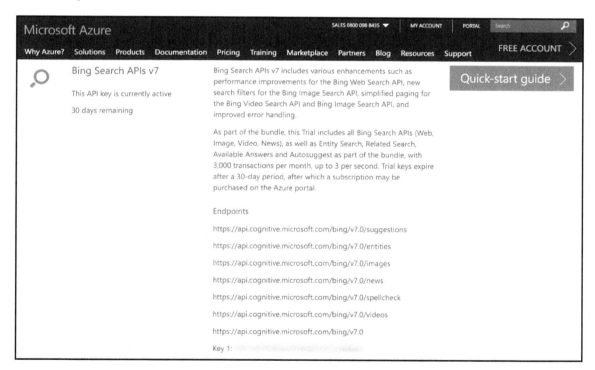

Return to the `SketchViewController` by selecting the `SketchViewController.swift` file from the left-hand panel, and locate the method `onQueryCompleted`:

```
func onQueryCompleted(status: Int, result:QueryResult?){
}
```

Recall that this is a method signature defined in the `QueryDelegate` protocol, which the `QueryFacade` uses to notify the delegate if the query fails or completes. It is here that we will present the matching images we have found through the process we just implemented. We do this by first checking the status. If deemed successful (greater than zero), we remove every item that is referenced in the `queryImages` array, which is the data source for our `UICollectionView` used to present the suggested images to the user. Once emptied, we iterate through all the images referenced within the `QueryResult` instance, adding them to the `queryImages` array before requesting the `UICollectionView` to reload the data. Add the following code to the body of the `onQueryCompleted` method:

```
guard status > 0 else{
    return
}

queryImages.removeAll()

if let result = result{
    for cimage in result.images{
        if let cgImage = self.ciContext.createCGImage(cimage,
from:cimage.extent){
            queryImages.append(UIImage(cgImage:cgImage))
        }
    }
}

toolBarLabel.isHidden = queryImages.count == 0
collectionView.reloadData()
```

There we have it; everything is in place to handle guessing of what the user draws and present possible suggestions. Now is a good time to build and run the application on either the simulator or the device to check whether everything is working correctly. If so, then you should see something similar to the following:

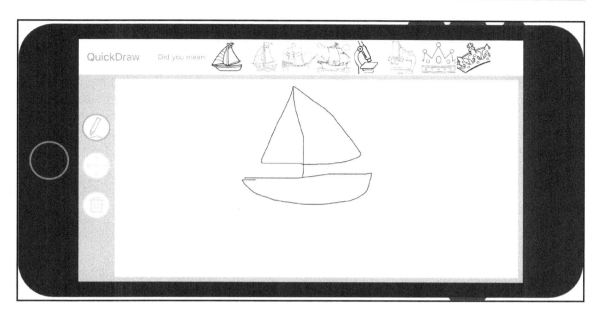

There is one more thing left to do before finishing off this section. Remembering that our goal is to assist the user to quickly sketch out a scene or something similar, our hypothesis is that guessing what the user is drawing and suggesting ready-drawn images will help them achieve their task. So far, we have performed prediction and provided suggestions to the user, but currently the user is unable to replace their sketch with any of the presented suggestions. Let's address this now.

Our SketchView currently only renders StrokeSketch (which encapsulates the metadata of the user's drawing). Because our suggestions are rasterized images, our choice is to either extend this class (to render strokes and rasterized images) or create a new concrete implementation of the Sketch protocol. In this example, we will opt for the latter and implement a new type of Sketch capable of rendering a rasterized image. Select the Sketch.swift file to bring it to focus in the editor area of Xcode, scroll to the bottom, and add the following code:

```
class ImageSketch : Sketch{
    var image : UIImage!
    var size : CGSize!
    var origin : CGPoint!
    var label : String!
     init(image:UIImage, origin:CGPoint, size:CGSize, label: String) {
        self.image = image
        self.size = size
        self.label = label
```

```
            self.origin = origin
        }
    }
```

We have defined a simple class that is referencing an image, origin, size, and label. The origin determines the top-left position where the image should be rendered, while the size determines its, well, size! To satisfy the `Sketch` protocol, we must implement the properties `center` and `boundingBox` along with the methods `draw` and `exportSketch`. Let's implement each of these in turn, starting with `boundingBox`.

The `boundingBox` property is a computed property derived from the properties `origin` and `size`. Add the following code to your `ImageSketch` class:

```
    var boundingBox : CGRect{
        get{
            return CGRect(origin: self.origin, size: self.size)
        }
    }
```

Similarly, `center` will be another computed property derived from the origin and size properties, simply translating the `origin` with respect to the `size`. Add the following code to your `ImageSketch` class:

```
    var center : CGPoint{
        get{
            let bbox = self.boundingBox
            return CGPoint(x:bbox.origin.x + bbox.size.width/2,
                           y:bbox.origin.y + bbox.size.height/2)
        } set{
            self.origin = CGPoint(x:newValue.x - self.size.width/2,
                                  y:newValue.y - self.size.height/2)
        }
    }
```

The `draw` method will simply use the passed-in `context` to render the assigned `image` within the `boundingBox`; append the following code to your `ImageSketch` class:

```
    func draw(context:CGContext){
        self.image.draw(in: self.boundingBox)
    }
```

Our last method, exportSketch, is also fairly straightforward. Here, we create an instance of CIImage, passing in the image (of type UIImage). Then, we resize it using the extension method we implemented back in Chapter 3, *Recognizing Objects in the World*. Add the following code to finish off the ImageSketch class:

```
func exportSketch(size:CGSize?) -> CIImage?{
    guard let ciImage = CIImage(image: self.image) else{
        return nil
    }
    if self.image.size.width == self.size.width && self.image.size.height
== self.size.height{
        return ciImage
    } else{
        return ciImage.resize(size: self.size)
    }
}
```

We now have an implementation of Sketch that can handle rendering of rasterized images (like those returned from our search). Our final task is to swap the user's sketch with an item the user selects from the UICollectionView. Return to SketchViewController class by selecting the SketchViewController.swift from the left-hand-side panel in Xcode to bring it up in the editor area. Once loaded, navigate to the method collectionView(_ collectionView:, didSelectItemAt:); this should look familiar to most of you. It is the delegate method for handling cells selected from a UICollectionView and it's where we will handle swapping of the user's current sketch with the selected item.

Let's start by obtaining the current sketch and associated image that was selected. Add the following code to the body of the collectionView(_collectionView:,didSelectItemAt:) method:

```
guard let sketch = self.sketchView.currentSketch else{
    return
}
self.queryFacade.cancel()
let image = self.queryImages[indexPath.row]
```

Now, with reference to the current sketch and image, we want to try and keep the size relatively the same as the user's sketch. We will do this by simply obtaining the sketch's bounding box and scaling the dimensions to respect the aspect ratio of the selected image. Add the following code, which handles this:

```
var origin = CGPoint(x:0, y:0)
var size = CGSize(width:0, height:0)
if bbox.size.width > bbox.size.height{
    let ratio = image.size.height / image.size.width
    size.width = bbox.size.width
    size.height = bbox.size.width * ratio
} else{
    let ratio = image.size.width / image.size.height
    size.width = bbox.size.height * ratio
    size.height = bbox.size.height
}
```

Next, we obtain the origin (top left of the image) by obtaining the center of the sketch and offsetting it relative to its width and height. Do this by appending the following code:

```
origin.x = sketch.center.x - size.width / 2
origin.y = sketch.center.y - size.height / 2
```

We can now use the image, size, and origin to create an `ImageSketch`, and replace it with the current sketch simply by assigning it to the `currentSketch` property of the `SketchView` instance. Add the following code to do just that:

```
self.sketchView.currentSketch = ImageSketch(image:image,
                                            origin:origin,
                                            size:size,
                                            label:"")
```

Finally, some housekeeping; we'll clear the `UICollectionView` by removing all images from the `queryImages` array (its data source) and request it to reload itself. Add the following block to complete the `collectionView(_ collectionView:,didSelectItemAt:)` method:

```
self.queryImages.removeAll()
self.toolBarLabel.isHidden = queryImages.count == 0
self.collectionView.reloadData()
```

Everything is now hooked up; we have implemented all of the functionality that guesses what the user is drawing, presents suggestions, and allows the user to swap their rough sketch with an alternative. Now is a good time to build and run to ensure that everything is working as planned. If so then, you should be able to swap out your sketch with one of the suggestions presented at the top, as shown in the following screenshot:

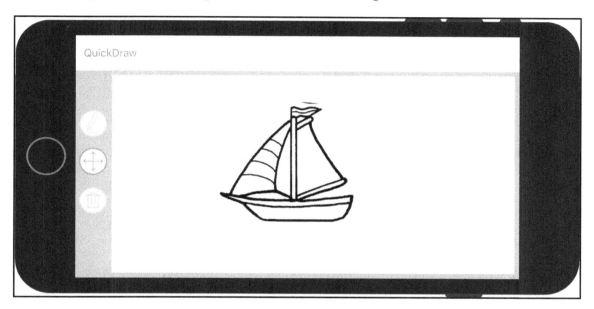

One last section before wrapping this chapter up. In this section, we will look at a technique to fine-tune our search results to better match what the user has drawn.

# Sorting by visual similarity

So far, we have achieved what we set out to do, that is, inferring what the user is trying to draw and providing them with suggestions that they can swap their sketch with. But our solution currently falls short of understanding the user. Sure, it may predict correctly and provide the correct category of what the user is drawing, but it dismisses any style or details of the user's drawing. For example, if the user is drawing, and only wanting, a cats head, our model may predict correctly that the user is drawing a cat but ignore the fact that their drawing lacks a body. It is likely to suggest images of full-bodied cats.

In this section, we will look at a technique to be more sensitive with respect to the user's input, and provide a very rudimentary solution but one that can be built upon. This approach will attempt to sort images by how similar they are with the user's sketch. Before jumping into the code, let's take a quick detour to discuss similarity metrics, by looking at how we can measure the similarity between something in a different domain, such as sentences. The following are three sentences we will base our discussion on:

- **"the quick brown fox jumped over the lazy dog"**
- **"the quick brown fox runs around the lazy farm dog"**
- **"machine learning creates new opportunities for interacting with computers"**

This exercise will be familiar to those withhttps://packt-type-cloud.s3.amazonaws.com/uploads/sites/1956/2018/06/B09544_08_14.p ngal representation. Here, we will create a vocabulary with all words that exist in our corpus (the three sentences, in this instance) and then create vectors for each sentence by incrementing the sentences words with their corresponding index in the vocabulary, as shown in the following screenshot:

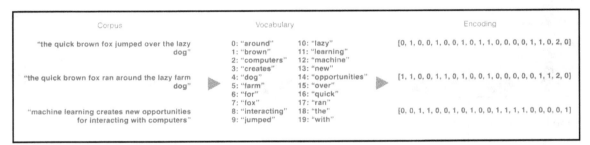

With our sentences now encoded as vectors, we can measure the similarity between each sentence by performing distance operations such as **Euclidean Distance** and **Cosine Distance**. The equations for each of these are as follows:

$$\sqrt{\sum_{i=0}^{n}(sentVecA_i - sentVecB_i)^2} \qquad 1 - \frac{\sum_{i=0}^{n} sentVecA_i \times sentVecB_i}{\sqrt{\sum_{i=0}^{n}(sentVecA_i)^2}\sqrt{\sum_{i=0}^{n}(sentVecB_i)^2}}$$

**Euclidean Distance**             **Cosine Distance**

Let's now calculate the distances between each of the sentences and compare the results. See the following screenshot for the results:

| | "the quick brown fox jumped over the lazy dog" | | "the quick brown fox ran around the lazy farm dog" | | "machine learning creates new opportunities for interacting with computers" | |
|---|---|---|---|---|---|---|
| | Euclidean Distance | Cosine Distance | Euclidean Distance | Cosine Distance | Euclidean Distance | Cosine Distance |
| "the quick brown fox jumped over the lazy dog" | 0.0 | 0.0 | 2.2 | 0.2 | 4.5 | 1.0 |
| "the quick brown fox ran around the lazy farm dog" | 2.2 | 0.2 | 0.0 | 0.0 | 4.6 | 1.0 |
| "machine learning creates new opportunities for interacting with computers" | 4.5 | 1.0 | 4.6 | 1.0 | 0.0 | 0.0 |

As you would expect, the sentences "**the quick brown fox jumped over the lazy dog**" and "**the quick brown fox ran around the lazy farm dog**" have a smaller distance between them compared to that for the sentence "**machine learning creates new opportunities for interacting with computers**". If you were to build a recommendation engine, albeit a naive one, you would likely rank the sentences with more words in common higher than the ones with less words in common. The same is true for images, but unlike sentences, where we are using words as features, we use the features derived from layers of the network.

Recall that our network for classifying sketches consists of a stack of convolution layers, with each layer building higher level patterns based on the patterns from the layers below it. Intuitively, we can think of these higher level patterns as our words (features) and the fully connected network as the sentences representing what words are present for a given image. To make this clearer, a simple illustration is shown here:

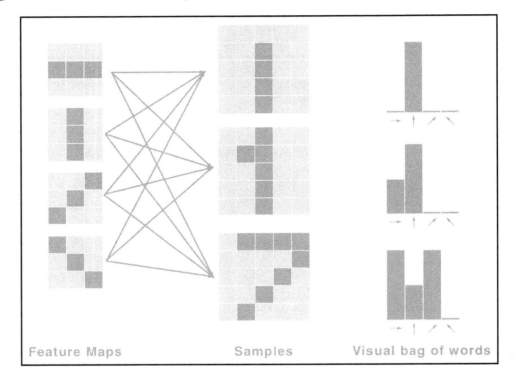

Examining the figure, we can see the set of feature maps on the left, which can be thought of as convolutional kernels used to extract horizontal, vertical, left, and right diagonal edges from the images.

In the middle are the samples from which we will be extracting these features. Finally, on the far right, we have the extracted features (histogram) of each of the samples. We use these extracted features as our feature vectors and can use them to calculate the distance between them, as we saw in the previous figure.

So, if we are able to extract this type of feature vector from an image, then we will also be able to sort them relative to the user's sketch (using its extracted feature vectors). But how do we get this feature vector? Recall that we already have a network that has learned high-level feature maps. If we are able to obtain a vector indicating which of these features are most active for a given image, then we can use this vector as our feature vector and use it to calculate the distance between other images, such as the user's sketch and downloaded images. This is exactly what we will do; instead of feeding the network through a softmax activation layer (to perform prediction on the classes), we will remove this layer from our network, leaving the last fully connected layer as the new output layer. This essentially provides us with a feature vector that we can then use to compare with other images. The following figure shows how the updated network looks diagrammatically:

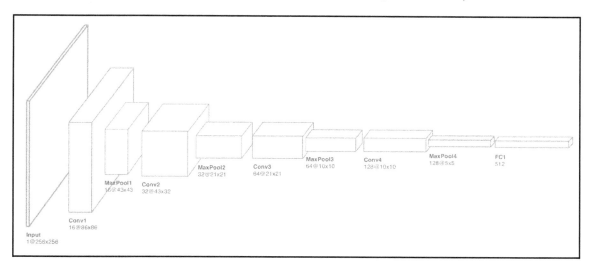

If you compare this with the network presented in the previous section, you will notice that the only change is the absence of the fully connected layer. The output of this network is now a feature vector of size 512. Let's make this concept more concrete by playing with it.

I assume you have already pulled down the accompanying code from the repository https://github.com/packtpublishing/machine-learning-with-core-ml. Navigate to the Chapter7/Start/QuickDraw/ directory and open the playground FeatureExtraction.playground. This playground includes the generated code and compiled model described earlier, along with some views and helper methods that we will make use of; all should be fairly self-explanatory. Let's begin by importing some dependencies and declaring some variables by adding the following code to the top of the playground:

```
import Accelerate
import CoreML

let histogramViewFrame = CGRect(
    x: 0, y: 0,
    width: 600, height: 300)

let heatmapViewFrame = CGRect(
    x: 0, y: 0,
    width: 600, height: 600)

let sketchFeatureExtractor = cnnsketchfeatureextractor()
let targetSize = CGSize(width: 256, height: 256)
let context = CIContext()
```

Here, we declare two rectangles; they will determine the frame of the views we will create later and, most importantly, instantiate our model, which we will use to extract features from each image. Talking about this, if you expand the Resources folder on the left-hand panel, then again in the Images folder, you'll see the images we will be using, as shown here:

As we discussed, we want to be able to sort the images so that the suggested images closely match what the user is drawing. Continuing on from our example from the user drawing just a cat's head, we want a way to sort out the images so that those with just a cat's head show up before those with a cat and its body. Let's continue on with our experiment; add the following methods, which we will use to extract the features from a given image:

```
func extractFeaturesFromImage(image:UIImage) -> MLMultiArray?{
    guard let image = CIImage(
        image: image) else{
        return nil
    }
    return extractFeaturesFromImage(image: image)
}

func extractFeaturesFromImage(image:CIImage) -> MLMultiArray?{
    guard let imagePixelBuffer = image.resize(
        size: targetSize)
        .rescalePixels()?
        .toPixelBuffer(context: context,
                       gray: true) else {
        return nil
    }

    guard let features = try? sketchFeatureExtractor.prediction(
        image: imagePixelBuffer) else{
        return nil
    }

    return features.classActivations
}
```

Most of the code should look familiar to you; we have an overloaded method for handling `UIImage`, which simply creates a `CIImage` instance of it before passing it to the other method. This will handle preparing the image and finally feed it into the model. Once inference has been performed, we return the model's property `classActiviations` as discussed previously. This is the output from the last fully connected layer, which we'll use as our feature vector for comparison.

Next, we will load all of our images and extract the features from each of them. Add the following code to your playground:

```
var images = [UIImage]()
var imageFeatures = [MLMultiArray]()
for i in 1...6{
    guard let image = UIImage(named:"images/cat_\(i).png"),
        let features = extractFeaturesFromImage(image:image) else{
            fatalError("Failed to extract features")
    }
    images.append(image)
    imageFeatures.append(features)
}
```

With our images and features now available, let's inspect a few of the images and their feature maps. We can do this by creating an instance of `HistogramView` and passing in the features. Here is the code to do just that:

```
let img1 = images[0]
let hist1 = HistogramView(frame:histogramViewFrame, data:imageFeatures[0])

let img2 = images[1]
let hist2 = HistogramView(frame:histogramViewFrame, data:imageFeatures[1])

// cat front view
let img3 = images[2]
let hist3 = HistogramView(frame:histogramViewFrame, data:imageFeatures[2])

let img4 = images[3]
let hist4 = HistogramView(frame:histogramViewFrame, data:imageFeatures[3])

// cats head
let img5 = images[4]
let hist5 = HistogramView(frame:histogramViewFrame, data:imageFeatures[4])

let img6 = images[5]
let hist6 = HistogramView(frame:histogramViewFrame, data:imageFeatures[5])
```

You can manually inspect each of them by clicking on the eye icon within the preview view associated with the state, as shown in the following screenshot:

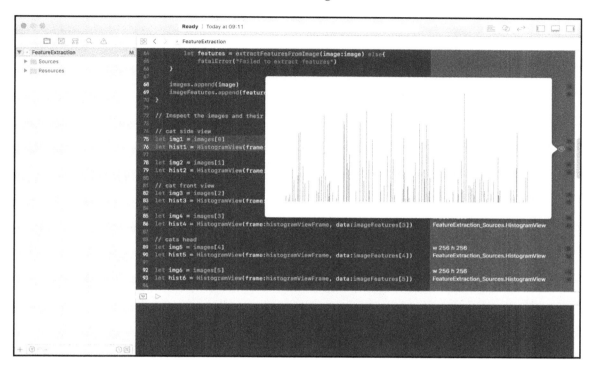

Inspecting each of them individually doesn't provide much insight. So in this figure, I have presented three images that we can inspect:

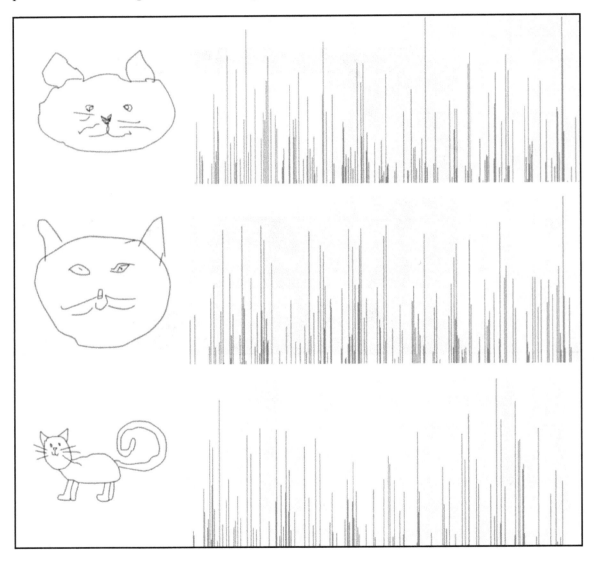

Without too much focus, you get a sense that the cat heads' feature vectors are more closely aligned than the feature vector of the side on view of the cat, especially on the right-hand of the plot.

Let's further explore this by calculating the cosine distance between each of the images and plotting them on a heat map. Start by adding the following code; it will be used to calculate the cosine distance:

```swift
func dot(vecA: MLMultiArray, vecB: MLMultiArray) -> Double {
    guard vecA.shape.count == 1 && vecB.shape.count == 1 else{
        fatalError("Expecting vectors (tensor with 1 rank)")
    }
    guard vecA.count == vecB.count else {
        fatalError("Excepting count of both vectors to be equal")
    }
    let count = vecA.count
    let vecAPtr =
UnsafeMutablePointer<Double>(OpaquePointer(vecA.dataPointer))
    let vecBPptr =
UnsafeMutablePointer<Double>(OpaquePointer(vecB.dataPointer))
    var output: Double = 0.0
    vDSP_dotprD(vecAPtr, 1, vecBPptr, 1, &output, vDSP_Length(count))
    var x: Double = 0
    for i in 0..<vecA.count{
        x += vecA[i].doubleValue * vecB[i].doubleValue
    }
    return x
}

func magnitude(vec: MLMultiArray) -> Double {
    guard vec.shape.count == 1 else{
        fatalError("Expecting a vector (tensor with 1 rank)")
    }
    let count = vec.count
    let vecPtr =
UnsafeMutablePointer<Double>(OpaquePointer(vec.dataPointer))
    var output: Double = 0.0
    vDSP_svsD(vecPtr, 1, &output, vDSP_Length(count))
    return sqrt(output)
}
```

The details of the equation were presented before and this is just a translation of these into Swift; what is important is the use of the **vector Digital Signal Processing (vDSP )** functions available within iOS's Accelerate framework. As described in the documentation, the vDSP API provides mathematical functions for applications such as speech, sound, audio, video processing, diagnostic medical imaging, radar signal processing, seismic analysis, and scientific data processing. Because it's built on top of Accelerate, it inherits the performance gains achieved through **single instruction, multiple data (SIMD)** running the same instruction concurrently across a vector of data—something very important when dealing with large vectors such as those from neural networks. Admittedly, at first it seems unintuitive, but the documentation provides most of what you'll need to make good use of it; let's inspect the `magnitude` method to get a feel for it.

We use the `vDSP_svsD` function to calculate the magnitude of our feature vectors; the function is expecting these arguments (in order): a pointer to the data (`UnsafePointer<Double>`), strides (`vDSP_Stride`), a pointer to the output variable (`UnsafeMutablePointer<Double>`), and finally the length (`vDSP_Length`). Most of the work is in preparing these arguments, as shown in this code snippet:

```
let vecPtr = UnsafeMutablePointer<Double>(OpaquePointer(vec.dataPointer))
var output: Double = 0.0
vDSP_svsD(vecPtr, 1, &output, vDSP_Length(vec.count))
```

After this function returns, we will have the calculated the magnitude of a given vector stored in the `output` variable. Let's now make use of this and calculate the distance between each of the images. Add the following code to your playground:

```
var similarities = Array(repeating: Array(repeating: 0.0, count:
images.count), count: images.count)

for i in 0..<imageFeatures.count{
    for j in 0..<imageFeatures.count{
        let sim = cosineSimilarity(
            vecA: imageFeatures[i],
            vecB: imageFeatures[j])
        similarities[i][j] = sim
    }
}
```

Here, we are iterating through each of the images twice to create a matrix (multi-dimensional array, in this case) to store the distances (similarities) between each of the images. We will now feed this, along with the associated images, to an instance of `HeatmapView`, which will visualize the distances between each of the images. Add the following code and then expand the view by clicking on the eye icon within the results panel to see the result:

```
let heatmap = HeatmapView(
    frame:heatmapViewFrame,
    images:images,
    data:similarities)
```

As mentioned previously, by previewing the view, you should see something similar to the following figure:

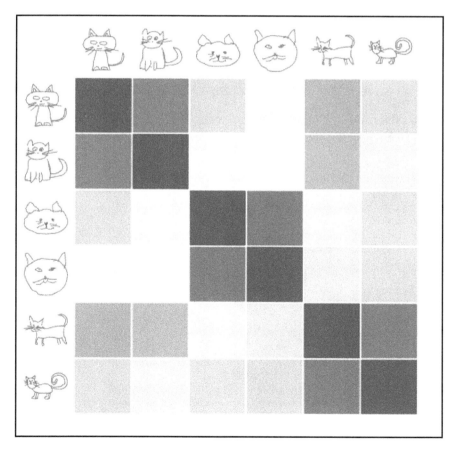

This visualization shows the distance between each of the images; the darker the cell, the closer they are. For example, if you look at cell 1 x 1, cell 2 x 2, and so on, you will see that each of these cells are darker (a distance of 0 because they are the same image). You'll also notice another pattern form: clusters of four cells diagonally down the plot. This, consequently, was our goal—to see whether we could sort sketches by their similarities, such as cats drawn front on, cat heads, and cats drawn side on.

Armed with our new knowledge, let's return to the iPhone project `QuickDraw.xcodeproj`, where we will copy this code across and implement sorting.

With the `QuickDraw` project now open, locate the feature extractor model from the project repositories folder `/CoreMLModels/Chapter7/cnnsketchfeatureextractor.mlmodel`. With the model selected, drag it onto your Xcode project, leaving the defaults for the import options.

With the model now imported, select the file `QueryFacade.swift` from the left-hand panel (within Xcode) to bring it up in the editor area. With the class open, add an instance variable to the top of the `QueryFacade` class, as shown here:

```
let sketchFeatureExtractor = cnnsketchfeatureextractor()
```

Next, copy across the methods `extractFeaturesFromImage`, `cosineSimilarity`, `dot`, and `magnitude` from your playground to the `QueryFacade` class, as shown here:

```
func extractFeaturesFromImage(image:CIImage) -> MLMultiArray?{
    // obtain the CVPixelBuffer from the image
    guard let imagePixelBuffer = image
        .resize(size: self.targetSize)
        .rescalePixels()?
        .toPixelBuffer(context: self.context, gray: true) else {
        return nil
    }
    guard let features = try? self.sketchFeatureExtractor
        .prediction(image: imagePixelBuffer) else{
        return nil
    }
    return features.classActivations
}

func cosineSimilarity(vecA: MLMultiArray,
                      vecB: MLMultiArray) -> Double {
    return 1.0 - self.dot(vecA:vecA, vecB:vecB) /
        (self.magnitude(vec: vecA) * self.magnitude(vec: vecB))
}
```

```
func dot(vecA: MLMultiArray, vecB: MLMultiArray) -> Double {
    guard vecA.shape.count == 1 && vecB.shape.count == 1 else{
        fatalError("Expecting vectors (tensor with 1 rank)")
    }
    guard vecA.count == vecB.count else {
        fatalError("Excepting count of both vectors to be equal")
    }
    let count = vecA.count
    let vecAPtr = UnsafeMutablePointer<Double>(
        OpaquePointer(vecA.dataPointer)
    )
    let vecBPptr = UnsafeMutablePointer<Double>(
        OpaquePointer(vecB.dataPointer)
    )
    var output: Double = 0.0
    vDSP_dotprD(vecAPtr, 1,
                vecBPptr, 1,
                &output,
                vDSP_Length(count))
    var x: Double = 0
    for i in 0..<vecA.count{
        x += vecA[i].doubleValue * vecB[i].doubleValue
    }
    return x
}

func magnitude(vec: MLMultiArray) -> Double {
    guard vec.shape.count == 1 else{
        fatalError("Expecting a vector (tensor with 1 rank)")
    }
    let count = vec.count
    let vecPtr = UnsafeMutablePointer<Double>(
        OpaquePointer(vec.dataPointer)
    )
    var output: Double = 0.0
    vDSP_svsD(vecPtr, 1, &output, vDSP_Length(count))
    return sqrt(output)
}
```

With our methods now it place, it's time to make use of them. Locate the method `sortByVisualSimilarity(images:[CIImage], sketchImage:CIImage)`; this method is already called within the `queryCurrentSketch` method, but currently it just returns the list that was passed in. It's within this method that we want to add some order by sorting the list so that the images most similar to the user's sketch are first. Let's build this up in chunks, starting with extracting the image features of the user's sketch. Add the following code to the body of the `sortByVisualSimilarity` method, replacing its current contents:

```
guard let sketchFeatures = self.extractFeaturesFromImage(
    image: sketchImage) else{
    return nil
}
```

Next, we want the features of all the other images, which we do simply by iterating over the list and storing them in an array. Add the following code to do just that:

```
var similatiryScores = Array<Double>(
    repeating:1.0,
    count:images.count)

for i in 0..<images.count{
    var similarityScore : Double = 1.0
    if let imageFeatures = self.extractFeaturesFromImage(
        image: images[i]){
        similarityScore = self.cosineSimilarity(
            vecA: sketchFeatures,
            vecB: imageFeatures)
    }
    similatiryScores[i] = similarityScore
    if self.isInterrupted{
        return nil
    }
}
```

As we did previously, after each image, we check whether the process has been interrupted by checking the property `isInterrupted`, before moving on to the next image. Our final task is to sort and return this images; add the following code to the body of the method `sortByVisualSimilarity`:

```
return images.enumerated().sorted { (elemA, elemB) -> Bool in
    return similatiryScores[elemA.offset] < similatiryScores[elemB.offset]
    }.map { (item) -> CIImage in
        return item.element
}
```

With that implemented, now is a good time to build and run your project to see that is everything is working, and compare the results with the previous build.

And this concludes the chapter; we will briefly wrap up in the summary before moving on to the next chapter.

# Summary

You are still here. I'm impressed, and congratulations! It was a long but fruitful chapter. We saw another example of how we can apply CNNs, and in doing so, we further developed our understanding of how they work, how to tune them, and ways in which we can modify them. We saw how we could use the learned features not just for classification but ranking, a technique used in many domains such as fashion discovery and recommendation engines. We also spent a significant amount of time building a drawing application, which we will continue to use in the next chapter. There, we will again explore how to perform sketch classification using a RNN trained on Google's `QuickDraw` dataset. Lots of fun ahead, so let's get started.

# Assisted Drawing with RNNs

# 8

In the previous chapter, we walked through building a simple drawing application that would try to infer what the user was drawing and present them with alternatives based on the most likely predicted categories; the intention of this application was to improve the efficiency of sketching tasks by giving the user completed sketches, obtained through Microsoft's Bing image search, rather than having to spend time fussing over the details.

In this chapter, we'll revisit this application but look at an alternative for inferring what the user is drawing, and, in doing so, we will be exposing ourselves to new types of data and machine learning models. Following the familiar format, we will first revise the task, explore the data and model, and then walk through building up the required functionality in a playground, before migrating it across to our application. Let's get started.

## Assisted drawing

In this section, we will briefly describe this chapter's project and what we aim to achieve. Recall from the previous chapter that we described an application capable of predicting what the user was trying to sketch, and fetched similar images based on the predicted categories, such as a sailboat. Based on this prediction, the application would search and download images of that category. After downloading, it would sort them based on their similarity with regards to the user's sketch. Then it would present the ordered alternatives to the user, which they could swap their sketch with.

The finished project is shown as follows:

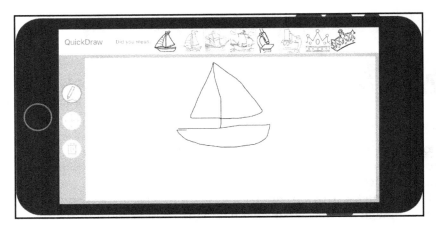

The model used for performing this classification was based on a **Convolutional Neural Network (CNN)**, a type of neural network well suited for understanding images owing to its ability to find local patterns and build on top of these lower patterns to find more complex and interesting patterns. We took advantage of these higher order patterns by using them as a basis to sort our downloaded images, such that those that were more similar in style to the user's sketch would be shown first. We reasoned how this worked by comparing it with measurements of similarities between sentences using words as features—words being analogous to our higher order patterns—and distance formulas to calculate the similarities.

But our approach suffered from a bit of overhead; to perform accurate classification, we needed a significant amount of the sketch completed, as well as needing to use memory and CPU cycles to rasterize the image before we could feed it into our model. In this chapter, we will be using an alternative that doesn't rely on pixels as its features but rather the **sequences of strokes** used to draw it. There are numerous reasons you may want to do this, including:

- Accessibility to the data or larger dataset
- Potential improvements to the accuracy of the predictions
- Generative capabilities, that is, being able to predict and generate the next set of strokes

But here, it gives us the opportunity to explore a type of data that encodes essentially the same thing—a sketch. Let's explore this further in the next section, where we introduce the dataset and model that will be used in this project.

# Recurrent Neural Networks for drawing classification

The model used in this chapter was trained on the dataset used in Google's AI experiment *Quick, Draw!*

*Quick, Draw!* is a game where players are challenged to draw a given object to see whether the computer can recognize it; an extract of the data is shown as follows:

The technique was inspired from the work done on handwritten recognition (Google Translate), where, rather than looking at the image as a whole, the team worked with data features describing how the characters were drawn. This is illustrated in the following image:

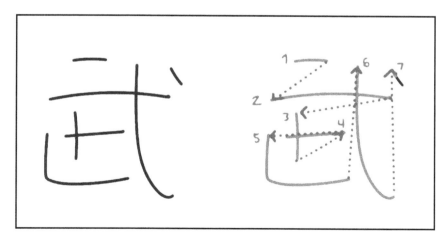

Source: https://experiments.withgoogle.com/ai/quick-draw

The hypothesis here is that there exists some consistent pattern of how people draw certain types of objects; but to discover those patterns, we would need a lot of data, which we do have. The dataset consists of over 50 million drawings across 345 categories obtained cleverly, from the players of the *Quick, Draw!* game. Each sample is described with timestamped vectors and associated metadata describing the country the player was based in and the category asked of the user. You can learn more about the dataset from the official website: https://github.com/googlecreativelab/quickdraw-dataset.

To make the dataset and training manageable, our model was only trained on 172 of the 345 categories, but the accompanying Notebook used to create and train the model is available for those wanting to delve into the details. To get a better understanding of the data, let's have a peek at a single sample, as shown here:

```
{
    "key_id":"5891796615823360",
    "word":"nose",
    "countrycode":"AE",
    "timestamp":"2017-03-01 20:41:36.70725 UTC",
    "recognized":true,
    "drawing":[[[129,128,129,129,130,130,131,132,132,133,133,133,133,...]]]
}
```

The details of the sketch are broken down into an array of strokes, each described by a three-dimensional array containing the x, y positions and timestamp that make up the path of the stroke:

```
[
    [ // First stroke
    [x0, x1, x2, x3, ...],
    [y0, y1, y2, y3, ...],
    [t0, t1, t2, t3, ...]
    ],
    [ // Second stroke
    [x0, x1, x2, x3, ...],
    [y0, y1, y2, y3, ...],
    [t0, t1, t2, t3, ...]
    ],
    ... // Additional strokes
]
```

As mentioned previously, this being an example from the **raw dataset**, the team behind *Quick, Draw!* has released many variants of the data, from raw samples to preprocessed and compressed versions. We are mostly interested in exploring the raw and simplified versions: the former because it's the closest representation we have that will represent the data we obtain from the user, and the latter because it was used to train the model.

**Spoiler**: Most of this chapter deals with preprocessing the user input.

Both raw and simplified versions have stored each category in an individual file in the NDJSON file format.

The NDJSON file format, short for newline delimited JSON, is a convenient format for storing and streaming structured data that may be processed one record at a time. As the name suggests, it stores multiple JSON-formatted objects in single lines. In our case, this means each sample is stored as a separate object delimited by a new line; you can learn more about the format at http://ndjson.org.

You may be wondering what the difference is between the raw and simplified versions. We will go into the details when we build the preprocessing functionality required for this application, but as the name implies, the simplified version reduces the complexity of each stroke by removing any unnecessary points, along with applying some level of standardization—a typical requirement when dealing with any data to make the samples more comparable.

Now that we have a better understanding of the data we are dealing with, let's turn our attention to building up some level of intuition of how we can learn from these sequences, by briefly discussing the details of the model used in this chapter.

In previous chapters, we saw many examples of how CNNs can learn useful patterns from local 2D patches, which themselves can be built upon to further abstract from raw pixels into something with more descriptive power. This is fairly intuitive given our understanding of images is not made up of independent pixels but rather a collection of pixels related to their neighbors, which in turn describe parts of an object. In Chapter 1, *Introduction to Machine Learning*, we introduced a **Recurrent Neural Network (RNN)**, a major component of building the **Sequence to Sequence (Seq2Seq)** model used for language translation, and we saw how its ability to remember made it well suited for data made up of sequences where order matters. As highlighted previously, our given samples are made up of sequences of strokes; the RNN is a likely candidate for learning to classify sketches.

As a quick recap, RNNs implement a type of **selective memory** using a feedback loop, which itself is adjusted during training; diagrammatically this is shown as follows:

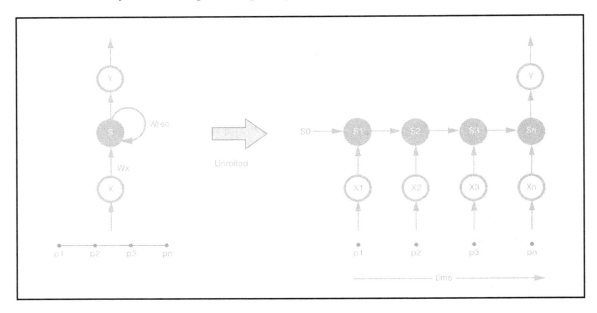

On the left is the actual network, and on the right we have the same network unrolled across four time steps. As the points of the sketch's strokes are fed in, they are multiplied by the layer's weight along with the current state before being fed back in and/or outputted. During training, this feedback allows the network to learn patterns of an ordered sequence. We can stack these recurrent layers on top of each other to learn more complex and abstract patterns as we did with CNN.

But recurrent layers are not the only way to learn patterns from sequential data. If you generalize the concept of CNNs as something being able to learn local patterns across any dimension (as opposed to just two dimensions), then you can see how we could use 1D convolutional layers to achieve a similar effect as our recurrent layers. Therein, similar to 2D convolutional layers, we learn 1D kernels across sequences (treating time as a spatial dimension) to find local patterns to represent our data. Using a convolutional layer has the advantage of being considerably computationally cheaper than its counterpart, making it ideal for processor- and power-constrained devices, such as mobile phones. It is also advantageous for its ability to learn patterns independent of order, similar to how 2D kernels are invariant of position. In this figure, we illustrate how the 1D convolutional layer operates on input data:

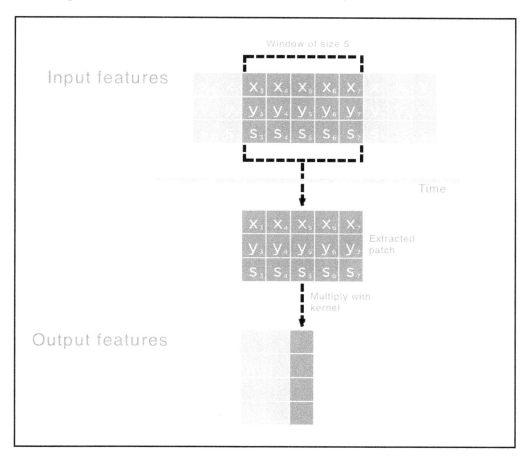

In this context, strokes (local to the window size) will be learned, independent of where they are in the sequence, and a compact representation will be outputted, which we can then feed into an RNN to learn ordered sequences from these strokes (rather than from raw points). Intuitively you can think of our model as initially learning strokes such as vertical and horizontal strokes (independent of time), and then learning (in our subsequent layers made up of RNNs) higher-order patterns such as shapes from the ordered sequence of these strokes. The following figure illustrates this concept:

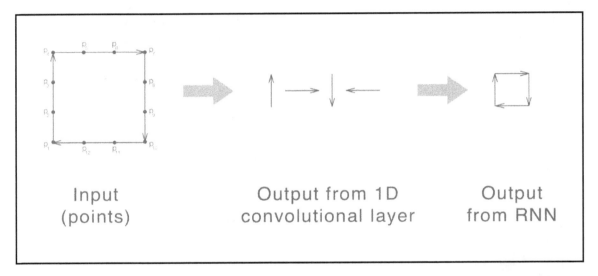

On the left, we have the raw points inputted into the model. The middle part shows how a 1D convolutional layer can learn local patterns from these points in a form of strokes. And finally, at the far right, we have the subsequent RNNs learning order-sensitive patterns from the sequence of these strokes.

One more concept to introduce before introducing the model, but, before doing so, I want you to quickly think of how you draw a square. Do you draw it in a clockwise direction or anti-clockwise direction?

The last concept I want to briefly introduce in this section is bidirectional layers; bidirectional layers attempt to make our network invariant to the previous question. We discussed earlier how RNNs are sensitive to order, which is precisely why they are useful here, but as I hope has been highlighted, our sketch may be drawn in the reverse order. To account for this, we can use a bidirectional layer, which, as the name implies, processes the input sequence in two directions (chronologically and anti-chronologically) and then merges their representations. By processing a sequence in both directions, our model can become somewhat invariant to the direction in which we draw.

We have now introduced all the building blocks used for this model; the following figure shows the model in its entirety:

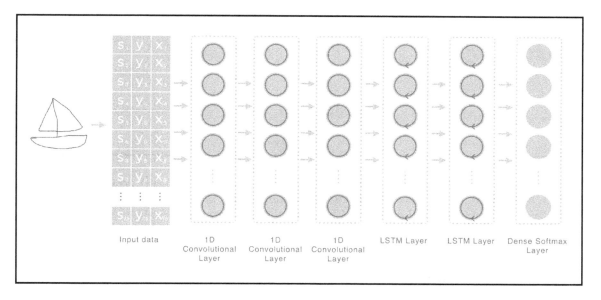

 As a reminder, this book is focused on the application of machine learning related to Core ML. Therefore we won't be going into the details of this (or any) model, but cover just enough to have an intuitive understanding of how the model works for you to use and explore further.

As shown previously, our model is comprised of a stack of 1D convolutional layers that feed into a stack of **Long Short-Term Memory** (**LSTM**), an implementation of an RNN, before being fed into a fully connected layer where our prediction is made. This model was trained on 172 categories, each using 10,000 training samples and 1,000 validation samples. After 16 epochs, the model achieved approximately 78% accuracy on both the training and validation data, as shown here:

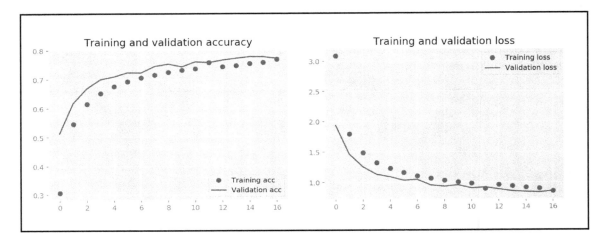

We now have our model but have skimmed across what we are actually feeding into our model. In the next section, we will discuss what our model was trained with (and therefore expecting) and implement the required functionality to prepare it.

# Input data and preprocessing

In this section, we will implement the preprocessing functionality required to transform our raw user input into something the model is expecting. We will build up this functionality in a playground project before migrating it across to our project in the next section.

If you haven't done so, pull down the latest code from the accompanying repository `https://github.com/PacktPublishing/Machine-Learning-with-Core-ML`. Once downloaded, navigate to the directory `Chapter8/Start/` and open the playground project `ExploringQuickDrawData.playground`. Once loaded, you will see the playground for this chapter, as shown:

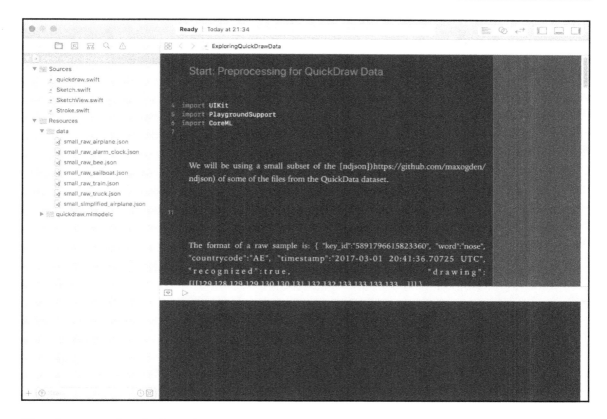

The playground includes a few samples of the raw *Quick, Draw!* dataset, a single simplified extract, as well as the complied model and supporting classes we created in the previous chapter to represent a sketch (`Stroke.swift`, `Sketch.swift`) and render it (`SketchView.swift`). Our goal for this section will be to better understand the data and the preprocessing required before feeding our model; in doing so, we will be extending our existing classes to encapsulate this functionality.

Let's start reviewing what code exists before we move forward; if you scroll down the opened source file, you will see the methods `createFromJSON` and `drawSketch`. The former takes in a JSON object (the format our samples are saved in) and returns a strongly typed object: `StrokeSketch`. As a reminder, each sample is made up of:

- `key_id`: Unique identifier
- `word`: Category label
- `countrycode`: Country code where the sample was drawn

- `timestamp`: Timestamp when the sample was created
- `recognized`: A flag indicating whether the sketch was currently recognized
- `drawing`: A multi-dimensional array consisting of arrays of *x*, *y* coordinates along with the elapsed time since the point was created

The `StrokeSketch` maps the word to the label property and *x*, *y* coordinates to the stroke points. We discard everything else as it is not deemed useful in classification and not used by our model. The `drawSketch` method is a utility method that handles scaling and centering the sketch before creating an instance of a `SketchView` to render the scaled and centered sketch.

The last block of code preloads the JSON files and makes them available through the dictionary `loadedJSON`, where the key is the associated filename and value is the loaded JSON object.

Let's start by taking a peek at the data, comparing the raw samples to the simplified samples; add the following code to your playground:

```
if let rJson = loadedJSON["small_raw_airplane"],
    let sJson = loadedJSON["small_simplified_airplane"]{
    if let rSketch = StrokeSketch.createFromJSON(json: rJson[0] as?
[String:Any]),
        let sSketch = StrokeSketch.createFromJSON(json: sJson[0] as?
[String:Any]){
        drawSketch(sketch: rSketch)
        drawSketch(sketch: sSketch)
    }
    if let rSketch = StrokeSketch.createFromJSON(json: rJson[1] as?
[String:Any]),
        let sSketch = StrokeSketch.createFromJSON(json: sJson[1] as?
[String:Any]){
        drawSketch(sketch: rSketch)
        drawSketch(sketch: sSketch)
    }
}
```

In the previous code snippet, we are simply getting a reference to our loaded JSON files and passing the samples at index 0 and 1 to our `createFromJSON` file, which will return their `StrokeSketch` representation. We then proceed to pass this into our `drawSketch` method to create the view to render them. After running, you can preview each of the sketches by clicking on the eye icon located to the right-hand panel on the same line as the call to the method `drawSketch`. The following image presents both outputs side by side for comparison:

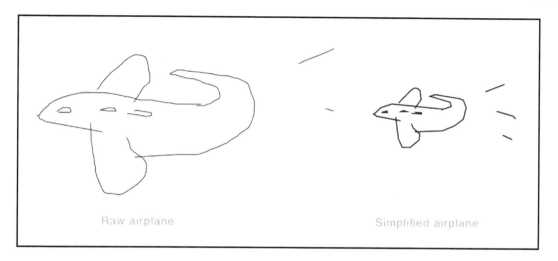

Raw airplane                                          Simplified airplane

The major differences between the samples from the raw dataset and simplified dataset can be seen in the preceding figure. The raw sample is much larger and smoother. What is not obvious from the previous image is that the simplified sample is positioned to the top left while the raw one consists of points in their original and absolute positions (recalling that our `drawSketch` method rescales, if required, and centers the sketch).

As a reminder, the raw samples resemble the input we are expecting to receive from the user, while on the other hand our model was trained on the samples from the simplified dataset. Therefore, we need to perform the same preprocessing steps that have been used to transform the raw data into its simplified counterparts before feeding our model. These steps, described in the repository for the data at `https://github.com/googlecreativelab/quickdraw-dataset`, are listed as follows, and this is what we will now implement in our playground:

- Align the drawing to the top-left corner to have minimum values of zero
- Uniformly scale the drawing to have a maximum value of 255
- Resample all strokes with a one pixel spacing
- Simplify all strokes using the Ramer-Douglas-Peucker algorithm with an epsilon value of 2.0

The Ramer–Douglas–Peucker algorithm takes a curve composed of line segments (strokes) and finds a simpler curve with fewer points. You can learn more about the algorithm here: `https://en.wikipedia.org/wiki/Ramer-Douglas-Peucker_algorithm`.

The rationale behind these steps should be fairly self-explanatory and is highlighted from the figure showing the two sketches of an airplane. That is, the airplane should be invariant to its actual position on the screen and invariant to the scale. And simplifying the stroke makes it easier for our model to learn as it helps ensure that we only capture salient features.

Start off by creating an extension of your StrokeSketch class and stubbing out the method simplify, as shown:

```
public func simplify() -> StrokeSketch{
    let copy = self.copy() as! StrokeSketch
}
```

We will be mutating a clone of the instance of itself, which is why we first create a copy. We next want to calculate the scale factor required to scale the sketch to have a maximum height and/or width of 255 while respecting its aspect ratio; add the following code to your simplify method, which does just this:

```
let minPoint = copy.minPoint
let maxPoint = copy.maxPoint
let scale = CGPoint(x: maxPoint.x-minPoint.x, y:maxPoint.y-minPoint.y)

var width : CGFloat = 255.0
var height : CGFloat = 255.0

// adjust aspect ratio
if scale.x > scale.y{
    height *= scale.y/scale.x
} else{
    width *= scale.y/scale.x
}
```

For each dimension (width and height), we have calculated the scale required to ensure that our sketch is either scaled up or down to a dimension of 255. We now need to apply this to each of the points associated with each of the strokes held by the StrokeSketch class; as we're iterating through each point, it also makes sense to align our sketch to the top-left corner (x= 0, y = 0) as a required preprocessing step. We can do this simply by subtracting the minimum value of each of the dimensions. Append the following code to your simplify method to do this:

```
for i in 0..<copy.strokes.count{
    copy.strokes[i].points = copy.strokes[i].points.map({ (pt) -> CGPoint in
        let x : CGFloat = CGFloat(Int(((pt.x - minPoint.x)/scale.x) * width))
```

```
        let y : CGFloat = CGFloat(Int(((pt.y - minPoint.y)/scale.y) *
   height))
        return CGPoint(x:x, y:y)
    })
}
```

Our final step is to simplify the curve using the Ramer-Douglas-Peucker algorithm; to do this, we will make the `Stroke` responsible for implementing the details and just delegate the task there. Add the final piece of code to your `simplify` method within your `StrokeSketch` extension:

```
copy.strokes = copy.strokes.map({ (stroke) -> Stroke in
    return stroke.simplify()
})

return copy
```

The Ramer-Douglas-Peucker algorithm recursively traverses the curve, initially starting with the first and last point and finding the point that is furthest from this line segment. If the point is closer than a given threshold, then any points currently marked to be kept can be discarded, but if the point is greater than our threshold then that point must be kept. The algorithm then recursively calls itself with the first point and furthest point as well as furthest point and last point. After traversing the whole curve, the result is a simplified curve that only consists of the points marked as being kept, as described previously. The process is summarized in the following figure:

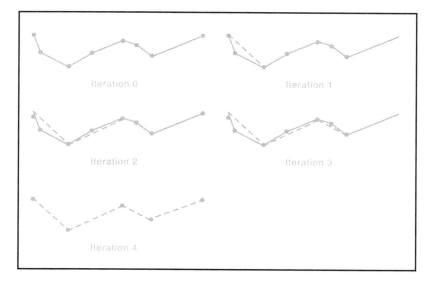

Let's start by extending the `CGPoint` structure to include a method for calculating the distance of a point given a line; add this code to your playground:

```
public extension CGPoint{
    public static func getSquareSegmentDistance(p0:CGPoint,
                                                p1:CGPoint,
                                                p2:CGPoint) -> CGFloat{
        let x0 = p0.x, y0 = p0.y
        var x1 = p1.x, y1 = p1.y
        let x2 = p2.x, y2 = p2.y
        var dx = x2 - x1
        var dy = y2 - y1
        if dx != 0.0 && dy != 0.0{
            let numerator = (x0 - x1)
                * dx + (y0 - y1)
                * dy
            let denom = dx * dx + dy * dy
            let t = numerator / denom
            if t > 1.0{
                x1 = x2
                y1 = y2
            } else{
                x1 += dx * t
                y1 += dy * t
            }
        }
        dx = x0 - x1
        dy = y0 - y1
        return dx * dx + dy * dy
    }
}
```

Here, we have added a static method to the `CGPoint` structure; it calculates the perpendicular distance of a point given a line (which is the value we compare with our threshold to simplify our line, as previously described). Next, we will implement the recursive method as described, which will be used to build up the curve by testing and discarding any points under our threshold. As mentioned, we will encapsulate this functionality within the `Stroke` class itself, so we start off by stubbing out the extension:

```
public extension Stroke{
}
```

Now, within the extension, add the recursive method:

```
func simplifyDPStep(points:[CGPoint], first:Int, last:Int,
                    tolerance:CGFloat, simplified: inout [CGPoint]){
    var maxSqDistance = tolerance
```

```
var index = 0
for i in first + 1..<last{
    let sqDist = CGPoint.getSquareSegmentDistance(
        p0: points[i],
        p1: points[first],
        p2: points[last])
    if sqDist > maxSqDistance {
        maxSqDistance = sqDist
        index = i
    }
}
if maxSqDistance > tolerance{
    if index - first > 1 {
        simplifyDPStep(points: points,
                       first: first,
                       last: index,
                       tolerance: tolerance,
                       simplified: &simplified)
    }
    simplified.append(points[index])
    if last - index > 1{
        simplifyDPStep(points: points,
                       first: index,
                       last: last,
                       tolerance: tolerance,
                       simplified: &simplified)
    }
}
}
```

Most of this should make sense as it's a direct implementation of the algorithm described. We start off by finding the furthest distance, which must be greater than our threshold; otherwise, the point is ignored. We add the point to the array of points to keep and then pass each end of the segment to our recursive method until we have traversed the whole curve.

The last method we need to implement is the method responsible for initiating this process, which we will also encapsulate within our Stroke extension; so go ahead and add the following method to your extension:

```
public func simplify(epsilon:CGFloat=3.0) -> Stroke{
    var simplified: [CGPoint] = [self.points.first!]
    self.simplifyDPStep(points: self.points,
                        first: 0, last: self.points.count-1,
                        tolerance: epsilon * epsilon,
                        simplified: &simplified)
    simplified.append(self.points.last!)
```

```
        let copy = self.copy() as! Stroke
        copy.points = simplified
        return copy
    }
```

The `simplify` method simply (excuse the pun) creates an array of points of our simplified curve, adding the first point, before kicking off the recursive method we had just implemented. Then, when the curve has been traversed, it finally adds the last point before returning the `Stroke` with the simplified points.

At this point, we have implemented the functionality required to transform raw input into its simplified form, as specified in the *Quick, Draw!* repository. Let's verify our work by comparing our simplified version of a raw sketch with an existing simplified version of the same sketch. Add the following code to your playground:

```
    if let rJson = loadedJSON["small_raw_airplane"],
       let sJson = loadedJSON["small_simplified_airplane"]{
        if let rSketch = StrokeSketch.createFromJSON(json: rJson[2] as?
[String:Any]),
           let sSketch = StrokeSketch.createFromJSON(json: sJson[2] as?
[String:Any]){
            drawSketch(sketch: rSketch)
            drawSketch(sketch: sSketch)
            drawSketch(sketch: rSketch.simplify())
        }
    }
```

As we did before, you can click on the eye icon within the right-hand-side panel for each of the `drawSketch` calls to preview each of the sketches. The first is the sketch from the raw dataset, the second is from the simplified dataset, and third is by using our simplified implementation, using the sample from the raw dataset. If everything goes as per the plan, then you should see something that resembles the following:

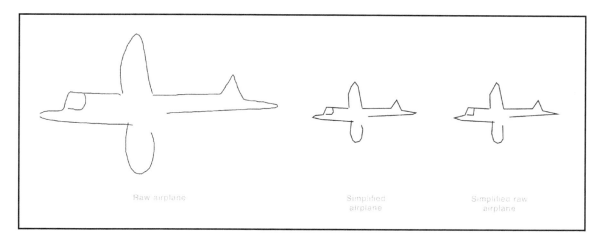

Raw airplane    Simplified airplane    Simplified raw airplane

At close inspection, our simplified version looks as though it is more aggressive than the sample from the simplified dataset, but we can easily tweak this by adjusting our threshold. However, for all intents and purposes, this will suffice for now. At this point, we have the required functionality to simplify our dataset, transforming it to something that resembles the training dataset. But before feeding our data into the model, we have more preprocessing to do; let's do that now, starting with a quick discussion of what our model is expecting.

Our model is expecting each sample to have three dimensions; point position *(x, y)* and a flag indicating whether the point is the last point for its associated stroke. The reason for having this flag is that we are passing in a fixed-length sequence of size 75. That is, each sketch will be either truncated to squeeze into this sequence or padded out with leading zeros to fill it. And using a flag is a way to add context indicating whether it is the end of the stroke or not (keeping in mind that our sequence represents our sketch and our sketch is made up of many strokes).

Next, as usual, we normalize the inputs to a range of *0.0 - 1.0* to avoid having our model fluctuate while training due to large weights. The last adjustment is converting our absolute values into deltas, which makes a lot of sense when you think about it. The first reason is that we want our model to be invariant to the actual position of each point; that is, we could draw the same sketch side by side, and ideally we want these to be classified as the same class. In the previous chapter, we achieved this by using a CNN operating on pixel data range and positions as we are doing here. The second reason for using deltas rather than absolute values is that the delta carries more useful information than the absolute position, that is, direction. After implementing this, we will be ready to test out our model, so let's get going; start by adding the following extension and method that will be responsible for this preprocessing step:

```
extension StrokeSketch{
    public static func preprocess(_ sketch:StrokeSketch)
        -> MLMultiArray?{
        let arrayLen = NSNumber(value:75 * 3)
        guard let array = try? MLMultiArray(shape: [arrayLen],
                                            dataType: .double)
            else{ return nil }
        let simplifiedSketch = sketch.simplify()
    }
}
```

Here we have added the static method `preprocess` to our `StrokeSketch` class via an extension; within this method, we begin by setting up the buffer that will be passed to our model. The size of this buffer needs to fit a full sequence, which is calculated simply by multiplying the sequence length (75) with the number of dimensions (3). We then call `simplify` on the `StrokeSketch` instance to obtain the simplified sketch, ensuring that it closely resembles the data we had trained our model on.

Next, we will iterate through each point for every stroke, normalizing the point and determining the value of the flag (one indicating the end of the stroke; otherwise it's zero). Append the following code to your `preprocess` method:

```
let minPoint = simplifiedSketch.minPoint
let maxPoint = simplifiedSketch.maxPoint
let scale = CGPoint(x: maxPoint.x-minPoint.x,
                    y:maxPoint.y-minPoint.y)

var data = Array<Double>()
for i in 0..<simplifiedSketch.strokes.count{
    for j in 0..<simplifiedSketch.strokes[i].points.count{
        let point = simplifiedSketch.strokes[i].points[j]
        let x = (point.x-minPoint.x)/scale.x
        let y = (point.y-minPoint.y)/scale.y
```

```
let z = j == simplifiedSketch.strokes[i].points.count-1
      ? 1 : 0
data.append(Double(x))
data.append(Double(y))
data.append(Double(z))
}
```

We start by obtaining the minimum and maximum values, which we will use when normalizing each point (using the equation $x^i-min(x)/max(x)-min(x)$, where $x_i$ is a single point and $x$ represents all points within that stroke). Then we create a temporary place to store the data before iterating through all our points, normalizing each one, and determining the value of the flag as described previously.

We now want to calculate the deltas of each point and finally remove the last point as we are unable to calculate its delta; append the following to your preprocess method:

```
let dataStride : Int = 3
for i in stride(from: dataStride, to:data.count, by: dataStride){
    data[i - dataStride] = data[i] - data[i - dataStride]
    data[i - (dataStride-1)] = data[i+1] - data[i - (dataStride-1)]
    data[i - (dataStride-2)] = data[i+2]
}

data.removeLast(3)
```

The previous code should be self-explanatory; the only notable point worth highlighting is that we are now dealing with a flattened array, and therefore we need to use a stride of 3 when traversing the data.

One last chunk of code to add! We need to ensure that our array is equal to 75 samples (our sequence length, that is, an array of length 225). We do this by either truncating the array if too large or padding it out if too small. We can easily do this while copying the data from our temporary array, data, across to the buffer that we will be passing to our model, array. Here we first calculate the starting index and then proceed to iterate through the whole sequence, copying the data across if the current index has passed our starting index, or else padding it with zeros. Add the following snippet to finish off your preprocess method:

```
var dataIdx : Int = 0
let startAddingIdx = max(array.count-data.count, 0)

for i in 0..<array.count{
    if i >= startAddingIdx{
        array[i] = NSNumber(value:data[dataIdx])
        dataIdx = dataIdx + 1
```

```
    } else{
        array[i] = NSNumber(value:0)
    }
}

return array
```

With our `preprocess` method now complete, we are ready to test out our model. We will start by instantiating our model (contained within the playground) and then feeding in a airplane sample we have used previously, before testing with the other categories. Append the following code to your playground:

```
let model = quickdraw()

if let json = loadedJSON["small_raw_airplane"]{
    if let sketch = StrokeSketch.createFromJSON(json: json[0] as?
[String:Any]){
        if let x = StrokeSketch.preprocess(sketch){
            if let predictions = try?
model.prediction(input:quickdrawInput(strokeSeq:x)){
                print("Class label \(predictions.classLabel)")
                print("Class label probability/confidence
\(predictions.classLabelProbs["airplane"] ?? 0)")
            }
        }
    }
}
```

If all goes well, your playground will output the following to the console:

```
Class label airplane
Class label probability/confidence 0.773365199565887
```

It has predicted the category of airplane and done so fairly confidently (with a probability of approximately 77%). Before we migrate our code into our application, let's test with some other categories; we will start by implementing a method to handle all the leg work and then proceed to pass some samples to perform inference. Add the following method to your playground, which will be responsible for obtaining and preprocessing the sample before passing it to your model for prediction and then returning the results as a formatted string containing the most likely category and probability:

```
func makePrediction(key:String, index:Int) -> String{
    if let json = loadedJSON[key]{
        if let sketch = StrokeSketch.createFromJSON(
            json: json[index] as? [String:Any]){
            if let x = StrokeSketch.preprocess(sketch){
                if let predictions = try?
model.prediction(input:quickdrawInput(strokeSeq:x)){
                    return "\(predictions.classLabel)
\(predictions.classLabelProbs[predictions.classLabel] ?? 0)"
                }
            }
        }
    }
    return "None"
}
```

With most of the work now done, we are just left with the nail-biting task of testing that our preprocessing implementation and model are sufficiently able to predict the samples we pass. Let's test with each category; add the following code to your playground:

```
print(makePrediction(key: "small_raw_airplane", index: 0))
print(makePrediction(key: "small_raw_alarm_clock", index: 1))
print(makePrediction(key: "small_raw_bee", index: 2))
print(makePrediction(key: "small_raw_sailboat", index: 3))
print(makePrediction(key: "small_raw_train", index: 4))
print(makePrediction(key: "small_raw_truck", index: 5))
print(makePrediction(key: "small_simplified_airplane", index: 0))
```

The output for each of these can be seen in this screenshot:

```
Class label airplane
Class label probability/confidence 0.773365199565887
airplane 0.773365199565887
alarm clock 0.929081261115799
bee 0.99956601858139
sailboat 0.999997138977051
train 0.989866809844971
truck 0.411328673362732
airplane 0.838698148727417
```

Not bad! We managed to predict all the categories correctly, albeit the truck was only given the probability of 41%. And interestingly, our simplified airplane sample was given a higher probability (84%) than its counterpart from the raw dataset (77%).

Out of curiosity, let's peek at the truck sample we asked our model to predict:

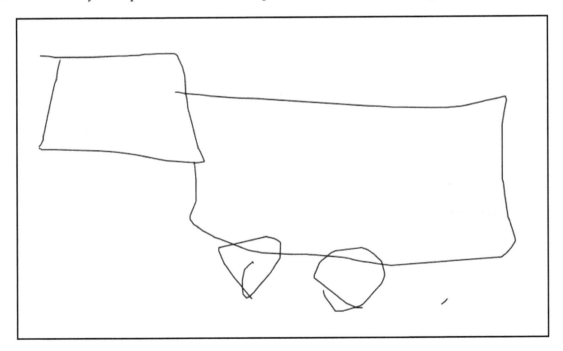

All due respect to the artist, but I would be pushed to predict a truck from this sketch, so full credit to our model.

We have now exposed our model to a variety of categories, and each one we are able to predict correctly, which implies that our preprocessing code has been satisfactorily implemented. We are now ready to migrate our code across to our application, but before doing so, one very last experiment. Let's think about how our model has been trained and how it will be used in the context of the application. The model was trained on sequences that are essentially strokes, the user made while drawing their sketch. This is precisely how users will be interacting with our application; they will be sketching something with a series (or sequence) of strokes; each time they finish a stroke, we want to try and predict what it is they are trying to draw. Let's mimic that behavior by building up a sample stroke by stroke, predicting after each subsequent stroke is added to evaluate how well the model performs in a more realistic setting. Add the following code to your playground:

```
if let json = loadedJSON["small_raw_bee"]{
    if let sketch = StrokeSketch.createFromJSON(json: json[2] as?
[String:Any]){
        let strokeCount = sketch.strokes.count
        print("\(sketch.label ?? "" ) sketch has \(strokeCount) strokes")
        for i in (0..<strokeCount-1).reversed(){
            let copyOfSketch = sketch.copy() as! StrokeSketch
            copyOfSketch.strokes.removeLast(i)
            if let x = StrokeSketch.preprocess(copyOfSketch){
                if let predictions = try?
model.prediction(input:quickdrawInput(strokeSeq:x)){
                    let label = predictions.classLabel
                    let probability = String(format: "%.2f",
predictions.classLabelProbs[predictions.classLabel] ?? 0)
                    print("Guessing \(label) with probability of
\(probability) using \(copyOfSketch.strokes.count) strokes")
                }
            }
        }
    }
}
```

Nothing new has being introduced here; we are just loading in a sketch, slowly building it up stroke by stroke as discussed, and passing up the partial sketch to our model to perform inference. Here are the results, with their corresponding sketches to give the results more context:

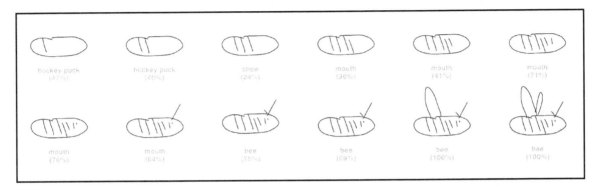

All reasonable predictions, possibly uncovering how a lot of people draw a **hockey puck**, **mouth**, and **bee**. Now, satisfied with our implementation, let's move on to the next section, where we will migrate this code and look at how we can obtain and compile a model at runtime.

# Bringing it all together

If you haven't done already, pull down the latest code from the accompanying repository: `https://github.com/packtpublishing/machine-learning-with-core-ml`. Once downloaded, navigate to the directory `Chapter8/Start/QuickDrawRNN` and open the project `QuickDrawRNN.xcodeproj`. Once loaded, you will see a project that should look familiar to you as it is almost a replica of the project we built in the previous chapter. For this reason, I won't be going over the details here, but feel free to refresh your memory by skimming through the previous chapter.

Rather I want to spend some time highlighting what I consider one of the most important aspects of designing and building the interface between people and machine learning systems. Let's start with this and then move on to migrating our code across from our playground project.

I consider Quick, Draw! a great example that highlights a major responsibility of the designer of any interface of a machine learning system. What makes it stand out is not the clever preprocessing that makes it invariant to scale and translation. Nor is it the sophisticated architecture that can effectively learn complex sequences, but rather the mechanism used to capture the training data. One major obstacle we have in creating intelligent systems is obtaining (enough) clean and labeled data that we can use to train our models. *Quick, Draw!* tackled this by, I assume, intentionally being a tool for capturing and labeling data through the façade of a compelling game—compelling enough to motivate a large number of users to generate sufficient amounts of labeled data. Although some of the sketches are questionable, the sheer number of sketches dilutes these outliers.

The point is that machine learning systems are not static, and we should design opportunities to allow the user to correct the system, where applicable, and capture new data, either implicitly (with the user's consent) and/or explicitly. Allowing a level of transparency between the user and system and allowing the user to correct the model when wrong not only provides us with new data to improve our model, but also—just as important—assists the user in building a useful mental model of the system. Thus it builds some intuition around the affordances of our system, which help them use it correctly.

In our example project, we can easily expose the predictions and provide the means for the user to correct the model. But to ensure that this chapter is concise, we will just look at how we obtain an updated model that typically (remembering that Core ML is suited for inference as opposed to training) we would train off the device. In such a case, you would upload the data to a central server and fetch an updated model when available. As mentioned before, here we will look at the latter: how we obtain the updated model. Let's see how.

Previously I mentioned, and implied, that you would typically upload new training data and train your model off the device. This, of course, is not the only option and it's reasonable to perform training on the device using the user's personal data to tune a model. The advantage of training locally is privacy and lower latency, but it has the disadvantage of diminishing collective intelligence, that is, improvement of the model from collective behavior. Google proposed a clever solution that ensured privacy and allowed for collaboration. In a post titled *Federated Learning: Collaborative Machine Learning without Centralized Training Data*, they described a technique of training locally on the device using personalized data and then uploading only the tuned model to the server, where it would average the weights from the crowd before updating a central model. I encourage you to read the post at `https://research.googleblog.com/2017/04/federated-learning-collaborative.html`.

As you may have come to expect when using Core ML, the bulk of the work is not interfacing with the framework but rather the activities before and after it. Compiling and instantiating a model can be done in just two lines of code, as follows:

```
let compiledUrl = try MLModel.compileModel(at: modelUrl)
let model = try MLModel(contentsOf: compiledUrl)
```

Where `modelUrl` is a URL of a locally stored `.mlmodel` file. Passing it to `compileModel` will return the `.mlmodelc` file. This can be used to initialize an instance of `MLModel`, which provides the same capabilities as a model bundled with your application.

Downloading and compilation are time consuming. So you not only want to do this off the main thread but also want to avoid having to perform the task unnecessary; that is, cache locally and only update when required. Let's implement this functionality now; click on the `QueryFacade.swift` file on the left-hand-side panel to bring it to focus in the main editor window. Then add a new extension to the `QueryFacade` class, which is where we will add our code responsible for downloading and compiling the model.

Our first task is to test whether we need to download the model. We do this by simply checking whether we have the model and our model is considered recent. We will use `NSUserDefaults` to keep track of the location of the compiled model as well as a timestamp of when it was last updated. Add the following code to your extension of `QueryFacade`, which is be responsible for checking whether we need to download the model:

```
private var SyncTimestampKey : String{
    get{
        return "model_sync_timestamp"
    }
}

private var ModelUrlKey : String{
    get{
        return "model_url"
    }
}

private var isModelStale : Bool{
    get{
        if let modelUrl = UserDefaults.standard.string(
            forKey: self.ModelUrlKey){
            if !FileManager.default.fileExists(atPath: modelUrl){
                return true
            }
        }
```

```
        let daysToUpdate : Int = 10
        let lastUpdated =
Date(timestamp:UserDefaults.standard.integer(forKey: SyncTimestampKey))

        guard let numberOfDaysSinceUpdate =
NSCalendar.current.dateComponents([.day], from: lastUpdated, to:
Date()).day else{
            fatalError("Failed to calculated elapsed days since the model
was updated")
        }
        return numberOfDaysSinceUpdate >= daysToUpdate
    }
}
```

As mentioned, we first check whether the model exists, and if so, then test how many days have elapsed since the model was last updated, testing this against some arbitrary threshold for which we consider the model to be stale.

The next method we implement will be responsible for downloading the model (the .mlmodel file); this should look familiar to most iOS developers, with the only notable piece of code being the use of a semaphore to make the task synchronous, as the calling method will be running this off the main thread. Append the following code to your QueryFacade extension:

```
private func downloadModel() -> URL?{
    guard let modelUrl = URL(
string:"https://github.com/joshnewnham/MachineLearningWithCoreML/blob/maste
r/CoreMLModels/Chapter8/quickdraw.mlmodel?raw=true") else{
            fatalError("Invalid URL")
    }
    var tempUrl : URL?
    let sessionConfig = URLSessionConfiguration.default
    let session = URLSession(configuration: sessionConfig)
    let request = URLRequest(url:modelUrl)
    let semaphore = DispatchSemaphore(value: 0)
    let task = session.downloadTask(with: request) { (tempLocalUrl,
response, error) in
        if let tempLocalUrl = tempLocalUrl, error == nil {
            tempUrl = tempLocalUrl
        } else {
            fatalError("Error downloading model \(String(describing:
error?.localizedDescription))")
        }
        semaphore.signal()
    }
    task.resume()
    _ = semaphore.wait(timeout: .distantFuture)
```

```
        return tempUrl
    }
```

I have highlighted the statements related to making this task synchronous; essentially, calling `semaphore.wait(timeout: .distantFuture)` will hold the current thread until it is signaled to move on, via `semaphore.signal()`. If successful, this method returns the local URL of the downloaded file.

Our last task is to tie this all together; the next method we implement will be called when `QueryFacade` is instantiated (which we will add just after this). It will be responsible for checking whether we need to download the model, proceeding to download and compile if necessary, and instantiating an instance variable `model`, which we can use to perform inference. Append the final snippet of code to your `QueryFacade` extension:

```
private func syncModel(){
    queryQueue.async {
        if self.isModelStale{
            guard let tempModelUrl = self.downloadModel() else{
                return
            }
            guard let compiledUrl = try? MLModel.compileModel(
                at: tempModelUrl) else{
                fatalError("Failed to compile model")
            }
            let appSupportDirectory = try! FileManager.default.url(
                for: .applicationSupportDirectory,
                in: .userDomainMask,
                appropriateFor: compiledUrl,
                create: true)
            let permanentUrl = appSupportDirectory.appendingPathComponent(
                compiledUrl.lastPathComponent)
            do {
                if FileManager.default.fileExists(
                    atPath: permanentUrl.absoluteString) {
                    _ = try FileManager.default.replaceItemAt(
                        permanentUrl,
                        withItemAt: compiledUrl)
                } else {
                    try FileManager.default.copyItem(
                        at: compiledUrl,
                        to: permanentUrl)
                }
            } catch {
                fatalError("Error during copy:
\(error.localizedDescription)")
            }
```

```
                UserDefaults.standard.set(Date.timestamp,
                                    forKey: self.SyncTimestampKey)
                UserDefaults.standard.set(permanentUrl.absoluteString,
                                    forKey:self.ModelUrlKey)
            }
        guard let modelUrl = URL(
            string:UserDefaults.standard.string(forKey: self.ModelUrlKey)
??  "")
            else{
            fatalError("Invalid model Url")
        }
        self.model = try? MLModel(contentsOf: modelUrl)
    }
}
```

We start by checking whether we need to download the model, and if so, proceed to download and compile it:

```
guard let tempModelUrl = self.downloadModel() else{
    return
}

guard let compiledUrl = try? MLModel.compileModel(
    at: tempModelUrl) else{
    fatalError("Failed to compile model")
}
```

To avoid having to perform this step unnecessarily, we then save the details somewhere permanently, setting the model's location and the current timestamp in NSUserDefaults:

```
let appSupportDirectory = try! FileManager.default.url(
    for: .applicationSupportDirectory,
    in: .userDomainMask,
    appropriateFor: compiledUrl,
    create: true)

let permanentUrl = appSupportDirectory.appendingPathComponent(
    compiledUrl.lastPathComponent)
do {
    if FileManager.default.fileExists(
        atPath: permanentUrl.absoluteString) {
        _ = try FileManager.default.replaceItemAt(
            permanentUrl,
            withItemAt: compiledUrl)
    } else {
        try FileManager.default.copyItem(
            at: compiledUrl,
```

```
            to: permanentUrl)
    }
} catch {
    fatalError("Error during copy: \(error.localizedDescription)")
}

UserDefaults.standard.set(Date.timestamp,
                    forKey: self.SyncTimestampKey)
UserDefaults.standard.set(permanentUrl.absoluteString,
                    forKey:self.ModelUrlKey)
```

Finally, we instantiate and assign an instance of MLModel to our instance variable model. The last task is to update the constructor of the QueryFacade class to kick off this process when instantiated; update the QueryFacade init method with the following code:

```
init() {
    syncModel()
}
```

At this stage, we have our model ready for performing inference; our next task is to migrate the code we developed in our playground to our project and then hook it all up. Given that we have spent the first part of this chapter discussing the details, I will skip the specifics here but rather include the additions for convenience and completeness.

Let's start with our extensions to the CGPoint structure; add a new swift file to your project called CGPointRNNExtension.swift and add the following code in it:

```
extension CGPoint{
    public static func getSquareSegmentDistance(
        p0:CGPoint,
        p1:CGPoint,
        p2:CGPoint) -> CGFloat{
        let x0 = p0.x, y0 = p0.y
        var x1 = p1.x, y1 = p1.y
        let x2 = p2.x, y2 = p2.y
        var dx = x2 - x1
        var dy = y2 - y1
        if dx != 0.0 && dy != 0.0{
            let numerator = (x0 - x1) * dx + (y0 - y1) * dy
            let denom = dx * dx + dy * dy
            let t = numerator / denom
            if t > 1.0{
                x1 = x2
                y1 = y2
            } else{
                x1 += dx * t
                y1 += dy * t
```

```
        }
    }
    dx = x0 - x1
    dy = y0 - y1
    return dx * dx + dy * dy
  }
}
```

Next, add another new swift file to your project called `StrokeRNNExtension.swift` and add the following code:

```
extension Stroke{
    public func simplify(epsilon:CGFloat=3.0) -> Stroke{
        var simplified: [CGPoint] = [self.points.first!]
        self.simplifyDPStep(points: self.points,
                            first: 0, last: self.points.count-1,
                            tolerance: epsilon * epsilon,
                            simplified: &simplified)
        simplified.append(self.points.last!)
        let copy = self.copy() as! Stroke
        copy.points = simplified
        return copy
    }
    func simplifyDPStep(points:[CGPoint],
                        first:Int,
                        last:Int,
                        tolerance:CGFloat,
                        simplified: inout [CGPoint]){
        var maxSqDistance = tolerance
        var index = 0
        for i in first + 1..<last{
            let sqDist = CGPoint.getSquareSegmentDistance(
                p0: points[i],
                p1: points[first],
                p2: points[last])
            if sqDist > maxSqDistance {
                maxSqDistance = sqDist
                index = i
            }
        }
        if maxSqDistance > tolerance{
            if index - first > 1 {
                simplifyDPStep(points: points,
                               first: first,
                               last: index,
                               tolerance: tolerance,
                               simplified: &simplified)
```

```
            }
            simplified.append(points[index])
            if last - index > 1{
                simplifyDPStep(points: points,
                               first: index,
                               last: last,
                               tolerance: tolerance,
                               simplified: &simplified)
            }
        }
    }
}
```

Finally, we will add a couple of methods that we implemented in the playground to our `StrokeSketch` class to handle the required preprocessing; start by adding a new `.swift` file called `StrokeSketchExtension.swift` and block out the extension as follows:

```
import UIKit
import CoreML

extension StrokeSketch{

}
```

Next, we copy and paste in the `simplify` method, which we implement in the playground as follows:

```
public func simplify() -> StrokeSketch{
    let copy = self.copy() as! StrokeSketch
    copy.scale = 1.0
    let minPoint = copy.minPoint
    let maxPoint = copy.maxPoint
    let scale = CGPoint(x: maxPoint.x-minPoint.x,
                        y:maxPoint.y-minPoint.y)
    var width : CGFloat = 255.0
    var height : CGFloat = 255.0
    if scale.x > scale.y{
        height *= scale.y/scale.x
    } else{
        width *= scale.y/scale.x
    }
    // for each point, subtract the min and divide by the max
    for i in 0..<copy.strokes.count{
        copy.strokes[i].points = copy.strokes[i].points.map({
            (pt) -> CGPoint in
            let x : CGFloat = CGFloat(
                Int(((pt.x - minPoint.x)/scale.x) * width)
```

```
            )
            let y : CGFloat = CGFloat(
                Int(((pt.y - minPoint.y)/scale.y) * height)
            )
            return CGPoint(x:x, y:y)
        })
    }
    copy.strokes = copy.strokes.map({ (stroke) -> Stroke in
        return stroke.simplify()
    })
    return copy
}
```

As a reminder, this method is responsible for the preprocessing of a sequence of strokes, as described previously. Next, we add our static method `preprocess` to the `StrokeSketch` extension, which takes an instance of `StrokeSketch` and is responsible for putting its simplified state into a data structure that we can pass to our model for inference:

```
public static func preprocess(_ sketch:StrokeSketch)
    -> MLMultiArray?{
    let arrayLen = NSNumber(value:75 * 3)
    let simplifiedSketch = sketch.simplify()
    guard let array = try? MLMultiArray(shape: [arrayLen],
                                        dataType: .double)
        else{ return nil }
    let minPoint = simplifiedSketch.minPoint
    let maxPoint = simplifiedSketch.maxPoint
    let scale = CGPoint(x: maxPoint.x-minPoint.x,
                        y:maxPoint.y-minPoint.y)
    var data = Array<Double>()
    for i in 0..<simplifiedSketch.strokes.count{
        for j in 0..<simplifiedSketch.strokes[i].points.count{
            let point = simplifiedSketch.strokes[i].points[j]
            let x = (point.x-minPoint.x)/scale.x
            let y = (point.y-minPoint.y)/scale.y
            let z = j == simplifiedSketch.strokes[i].points.count-1 ?
                1 : 0
            data.append(Double(x))
            data.append(Double(y))
            data.append(Double(z))
        }
    }
    let dataStride : Int = 3
    for i in stride(from: dataStride, to:data.count, by: dataStride){
        data[i - dataStride] = data[i] - data[i - dataStride]
        data[i - (dataStride-1)] = data[i+1] - data[i - (dataStride-1)]
```

```
        data[i - (dataStride-2)] = data[i+2] // EOS
    }

    data.removeLast(3)
    var dataIdx : Int = 0
    let startAddingIdx = max(array.count-data.count, 0)
    for i in 0..<array.count{
        if i >= startAddingIdx{
            array[i] = NSNumber(value:data[dataIdx])
            dataIdx = dataIdx + 1
        } else{
            array[i] = NSNumber(value:0)
        }
    }
    return array
}
```

If anything looks unfamiliar, then I encourage you to revisit the previous section, where we delve into the details of what these methods do (and why).

We now have our model and functionality for preprocessing the input; our last task is to tie this all together. Head back to the `QueryFacade` class and locate the method `classifySketch`. As a reminder, this method is called via `queryCurrentSketch`, which in turn is triggered anytime the user completes a stroke. The method is expected to return a dictionary of category and probability pairs, which is then used to search and download related drawings of most likely categories. At this point, it's simply a matter of using the work we have previously done, with one little caveat. If you recall from previous chapters, when we imported our model into the project, Xcode would conveniently generate a strongly typed wrapper for our model and its associated inputs and outputs. A disadvantage of downloading and importing at runtime is that we forgo these generated wrappers and are left to do it manually.

Starting backwards, after making the prediction, we are expecting an instance of `MLFeatureProvider` to be returned, which in turn has a method called `featureValue`. This returns an instance of `MLFeatureValue` for a given output key (`classLabelProbs`). The returned instance of `MLFeatureValue` exposes properties set by the model during inference; here we are interested in the `dictionaryValue` property of type `[String:Double]` (category and its associated probability).

Obviously, to obtain this output, we need to call `predict` on our model, which is expecting an instance adhering to the `MLFeatureProvider` protocol that was generated for us, as mentioned previously. Given that in most instances you will have access and knowledge of the model, the easiest way to generate this wrapper is to import the model and extract the generated input, which is exactly what we will do.

Locate the file `CoreMLModels/Chapter8/quickdraw.mlmodel` in the accompanying repository `https://github.com/packtpublishing/machine-learning-with-core-ml`, and drag the file into your project as we have done in previous chapters. Once imported, select it from the left-hand-side panel and click on the arrow button within the **Model Class** section, as shown in the following screenshot:

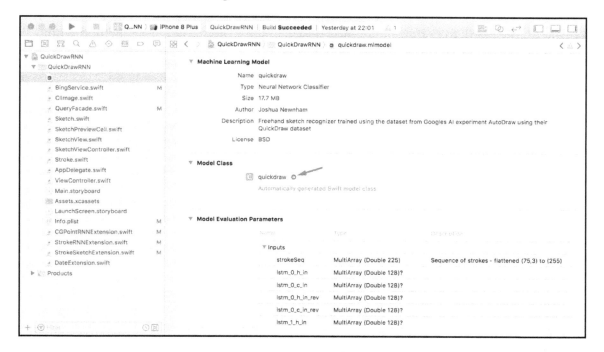

This will open up the generated classes; locate the class `quickdrawInput` and copy and paste it to your `QueryFacade.swift`, ensuring that it's outside the `QueryFacade` class (or extensions). Because we are only concerned with the `strokeSeq` input, we can strip all other variables; clean it up such that you are left with something like the following:

```
class quickdrawInput : MLFeatureProvider {
    var strokeSeq: MLMultiArray
    var featureNames: Set<String> {
        get {
            return ["strokeSeq"]
        }
    }
    func featureValue(for featureName: String) -> MLFeatureValue? {
        if (featureName == "strokeSeq") {
            return MLFeatureValue(multiArray: strokeSeq)
```

```
        }
        return nil
    }
    init(strokeSeq: MLMultiArray) {
        self.strokeSeq = strokeSeq
    }
}
```

We are finally ready to perform inference; return to the `classifySketch` method within the `QueryFacade` class and add the following code:

```
if let strokeSketch = sketch as? StrokeSketch, let
    x = StrokeSketch.preprocess(strokeSketch){
    if let modelOutput = try!
model?.prediction(from:quickdrawInput(strokeSeq:x)){
        if let classPredictions = modelOutput.featureValue(
            for: "classLabelProbs")?.dictionaryValue as? [String:Double]{
            let sortedClassPredictions = classPredictions.sorted(
                by: { (kvp1, kvp2) -> Bool in
                kvp1.value > kvp2.value
            })
            return sortedClassPredictions
        }
    }
}

return nil
```

No doubt most of this will look familiar to you; we start by extracting the features via the `preprocess` method we implemented at the start of this chapter. Once we have obtained these features, we wrap them in an instance of `quickdrawInput`, before passing them to our model's `prediction` method to perform inference. If successful, we are returned the output, with which we proceed to extract the appropriate output, as discussed previously. Finally we sort the results before returning them to the caller.

With that complete, you are now in a good position to test. Build and deploy to the simulator or device, and if everything goes as planned, you should be able to test the accuracy of your mode (or drawing, depending on how you look at it):

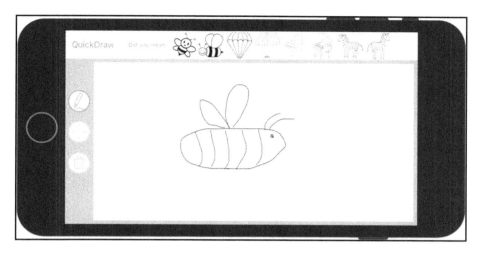

Let's wrap up this chapter by reviewing what we have covered.

# Summary

In this chapter, we revisited a previous problem (sketch recognition) but used a different dataset and different approach. Previously, we tackled the problem using CNN, but in this chapter, we identified nuances of how the data was collected, which in turn allowed us to take a different approach using an RNN. As usual, most of the effort was spent in preparing the data for the model. This, in doing so, highlighted some techniques we can use to make our data invariant to scale and translation, as well as the usefulness of reducing details of the inputs (through simplification) to assist our model in more easily finding patterns.

Finally, we highlighted an important aspect of designing interfaces for machine learning systems, that is, adding a layer of transparency and control for the user to help them build a useful mental model of the system and improve the model through explicit user feedback, such as corrections.

Let's continue our journey into the world of machine learning applications and dive into the next chapter, where we will look at our final visual application: image segmentation.

# Object Segmentation Using CNNs

9

Throughout the chapters in this book, we have seen various machine learning models, each progressively increasing their perceptual abilities. By this, I mean that we were first introduced to a model capable of classifying a single object present in an image. Then came a model that was able to classify not only multiple objects but also their corresponding bounding boxes. In this chapter, we continue this progression by introducing semantic segmentation, in other words, being able to assign each pixel to a specific class, as shown in the following figure:

Source: http://cocodataset.org/#explore

This allows for a greater understanding of the scene and, therefore, opportunities for more intelligible interfaces and services. But this is not the main focus of this chapter. In this chapter, we will use semantic segmentation to create an image effects application as a way to demonstrate imperfect predictions. We'll be using this to motivate a discussion on one of the most important aspects of designing and building machine learning (or artificial intelligence) interfaces—dealing with probabilistic, or imperfect, outcomes from models.

By the end of this chapter, you will have:

- An understanding semantic of segmentation
- Built an intuitive understanding of how it is achieved (learned)
- Learned how it can be applied in a novel way for real life applications by building an action shot photo effects application
- Gained appreciation and awareness for dealing with probability outcomes from machine learning models

Let's begin by better understanding what semantic segmentation is and get an intuitive understanding of how it is achieved.

# Classifying pixels

As we have already discussed, the desired output of a model performing semantic segmentation is an image with each of its pixels assigned a label of its most likely class (or even a specific instance of a class). Throughout this book, we have also seen that layers of a deep neural network learn features that are activated when a corresponding input that satisfies the particular feature is detected. We can visualize these activations using a technique called **class activation maps** (**CAMs**). The output produces a heatmap of class activations over the input image; the heatmap consists of a matrix of scores associated with a specific class, essentially giving us a spatial map of how intensely the input region activates a specified class. The following figure shows an output of a CAM visualization for the class cat. Here, you can see that the heatmap portrays what the model considers important features (and therefore regions) for this class:

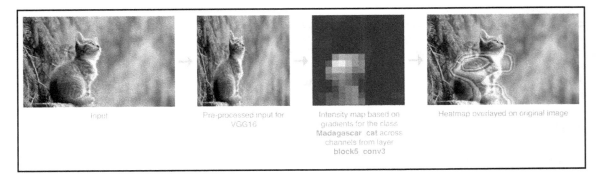

The preceding figure was produced using the implementation described in the paper *Grad-CAM: Visual Explanations from Deep Networks via Gradient-based Localization* by R. Selvaraju. The approach is to take the output feature map of a convolutional layer and weigh every channel in that feature map by the gradient of the class. For more details of how it works, please refer to the original paper: https://arxiv.org/abs/1610.02391.

Early attempts of semantic segmentation were made using slightly adapted classification models such as VGG and Alexnet, but they only produced coarse approximations. This can be seen in the preceding figure and is largely due to the network using repetitive pooling layers, which results in loss of spatial information.

U-Net is one architecture that addresses this; it consists of an **encoder** and **decoder**, with the addition of **shortcuts** between the two to preserve spatial information. Released in 2015 by *O. Ronneberger*, *P. Fischer*, and *T. Brox* for biomedical image segmentation, it has since become one of the go-to architectures for segmentation due to its effectiveness (it can be trained on a small dataset) and performance. The following figure shows the modified U-Net we will be using in this chapter:

U-Net is one of many architectures for semantic segmentation. Sasank Chilamkurthy's post *A 2017 Guide to Semantic Segmentation with Deep Learning* provides a great overview and comparison of the most popular architectures, available at http://blog.qure.ai/notes/semantic-segmentation-deep-learning-review. For further details on U-Net, please refer to the original paper mentioned earlier. It is available at https://arxiv.org/pdf/1505.04597.pdf.

On the left in the preceding figure, we have the full network used in this chapter's project, and on the right we have an extract of blocks used in the encoder and decoder parts of the network. As a reminder, the focus of this book is on applying machine learning rather than the details of the models themselves. So for this reason, we won't be delving into the details, but there are a few interesting and useful things worth pointing out.

The first is the general structure of the network; it consists of an encoder and decoder. The encoder's role is to capture context. The decoder's task is to use this context and features from the corresponding shortcuts to project its understanding onto pixel space, to get a dense and precise classification. It's a common practice to bootstrap the encoder using an architecture and weights from a trained classification model, such as VGG16. This not only speeds up training but also is likely to increase performance as it brings with it a depth (pun intended) of understanding of images it has been trained on, which is typically from a larger dataset.

Another point worth highlighting is those shortcuts between the encoder and decoder. As mentioned previously, they are used to preserve spatial information outputted from convolutional layers from each encoding block before being lost when its downsampled using max pooling. This information is used to assist the model in precise localization.

It's the first time in this book that we have seen an upsampling layer. As the name implies, it's a technique that upsamples your image (or feature maps) to a higher resolution. One of the easiest ways is to use the same techniques we use with image upsampling, that is, rescaling the input to a desired size and calculating the values at each point using an interpolation method, such as bilinear interpolation.

Lastly, I wanted to bring to your attention the input and outputs of the model. The model is expecting a 448 x 448 color image as its input and outputs a 448 x 448 x 1 (single channel) matrix. If you inspect the architecture, you will notice that the last layer is a sigmoid activation, where a sigmoid function is typically used for binary classification, which is precisely what we are doing here. Typically, you would perform multi-class classification for semantic segmentation tasks, in which case you would replace the sigmoid activation with a softmax activation. An example commonly used when introducing semantic segmentation is scene understanding for self-driving cars. The following is an example of a labeled scene from Cambridge University's Motion-based Segmentation and Recognition Dataset where each color represents a different class:

Source: http://mi.eng.cam.ac.uk/research/projects/VideoRec/CamVid/

But in this example, a binary classifier is sufficient, which will become apparent as we go into the details of the project. However, I wanted to highlight it here as the architecture will scale to multi-class classification by simply swapping the last layer with a softmax activation and changing the loss function.

You have thus seen the architecture we will be using in this chapter. Let's now look at how we will use it and the data used to train the model.

# Data to drive the desired effect – action shots

Now would be a good time to introduce the photo effect we want to create in this chapter. The effect, as I know it, is called an **action shot.** It's essentially a still photograph that shows someone (or something) in motion, probably best illustrated with an image - like the one shown here:

As previously mentioned, the model we used in this chapter performs binary (or single-class) classification. This simplification, using a binary classifier instead of a multi-class classifier, has been driven by the intended use that is just segmenting people from the background. Similar to any software project, you should strive for simplicity where you can.

To extract people, we need a model to learn how to recognize people and their associated pixels. For this, we need a dataset consisting of images of people and corresponding images with those pixels of the persons labeled—and lots of them. Unlike datasets for classification, datasets for object segmentation are not so common nor as vast. This is understandable given the additional effort that would be required to label such a dataset. Some common datasets for object segmentation, and ones that are considered for this chapter, include:

- **PASCAL VOC**: A dataset with 9,993 labeled images across 20 classes. You can find the dataset at `http://host.robots.ox.ac.uk/pascal/VOC/voc2012/index.html`.

- **Labeled Faces in the Wild (LFW) from University of Massachusetts Amherst**: A dataset comprising 2,927 faces. Each has the hair, skin, and background labeled (three classes). You can find the dataset at `http://vis-www.cs.umass.edu/lfw/part_labels/`.

- **Common Objects in Context (COCO) dataset**: A popular dataset for all things related to computer vision, including segmentation. Its segmented datasets comprise approximately 200,000 labeled images across 80 classes. It's the dataset that was used and which we will be briefly exploring in this section. You can find the dataset at `http://cocodataset.org/#home`.

- Not considered for this project but good to be aware of is the **Cambridge-driving Labeled Video Database** (**CamVid**) from Cambridge University. As is clear from the name, the dataset is made up of frames from a video feed from a car camera—ideal for anyone interested in training their own self-driving car. You can find the dataset at `http://mi.eng.cam.ac.uk/research/projects/VideoRec/CamVid/`.

 Listing the datasets here is possibly superfluous, but semantic segmentation is such an exciting opportunity with huge potential that I hope listing these here will encourage you to explore and experiment with new applications of it.

Luckily for us, COCO's 13+ GB dataset contains many labeled images of people and a convenient API to make finding relevant images easy. For this chapter, COCO's API was used to find all images including people. Then, these were filtered further, only keeping those that contained either one or two people and whose area covered between 20% and 70% of the image, discarding those images where the person was too small or too large. For each of these images, the contours of each of the persons were fetched and then used to create a binary mask, which then became our labels for our training. The following figure illustrates this process for a single image:

Source: The COCO dataset (http://cocodataset.org)

After training on 8,689 images over 40 epochs, an **Intersection over Union (IoU)** coefficient (also known as the **dice coefficient**) of 0.8192 was achieved on the validation data (approximately 300).

Hopefully, IoU sounds familiar as it was what we used back in Chapter 5, *Locating Objects in the World*. As a reminder, IoU is an evaluation metric used to measure how well two bounding boxes overlap each other. A perfect overlap, where both bounding boxes overlap each other perfectly, would return 1.0 (which is why the loss is negated for training).

In the following image, we get to see what this looks like, starting with random examples from the validation set. Then, some are manually searched for, like the ones that portray actions:

Source: The COCO dataset (http://cocodataset.org)

And here are some examples of action images where the model was able to sufficiently segment the person from the image:

Finally, here are some, out of many, examples of action images where the model was less successful:

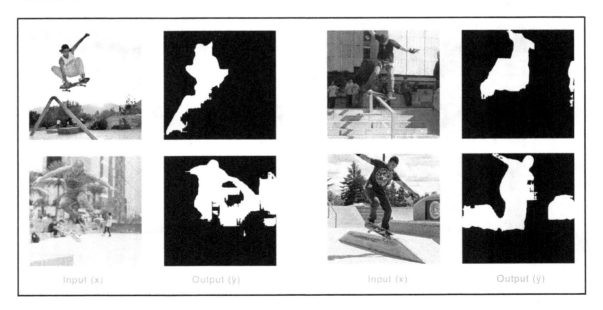

We have covered the model and training data and examined the outputs of the model. It's now time to turn our attention to the application in this chapter, which we will begin working on in the next section.

# Building the photo effects application

In this section, we will be looking briefly at the application and highlighting some of the interesting pieces of the code, omitting most of it as it has already been discussed in previous chapters. As mentioned in the introduction, this example is to provide a case study for a later section, where we will discuss some broad strategies to use when building intelligent interfaces and services.

If you haven't already, pull down the latest code from the accompanying repository at `https://github.com/packtpublishing/machine-learning-with-core-ml`. Once downloaded, navigate to the `Chapter9/Start/` directory and open the project `ActionShot.xcodeproj`.

As mentioned in the previous section, the example for this chapter is an photo effects application. In it, the user is able to take an *action shot*, have the application extract each person from the frames, and compose them onto the final frame, as illustrated in the following figure:

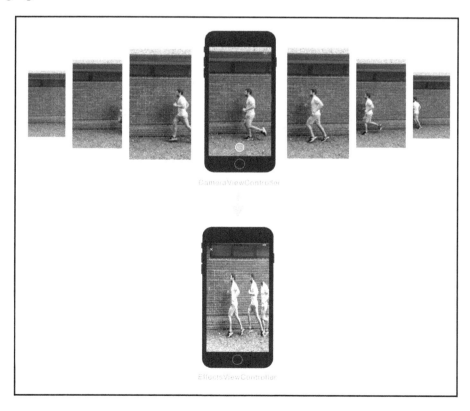

The application consists of two view controllers; one is responsible for capturing the frames and the other for presenting the composite image. The workhorse for the processing, once again, has been delegated to the ImageProcessor class and it is the perspective from which we will be reviewing this project.

ImageProcessor acts as both the sink and processor; by sink I refer to it being the class that is passed captured frames from the camera, using the CameraViewController, and holding them in memory for processing. Let's see what the code for this looks like; select ImageProcessor.swift from the left panel to bring the source code into focus. Let's see what exists; initially paying particular attention to the properties and methods responsible for handling received frames and then move on to their processing.

At the top of the file, you will notice that a protocol has been declared, which is implemented by the EffectViewController; it is used to broadcast the progress of the tasks:

```
protocol ImageProcessorDelegate : class{

    func onImageProcessorFinishedProcessingFrame(
        status:Int, processedFrames:Int, framesRemaining:Int)

    func onImageProcessorFinishedComposition(
        status:Int, image:CIImage?)
}
```

The first callback, onImageProcessorFinishedProcessingFrame, is used to notify the delegate of frame-by-frame processing progress while the other, onImageProcessorFinishedComposition, is used to notify the delegate once the final image has be created. These discrete callbacks are intentionally split as the processing has been broken down into segmentation and composition. Segmentation is responsible for segmenting each of the frames using our model, and composition is responsible for generating the final image using the processed (segmented) frames. This structure is also mimicked in the layout of the class, with the class broken down into four parts and the flow we will follow in this section.

The first part declares all the variables. The second implements the properties and methods responsible for retrieving the frames while they're being captured. The third contains all the methods for processing the frames, whereby the delegate is notified using the `onImageProcessorFinishedProcessingFrame` callback. The final part, and the one we will focus on the most, contains the methods responsible for generating the final image, that is, it composites the frames. Let's peek at the first part to get a sense of what variables are available, which are shown in the following code snippet:

```
class ImageProcessor{
    weak var delegate : ImageProcessorDelegate?
    lazy var model : VNCoreMLModel = {
        do{
            let model = try VNCoreMLModel(
                for: small_unet().model
            )
            return model
        } catch{
            fatalError("Failed to create VNCoreMLModel")
        }
    }()
    var minMaskArea:CGFloat = 0.005
    var targetSize = CGSize(width: 448, height: 448)
    let lock = NSLock()
    var frames = [CIImage]()
    var processedImages = [CIImage]()
    var processedMasks = [CIImage]()
    private var _processingImage = false
    init(){
    }
}
```

Nothing extraordinary. We first declare a property that wraps our model in an instance of `VNCoreMLModel` so that we can take advantage of the Vision framework's preprocessing functionality. We then declare a series of variables to deal with storing the frames and handling the processing; we make use of an `NSLock` instance to avoid different threads reading stale property values.

The following code snippet, and part of the `ImageProcessor` class, includes variables and methods for handling retrieving and releasing the captured frames:

```
extension ImageProcessor{
    var isProcessingImage : Bool{
        get{
            self.lock.lock()
            defer {
                self.lock.unlock()
```

```
            }
            return _processingImage
        }
        set(value){
            self.lock.lock()
            _processingImage = value
            self.lock.unlock()
        }
    }

    var isFrameAvailable : Bool{
        get{
            self.lock.lock()
            let frameAvailable =
                    self.frames.count > 0
            self.lock.unlock()
            return frameAvailable
        }
    }
    public func addFrame(frame:CIImage){
        self.lock.lock()
        self.frames.append(frame)
        self.lock.unlock()
    }
    public func getNextFrame() -> CIImage?{
        self.lock.lock()
        let frame = self.frames.removeFirst()
        self.lock.unlock()
        return frame
    }
    public func reset(){
        self.lock.lock()
        self.frames.removeAll()
        self.processedImages.removeAll()
        self.processedMasks.removeAll()
        self.lock.unlock()
    }
}
```

Although fairly verbose, it should all be self-explanatory; probably the only method worth outlying is the method `addFrame`, which is called each time a frame is captured by the camera. To give some bearing of how everything is tied together, the following diagram illustrates the general flow whilst capturing frames:

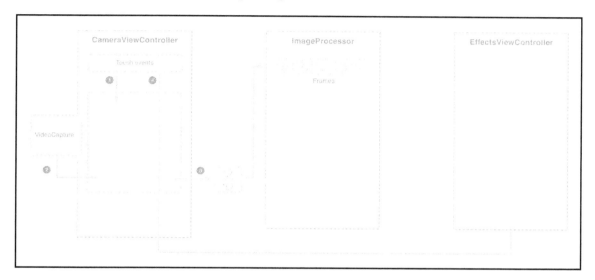

The details of the flow are covered in the following points:

1. Although capturing of the frames is persistent throughout the lifetime of the `CameraViewController`, they are only passed to the `ImageProcessor` once flagged once the user taps (and holds) their finger on the action button
2. During this time, each frame that is captured (at the throttled rate—currently 10 frames per second) is passed to the `CameraViewController`
3. This subsequently passes it to the `ImageProcessor` using the `addFrame` method shown earlier
4. The capturing stops when the user lifts their finger from the action button and, once finished, the `EffectsViewController` is instantiated and presented, along with passing it a reference to the `ImageProcessor` with the reference to the captured frames

The next part of the `ImageProcessor` class is responsible for processing each of these images; this is initiated using the `processFrames` method, which is called by the `EffectsViewController` once it has loaded. This part has a lot more code, but most of it should be familiar to you as it's the boilerplate code we've used in many of the projects during the course of this book. Let's start by inspecting the `processFrames` method, as shown in the following snippet:

 All of the remaining code is assumed to be inside the `ImageProcessor` class for the rest of this chapter unless stated otherwise; that is, the class and class extension declaration will be omitted to make the code easier to read.

```
public func processFrames(){
    if !self.isProcessingImage{
        DispatchQueue.global(qos: .background).async {
            self.processesingNextFrame()
        }
    }
}
```

This method simply dispatches the method call `processingNextFrame` to the background thread. This is mandatory when performing inference with Core ML and also a good practice when performing compute-intensive tasks to avoid locking up the user interface. Let's continue the trail by inspecting the `processingNextFrame` method along with the method responsible for returning an instance of a `VNCoreMLRequest`, which is shown in the following code snippet:

```
func getRequest() -> VNCoreMLRequest{
    let request = VNCoreMLRequest(
        model: self.model,
        completionHandler: { [weak self] request, error in
            self?.processRequest(for: request, error: error)
    })
    request.imageCropAndScaleOption = .centerCrop
    return request
}

func processesingNextFrame(){
    self.isProcessingImage = true
    guard let nextFrame = self.getNextFrame() else{
        self.isProcessingImage = false
        return
    }
    var ox : CGFloat = 0
    var oy : CGFloat = 0
```

```
let frameSize = min(nextFrame.extent.width, nextFrame.extent.height)
if nextFrame.extent.width > nextFrame.extent.height{
    ox = (nextFrame.extent.width - nextFrame.extent.height)/2
} else if nextFrame.extent.width < nextFrame.extent.height{
    oy = (nextFrame.extent.height - nextFrame.extent.width)/2
}
guard let frame = nextFrame
    .crop(rect: CGRect(x: ox,
                       y: oy,
                       width: frameSize,
                       height: frameSize))?
    .resize(size: targetSize) else{
        self.isProcessingImage = false
        return
}
self.processedImages.append(frame)
let handler = VNImageRequestHandler(ciImage: frame)
do {
    try handler.perform([self.getRequest()])
} catch {
    print("Failed to perform
classification.\n\(error.localizedDescription)")
    self.isProcessingImage = false
    return
}
}
```

We start off by setting the property `isProcessingImage` to `true` and checking that we have a frame to process, otherwise exiting early from the method.

The following might seem a little counter-intuitive (because it is); we have seen from previous chapters that `VNCoreMLRequest` handles the preprocessing task of resizing the cropping of our images. So, why are we doing it manually here? The reason has more to do with keeping the code simpler and meeting publishing deadlines. In this example, the final image is composited using the resized frames to avoid scaling and offsetting the output from the model, which I'll leave as an exercise for you. So here, we are performing that operation and persisting the result in the array `processedImages` to be used in the final stage. Finally, we execute the request, passing in the image, which calls our method `processRequest` once finished, passing in the results from the model.

Continuing on our trail, we will now inspect the `processRequest` method; as this method is quite long, we will break it down into chunks, working top to bottom:

```
func processRequest(for request:VNRequest, error: Error?){
    self.lock.lock()
    let framesReaminingCount = self.frames.count
    let processedFramesCount = self.processedImages.count
    self.lock.unlock()
    ...
}
```

We start off by getting the latest counts, which will be broadcast to the delegate when this method finishes or fails. Talking of which, the following block verifies that a result was returned of type [VNPixelBufferObservation], otherwise notifying the delegate and returning, as shown in the following snippet:

```
func processRequest(for request:VNRequest, error: Error?){
    ...

    guard let results = request.results,
        let pixelBufferObservations = results as?
[VNPixelBufferObservation],
        pixelBufferObservations.count > 0 else {
            print("ImageProcessor", #function, "ERROR:",
                String(describing: error?.localizedDescription))
            self.isProcessingImage = false
            DispatchQueue.main.async {
                self.delegate?.onImageProcessorFinishedProcessingFrame(
                    status: -1,
                    processedFrames: processedFramesCount,
                    framesRemaining: framesReaminingCount)
            }
            return
    }

    ...
}
```

With reference to our result (CVBufferPixel), our next task is to create an instance of CIImage, passing in the buffer and requesting the color space to be grayscale to ensure that a single channel image is created. Then, we will be adding it to our processedMasks array, shown in the following snippet:

```
func processRequest(for request:VNRequest, error: Error?){
    ...
    let options = [
        kCIImageColorSpace:CGColorSpaceCreateDeviceGray()
        ] as [String:Any]
    let ciImage = CIImage(
        cvPixelBuffer: pixelBufferObservations[0].pixelBuffer,
        options: options)
    self.processedMasks.append(ciImage)
    ...
}
```

Only two more things left to do! We notify the delegate that we have finished a frame and proceed to process the next frame, if available:

```
func processRequest(for request:VNRequest, error: Error?){
    ...
    DispatchQueue.main.async {
        self.delegate?.onImageProcessorFinishedProcessingFrame(
            status: 1,
            processedFrames: processedFramesCount,
            framesRemaining: framesReaminingCount)
    }
    if self.isFrameAvailable{
        self.processesingNextFrame()
    } else{
        self.isProcessingImage = false
    }
}
```

This concludes the third part of our `ImageProcessor`; at this point, we have two arrays containing the resized captured frames and the segmented images from our model. Before moving on to the final part of this class, let's get a bird's-eye view of what we just did, illustrated in this flow diagram:

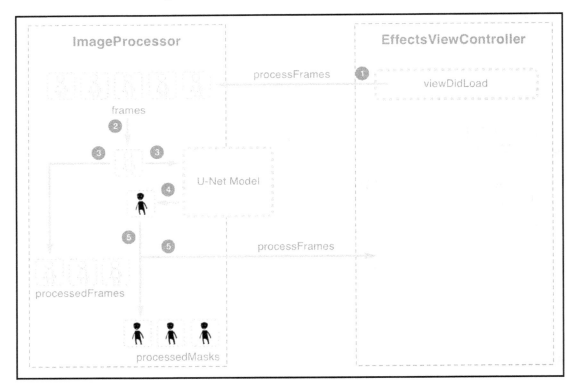

The details of the flow are shown in the following points:

1. As mentioned in the preceding diagram, processing is initiated once the `EffectsViewController` is loaded, which kicks off the background thread to process each of the captured frames
2. Each frame is first resized and cropped to match the output of the model
3. Then, it is added to the `processedFrames` array and passed to our model for interference (segmentation)
4. Once the model returns with the result, we instantiate a single color instance of `CIImage`
5. This instance is stored in the array `processedMasks` and the delegate is notified of the progress

What happens when all frames have been processed? This is what we plan on answering in the next part, where we will discuss the details of how to create the effect. To start with, let's discuss how the process is initiated.

Once the delegate (EffectsViewController) receives a callback, using onImageProcessorFinishedProcessingFrame, where all of the frames have been processed, it calls the compositeFrames method from the ImageProcessor to start the process of creating the effect. Let's review this and the existing code within this part of the ImageProcessor class:

```
func compositeFrames(){
    var selectedIndicies = self.getIndiciesOfBestFrames()
    if selectedIndicies.count == 0{
        DispatchQueue.main.async {
            self.delegate?.onImageProcessorFinishedComposition(
                status: -1,
                image: self.processedImages.last!)
        }
        return
    }
    var finalImage = self.processedImages[selectedIndicies.last!]
    selectedIndicies.removeLast()

    // TODO Composite final image using segments from intermediate frames
    DispatchQueue.main.async {
        self.delegate?.onImageProcessorFinishedComposition(
            status: 1,
            image: finalImage)
    }
}

func getIndiciesOfBestFrames() -> [Int]{
    // TODO; find best frames for the sequence i.e. avoid excessive
overlapping
    return (0..<self.processedMasks.count).map({ (i) -> Int in
        return i
    })
}

func getDominantDirection() -> CGPoint{
    var dir = CGPoint(x: 0, y: 0)
    // TODO detected dominate direction
    return dir
}
```

I have bolded the important/interesting parts, essentially the parts we will be implementing, but before writing any more code, let's review what we currently have (in terms of processed images) and an approach to creating our effect.

At this stage, we have an array of `processedFrames` that contains the resized and cropped versions of the captured images, and we have another array, `processedMasks`, containing the single-channel images from our segmentation model. Examples of these are shown in the following figure:

If we were to composite each of the frames as they are, we would end up with a lot of unwanted artifacts and excessive overlapping. One approach could be to adjust the frames that have been processed (and possibly captured), that is, skip every *n* frames to spread out the frames. The problem with this approach is that it assumes all subjects will be moving at the same speed; to account for this, you would need to expose this tuning to the user for manual adjustment (which is an reasonable approach). The approach we will take here will be to extract the bounding box for each of the frames, and using the displacement and relative overlap of these to determine when to insert a frame and when to skip a frame.

To calculate the bounding box, we simply scan each line from each of the edges of the image, that is, from **top to bottom**, to determine the top of the object. Then, we do it **bottom to top** to determine the bottom of the object. Similarly, we do it on the horizontal axis, illustrated in the following figure:

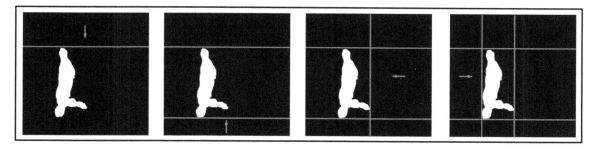

Even with bounding boxes, we still need to determine how far the object should move before inserting a frame. To determine this, we first determine the dominant direction, which is calculated by finding the direction between the first and last frames of the segmented object. This is then used to determine what axis to compare displacement on; that is, if the dominant direction is in the horizontal axis (as shown in the preceding figure), then we measure the displacement across the $x$ axis, ignoring the $y$ axis. We then simply measure the distance between the frames against some predetermined threshold to decide whether to composite the frame or ignore it. This is illustrated in the following figure:

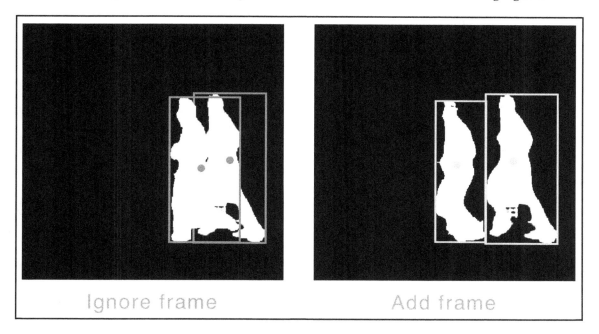

Let's see what this looks like in code, starting from determining the dominant direction. Add the following code to the getDominantDirection method:

```
var dir = CGPoint(x: 0, y: 0)

var startCenter : CGPoint?
var endCenter : CGPoint?

// Find startCenter
for i in 0..<self.processedMasks.count{
    let mask = self.processedMasks[i]
    guard let maskBB = mask.getContentBoundingBox(),
    (maskBB.width * maskBB.height) >=
        (mask.extent.width * mask.extent.height) * self.minMaskArea
    else {
        continue
    }
    startCenter = maskBB.center
    break
}

// Find endCenter
for i in (0..<self.processedMasks.count).reversed(){
    let mask = self.processedMasks[i]
    guard let maskBB = mask.getContentBoundingBox(),
    (maskBB.width * maskBB.height) >=
        (mask.extent.width * mask.extent.height) * self.minMaskArea
    else {
        continue
    }
    endCenter = maskBB.center
    break
}

if let startCenter = startCenter, let endCenter = endCenter, startCenter !=
endCenter{
    dir = (startCenter - endCenter).normalised
}

return dir
```

As described earlier, we first find the bounding boxes of the start and end of our sequence of frames, and use their centers to calculate the dominate direction.

The implementation of the `CIImage` method `getContentBoundingBox` is omitted here, but it can be found in the accompanying the source code within the `CIImage+Extension.swift` file.

Armed with the dominant direction, we can now proceed with determining what frames to include and what frames to ignore. We will implement this in the method `getIndiciesOfBestFrames` of the `ImageProcessor` class, which iterates over all frames, measuring the overlap and ignoring those that don't meet a specific threshold. The method returns an array of indices that satisfy this threshold to be composited onto the final image. Add the following code to the `getIndiciesOfBestFrames` method:

```
var selectedIndicies = [Int]()
var previousBoundingBox : CGRect?
let dir = self.getDominateDirection()

for i in (0..<self.processedMasks.count).reversed(){
    let mask = self.processedMasks[i]
    guard let maskBB = mask.getContentBoundingBox(),
        maskBB.width < mask.extent.width * 0.7,
        maskBB.height < mask.extent.height * 0.7 else {
        continue
    }
    if previousBoundingBox == nil{
        previousBoundingBox = maskBB
        selectedIndicies.append(i)
    } else{
        let distance = abs(dir.x) >= abs(dir.y)
            ? abs(previousBoundingBox!.center.x - maskBB.center.x)
            : abs(previousBoundingBox!.center.y - maskBB.center.y)
        let bounds = abs(dir.x) >= abs(dir.y)
            ? (previousBoundingBox!.width + maskBB.width) / 4.0
            : (previousBoundingBox!.height + maskBB.height) / 4.0
        if distance > bounds * 0.5{
            previousBoundingBox = maskBB
            selectedIndicies.append(i)
        }
    }
}

return selectedIndicies.reversed()
```

We begin by getting the dominant direction, as discussed earlier, and then proceed to iterate through our sequence of frames in reverse order (reverse as it is assumed that the user's hero shot is the last frame). With each frame, we obtain the bounding box, and if it's the first frame to be checked, we assign it to the variable `previousBoundingBox`. This will be used to compare subsequent bounding boxes (and updated to the latest included frame). If `previousBoundingBox` is not null, then we calculate the displacement between the two based on the dominant direction, as shown in the following snippet:

```
let distance = abs(dir.x) >= abs(dir.y)
    ? abs(previousBoundingBox!.center.x - maskBB.center.x)
    : abs(previousBoundingBox!.center.y - maskBB.center.y)
```

We then calculate the minimum length needed to separate the two objects, which is calculated by the combined size of the relative axis divided by 2. This gives us a distance of half of the combined frame, as shown in the following snippet:

```
let bounds = abs(dir.x) >= abs(dir.y)
    ? (previousBoundingBox!.width + maskBB.width) / 2.0
    : (previousBoundingBox!.height + maskBB.height) / 2.0
```

We then compare the distance with the bounds along with a threshold and proceed to add the frame to the current index if the distance satisfies this threshold:

```
if distance > bounds * 0.15{
    previousBoundingBox = maskBB
    selectedIndicies.append(i)
}
```

Returning to the `compositeFrames` method, we are now ready to composite the selected frames. To achieve this, we will leverage `CoreImages` filters; but before doing so, let's quickly review what it is exactly that we want to achieve.

For each selected (processed) image and mask pair, we want to clip out the image and overlay it onto the final image. To improve the effect, we will apply a progressively increasing alpha so that frames closer to the final frame will have an opacity closer to 1.0 while the frames further away will be progressively transparent; this will give us a faded trailing effect. This process is summarized in the following figure:

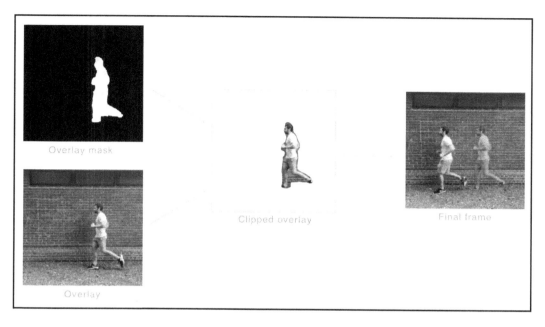

Overlay mask

Clipped overlay

Final frame

Overlay

Let's turn this into code by first implementing the filter. As shown earlier, we will be passing the kernel the output image, the overlay and its corresponding mask, and an alpha. Near the top of the ImageProcessor class, add the following code:

```
lazy var compositeKernel : CIColorKernel? = {
    let kernelString = """
        kernel vec4 compositeFilter(
            __sample image,
            __sample overlay,
            __sample overlay_mask,
            float alpha){
            float overlayStrength = 0.0;

            if(overlay_mask.r > 0.0){
                overlayStrength = 1.0;
            }

            overlayStrength *= alpha;
            return vec4(image.rgb * (1.0-overlayStrength), 1.0)
                + vec4(overlay.rgb * (overlayStrength), 1.0);
        }
    """
    return CIColorKernel(source:kernelString)
}()
```

Previously, we have implemented the CIColorKernel, which is responsible for compositing all of our frames onto the final image as discussed. We start by testing the mask's value, and if it is 1.0, we assign the strength 1.0 (meaning we want to replace the color at that location of the final image with that of the overlay). Otherwise, we assign 0, ignoring it. Then, we multiply the strength with the blend argument passed to our kernel. Finally, we calculate and return the final color with the statement vec4(image.rgb * (1.0-overlayStrength), 1.0) + vec4(overlay.rgb * (overlayStrength), 1.0). With our filter now implemented, let's return the compositeFrames method and put it to use. Within compositeFrames, replace the comment // TODO Composite final image using segments from intermediate frames with the following code:

```
let alphaStep : CGFloat = 1.0 / CGFloat(selectedIndicies.count)

for i in selectedIndicies{
    let image = self.processedImages[i]
    let mask = self.processedMasks[i]
    let extent = image.extent
    let alpha = CGFloat(i + 1) * alphaStep
    let arguments = [finalImage, image, mask, min(alpha, 1.0)] as [Any]
    if let compositeFrame = self.compositeKernel?.apply(extent: extent,
arguments: arguments){
        finalImage = compositeFrame
    }
}
```

Most of this should be self-explanatory; we start by calculating an alpha stride that will be used to progressively increase opacity as we get closer to the final frame. We then iterate through all the selected frames, applying the filter we just implemented in the preceding snippet, compositing our final image.

With that done, we have now finished this method and the coding for this chapter. Well done! It's time to test it out; build and run the project to see your hard work in action. The following is a result from a weekend park visit:

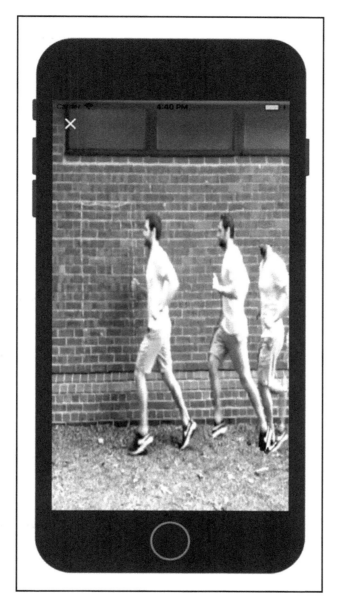

Before wrapping up this chapter, let's briefly discuss some strategies when working with machine learning models.

# Working with probabilistic results

As alluded to at the beginning of this chapter and seen firsthand in the previous section, working with machine learning models requires a set of new techniques and strategies to deal with uncertainty. The approach taken will be domain-specific, but there are some broad strategies that are worth keeping in mind, and that's what we will cover in this section in the context of the example project of this chapter.

# Improving the model

The first is improving the model. Of course, there may be limitations depending on the source of the model and dataset, but it's important to be able to understand ways in which the model can be improved as its output directly correlates to the quality of the user experience.

In the context of this project, we can augment the model using an existing pre-trained image classifier as the encoder, as mentioned earlier. This not only fast-tracks training, providing more opportunities to iterate, but also is likely to improve performance by having the model transfer existing knowledge from a more comprehensive dataset.

Another is tuning the dataset that the model was trained on. A simple, and relevant, example of how the model can be improved can be seen by any image in which the user is holding an object (which has been labeled). An example of this can be seen in the following figure, in which the guitar is cropped from the person:

How you deal with this is dependent on the desired characteristics of your model. In the context of the application presented in this chapter, it would make sense to either perform multi-class classification, including objects normally held by people, or including them in the mask.

Another common technique is **data augmentation**. This is where you artificially adjust the image (input) to increase variance in your dataset, or even adjust it to make it more aligned with the data for your particular use case. Some example augmentations include blurring (useful when dealing with fast moving objects), rotation, adding random noise, color adjustment - essentially any image manipulation effect that introduces nuances that you are likely to get in the real world.

Of course, there are many more techniques and tools to improve the model and data; here, our intention is just to highlight the main areas rather than delve into the details.

# Designing in constraints

This is somewhat unavoidable and how we design intelligent interfaces is still in its infancy. That is, how much transparency do you expose to the user? And how do you effectively assist them in building a useful mental model of your system without being distracting or losing the convenience of using the model in the first place? But here, I am simply referring to designing constraints within the experience to increase the chances of the model's success. A great, although slightly unrelated, example of this is household robots and the dishwasher. Despite its non-robotic characteristics, the faithful dishwasher can be considered a first generation robot for household tasks, like Rosie from Jetsons. Unlike Rosie, however, we had not been able to get the dishwasher to adapt to our environment. So, we adapted the environment for the dishwasher, that is, we encapsulated it in a box environment rather than using the existing kitchen sink we're accustomed to.

One simple approach is making the user aware of how to achieve the best results; in this example, it could be as simple as asking them to use a wall as their background. These hints can be delivered before use or delivered when there are signs of poor performance (or both). One approach for automatically detecting poor performance would be to measure the bounding box and its center of mass, comparing it with the expected center of mass, as illustrated in the following figure:

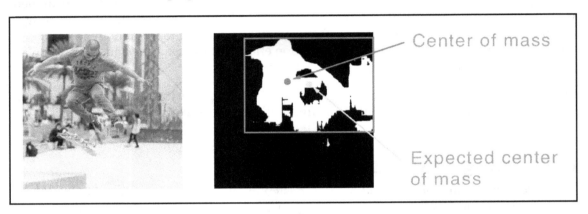

Which brings us nicely to the next strategy: embedding heuristics.

# Embedding heuristics

Heuristics is essentially codifying rules you have in your head to solve a particular task, typically implemented using a function that returns a score. This is used to rank a set of alternatives. In the previous section, *Designing in constraints*, we saw how we could use the center of mass and the bounding box to determine how well distributed the pixels are for a segmented image. This in turn could be used to rank each frame, by favoring those with a center of mass near the center of the bounding box. We also implemented a type of heuristic in the application when determining which frames to keep and which ones to ignore by measuring the overlap.

Heuristics can be a powerful ally, but be careful to ensure that the heuristics you derive can generalize well to your problem, just as you would expect a good model to. Also, be mindful of the additional computational cost incurred from using them.

# Post-processing and ensemble techniques

Techniques from image processing, computer vision, and computer graphics can be borrowed to improve the quality of the output as well as detection. As an example, a typical image processing task is performing the morphology operations of opening and closing. This combination is commonly used to remove noise and fill in small holes in a binary image. Another useful post-processing task we could borrow from computer vision is watersheds, a segmentation technique that treats the image as a topographical map, where the intensity of change defines the ridges and the boundary of the fill (or segmentation).

Another tool to use for post-processing is another model. You're familiar with YOLO for object detection. We can apply it to obtain its predicted boundaries of the object, which we can then use to refine our segmentation. Another model, and one being adopted for this task, is **conditional random fields** (**CRF**), which is capable of smoothing out the edges of our mask.

There are a vast number of techniques available from the fields of image processing, computer vision, and computer graphics, and I strongly encourage you to explore each area to build up your tool set.

 If you are new to computer vision, then I recommend the books *Computer Vision and Image Processing* by T. Morris and *Algorithms for Image Processing and Computer Vision* by J. Parker for a pragmatic introduction to the field.

# Human assistance

Sometimes it's unavoidable or even desirable to include the human in tuning the output from the model. In these instances, the model is used to assist the user rather than completely automating the task. A few approaches that could be employed for the project in this chapter include the following:

- Provide an intermediate step where the user can tidy up the masks. By this, I mean allowing the user to erase parts of the mask that have been incorrectly classified or are unwanted by the user.
- Present the user with a series of frames and have them select the frames for composition.
- Present the user with variations of the final composited image and have them select the one with the most appeal.

Another related concept is introducing human-in-the-loop machine learning. This has a human intervening when the model is not confident in its prediction, and it passes the responsibility over to the user for classification and/or correction. The amendments from the user are then stored and used for training the model to improve performance. In this example, we could let the user (or crowd-source this task) segment the image and use this data when re-training the model. Eventually, given sufficient data, the model will improve its performance relevant to the context it is being used in.

I hope this section highlighted the importance of handling uncertainty when working with machine models and provided enough of a springboard so that you can approach designing intelligent applications from the perspectives outlined here. Let's now conclude this chapter by reviewing what we have covered.

# Summary

In this chapter, we introduced the concept of semantic segmentation, an approach that gives our applications increased perceptual understanding of our photos and videos. It works by training a model to assign each pixel to a specific class. One popular architecture for this is U-Net, which achieves high-precision localization by preserving spatial information, by bridging the convolutional layers. We then reviewed the data used for training along with some example outputs of the model, including examples that highlight the limitations of the model.

We then saw how this model could be used by creating an image effects application, where the segmented images were used to clip people from a series of frames and composite them together to create an action shot. But this is just one example of how semantic segmentation can be applied; it's frequently used in domains such as robotics, security surveillance, and quality assurance in factories, to name a few. How else it can be applied is up to you.

In the final section, we spent some time discussing strategies when dealing with models, specifically, their probabilistic (or level of uncertainty) outputs, to improve user experience.

This is the last of our examples of applying machine learning. In the next, and last, chapter, we'll shift gears and provide a primer into building your own models with the help of Create ML. Let's get started.

# An Introduction to Create ML 10

The intention of this book has been to explore ways to apply machine learning on the iPhone, specifically focusing on computer vision tasks. Even with this narrow focus, we have only scratched the surface of what is currently possible. But, hopefully, we've covered enough to spark your curiosity and provided enough intuition behind the details of machine learning models to help you on your journey to build intelligent apps.

This chapter is intended as a primer into continuing that journey by introducing **Create ML**, a tool released with Core ML 2 that provides an easy way to create some common models using custom data. Even though we only provide a high-level introduction, specifically around computer vision, it still should be enough to help you make use of it in your own applications.

By the end of this chapter, you will have:

- Revised the machine learning workflow
- Appreciated the importance of splitting your data into sets for training and validation
- Used Create ML to create a custom image classifier
- Seen other tools and frameworks to continue your journey

Let's begin by reviewing a typical machine learning workflow.

## A typical workflow

As with any project, you enter the process with some understanding of what you are trying to build. The better you understand this (the problem), the better you are able to solve it.

After understanding what it is that you're trying to do, your next question (in the context of building a machine learning model) is *what data do I need?* This includes an exploration into what data is available and what data you may need to generate yourself.

Once you've understood what you're trying to do and what data you need, your next question/task is to decide on what algorithm (or model) is needed. This is obviously dependent on your task and the data you have; in some instances, you may be required to create your own model, but more often than not, there will be an adequate model available for you to use, or at least an architecture you can use with your own data. The following table shows some typical computer vision tasks and their related machine learning counterparts:

| Task | Machine learning algorithm |
| --- | --- |
| Label images | Image classification |
| Recognize multiple objects and their location | Object detection and semantic segmentation |
| Find similar images | Image similarity |
| Creating stylized images | Style transfer |

The next step is to train your model; typically, this is an iterative process with a lot of fine-tuning until you have a model that sufficiently achieves its task on data it hadn't been trained on.

Finally, with a trained model, you can deploy and use your model in your application. This process is summarized in the following diagram:

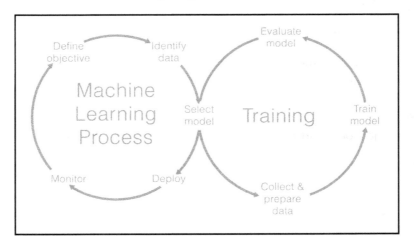

 The previous diagram is an oversimplification of the process; typically the workflow is more cyclic, with multiple iterations between training and selecting and tuning your model. It is also common to run multiple models (and model parameters) concurrently.

To make the concepts of this chapter more concrete, let's work with the hypothetical brief of having to build a fun application to assist toddlers to learn the names of fruits. You and your team have come up with the concept of a game that asks the toddler to find a specific fruit. The toddler earns points when they correctly identify the fruit using the device's camera. With our task now defined, let's discuss what data we need.

# Preparing the data

For our task, we require a collection of labeled photos of fruits. As you may recall from Chapter 1, *Introduction to Machine Learning*, this type of machine learning problem is known as **supervised learning**. We need our model to take in an image and return the label of what it thinks the image is, also known as **multi-class classification**.

Go ahead and collect photos of fruits. Create ML allows for multiple ways of organizing your data, but I find that ad hoc collection is easiest done by organizing it in folders, as shown here:

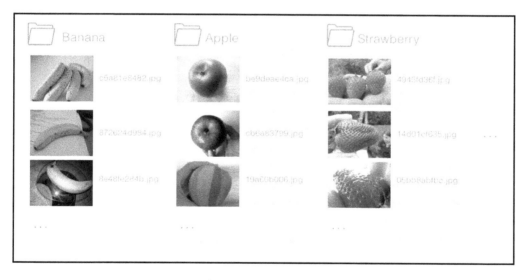

Source: http://www.image-net.org/

Here, we have organized our data into folders, where the folder name is used as a label for its contents. An alternative is labeling each image, where each instance of a specific class has a suffix number, for example `banana.0.jpg`, `banana.1.jpg`, and so on. Or you can simply pass in a dictionary of labels with their associated list of image URLs.

At this stage, you may be wondering how many images you should get. Apple has suggested a minimum of 10 images per class, but you typically want to collect as many as possible, to help the model generalize by ensuring that it sees a lot of variations during training. It's also important to, wherever possible, obtain images that are as close as possible to the real data the model will be used on (in the real world). This is because the model is not biased according to what it learns. It just learns what it needs to. That is, if all your apple examples were of red apples with a white background, then it's likely that your model will learn to associate these colors with apples, and any time it sees these colors, it will predict that the image contains an apple.

As mentioned previously, Apple has suggested a minimum of 10 images; this should have somewhat surprised you. Typically, when you talk about training deep neural networks, you expect the dataset to be large, very large. For example, a standard dataset used for training image classifiers is ImageNet. This dataset consists of over 14 million images; and this is part of the secret. As we've discussed throughout this book, layers of a CNN learn how to extract meaningful features from images, which they then use to infer an image's class. A common practice for specialized classifiers, like our fruit classifier, is to borrow these learnings from a model that has trained on millions of images and use the features it extracts to train a classifier on our smaller dataset—a technique known as **transfer learning**.

The following two diagrams provide an illustrative example of this, with the first showing a network that has been trained on a large dataset and the second using what it has learnt to train on a more specialized dataset:

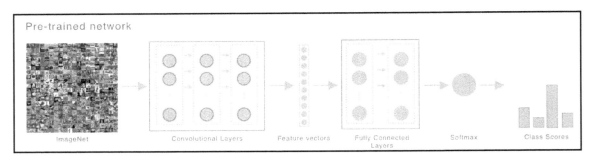

We are interested in the feature vectors that the convolutional layers learn; you can think of this as an encoding of its understanding of the input image. This is what we want to use to train our own classifier, shown in the following diagrams:

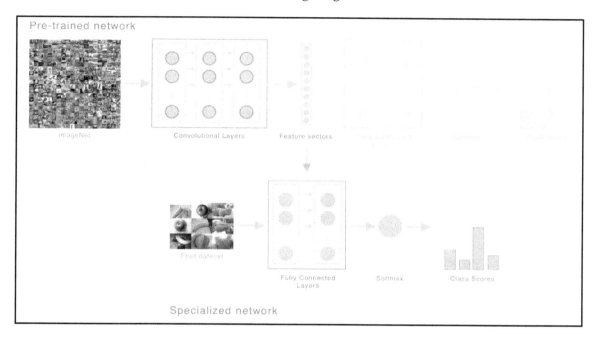

With this approach, we forgo having to learn how to extract features and are left with just having to train the weights of a fully connected network for classification, taking advantage of the previous network's ability to extract meaningful features. Create ML uses this technique for its image classifiers. Using a pre-trained model that resides on the device and has been trained over 1,000 categories means that we are left just having to train a relatively small network for classification. This is done using the features provided by the pre-trained network. This not only allows us to learn from a smaller dataset but also reduces the amount of time required for training.

Another feature Create ML offers, and performs on our behalf, to train effectively on small datasets is something called data augmentation. Data augmentation is simply a way of increasing the variance of our dataset by applying a number of random transformations to each image before the image is passed into the network during training, for example, horizontally flipping an image. The goal is that at training time, your model will see many variations of an image so as to improve your model's ability to generalize, that is, learn meaningful features that work on data it hasn't seen before. The following figure illustrates some of the transformations typically performed for data augmentation:

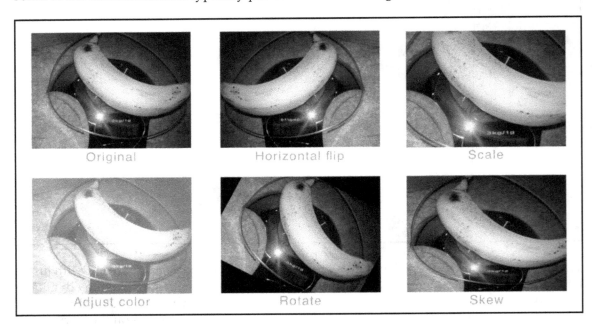

Another convenience offered by Create ML out of the box is that it handles the typical preprocessing tasks required when working with images, such as cropping and resizing. They typically have fixed-size inputs and outputs, requiring you to either explicitly preprocess the images to match the model or use the Vision framework to handle this for you. An extra consequence of Create ML being built on top of Vision is that it handles a lot of the pipeline you would typically need to do manually when training models.

There is just one more important topic I would like to highlight before moving on to creating and training our model; this has to do with balanced datasets, or the effects of imbalanced datasets. Balanced datasets refer to having an equal amount of examples for each class; that is, you avoid having a large variance between the number of examples you have in each of your classes. Why is this important? To answer this, let's remind ourselves of how a model is trained and what it learns. The following figure illustrates the process of training, where training is an iterative process of performing inference (forward pass) for a given input. Then, small adjustments are made to the weights of the model so that they reduce any discrepancies between the prediction and expected value (loss):

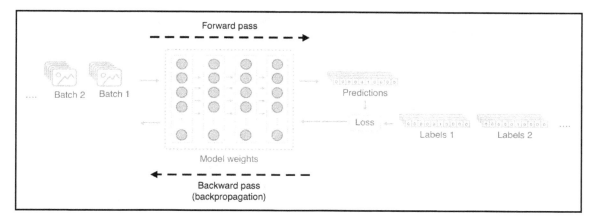

Put another way, overexposing a class will dominate this process of adjusting weights such that the weights will better fit their own class over others. This is especially true when training with batches, as the error is typically the average over all samples in the batch. So, if your model can effectively predict the dominant class, it's likely to achieve a reasonable loss and be unable to learn anything useful for the other classes.

At this point, we know what we are trying to achieve, have our balanced training set, and know what machine learning task we need; we are now ready to build and train our model.

# Creating and training a model

Thanks to the great effort by Apple's engineers, the process of creating common machine learning models is incredibly easy and will no doubt spark a new wave of intelligent apps over the coming months.

In this section, you will see just how easy it is as we walk through creating an image classifier for our application using Create ML.

Create ML is accessible using Xcode Playground, so there is a good place to start. Open up Xcode and create a new Playground, ensuring that you select **macOS** as the platform, as shown here:

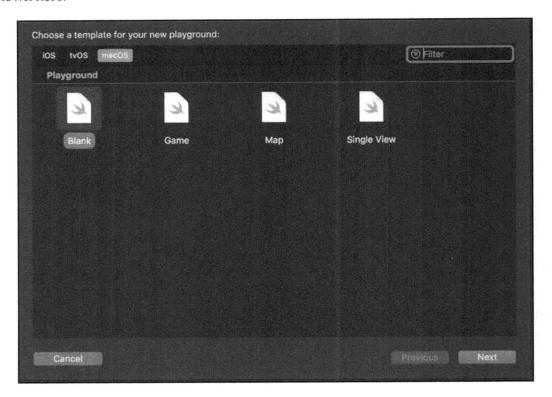

Once in the playground, import `CreateML` and `Foundation` as follows:

```
import CreateML
import Foundation
```

Next, create a `URL` that points to the directory that contains your training data:

```
let trainingDir = URL(fileURLWithPath: "/<PATH TO DIRECTORY WITH TRAINING
DATA>")
```

The only thing left to do is to create an instance of our model, passing in the path to our training data (I did say it was incredibly easy):

```
let model = try MLImageClassifier(
    trainingData: .labeledDirectories(at: trainingDir))
```

Create ML offers you the flexibility of providing a custom dictionary of labels and their associated files or through the convenience of a `MLImageClassifier.DataSource`. This can either be a hierarchical directory structure where classes are organized into their respective folders, `MLImageClassifier.DataSource.labeledDirectories` (as we have done in this example), or one where each file has been named with respect to their associated class, `MLImageClassifier.DataSource.labeledFiles`.

As soon as the model is instantiated, it will begin training. Once finished, it will output the accuracy achieved on your training set to the console, as shown in the following screenshot:

```
Extracting image features from full data set.
Analyzing and extracting image features.
+------------------+--------------+------------------+
| Images Processed | Elapsed Time | Percent Complete |
+------------------+--------------+------------------+
| 1                | 15.95s       | 2%               |
| 2                | 16.05s       | 4.25%            |
| 3                | 16.16s       | 6.25%            |
| 4                | 16.27s       | 8.5%             |
| 5                | 16.38s       | 10.5%            |
| 10               | 16.93s       | 21.25%           |
| 47               | 20.93s       | 100%             |
+------------------+--------------+------------------+
Skipping automatic creation of validation set; training set has fewer than 50 points.
Beginning model training on processed features.
Calibrating solver; this may take some time.
+-----------+--------------+-------------------+
| Iteration | Elapsed Time | Training-accuracy |
+-----------+--------------+-------------------+
| 1         | 0.231359     | 0.297872          |
| 2         | 0.328348     | 0.680851          |
| 3         | 0.405243     | 0.851064          |
| 4         | 0.469038     | 0.978723          |
| 5         | 0.534865     | 0.978723          |
| 10        | 0.854753     | 1.000000          |
+-----------+--------------+-------------------+
SUCCESS: Optimal solution found.
```

We are almost done; this tells us that our model has fit our training data well, but it doesn't tell us how well it will generalize, that is, how well it will work on images it hasn't seen before. It's possible (and common) for deep neural networks to remember their training data, commonly referred to as overfitting. To avoid overfitting, and therefore make it more likely to produce something usable in the real world, it's a common practice to split your data into three buckets. The first bucket is used to train your model. The second bucket, called validation data, is used during training (typically at the end of each iteration/epoch) to see how well the model is generalizing. It also provides clues as to when the model starts overfitting (when the training accuracy and validation accuracy begin to diverge). The last bucket is only used once you are satisfied with how your model performs on the validation data and is the determinant of how well your model actually works; this bucket is known as the test data.

 How much data do you reserve for validation and testing? For shallow learners, it was common to have a 70/20/10 (training, validation, and test) split. But deep learning normally implies big datasets, in which case the reserved data for validation and test may be excessive. So the answer really depends on how much data you have and what type of data it is.

Therefore, before deploying our model, we evaluate it on a dataset it hasn't seen during training. Once again, collect an equal amount of data for each of your classes and return here once you've done so.

As we had done before, create a URL that points to the directory that contains your validation data:

```
let validationDir = URL(fileURLWithPath: "/<PATH TO DIRECTORY WITH
VALIDATION DATA>")
```

Now it's simply a matter of calling `evaluation` on the model, as shown here:

```
model.evaluation(on: .labeledDirectories(at: validationDir))
```

This will perform inference on each of our validation samples and report the accuracy, which you can access via quick looks:

```
model.evaluation(on: .labeledDirectories(at: validationDir))          "Number of exampl...

    Number of examples: 26
    Number of classes: 6
    Accuracy: 100.00%
```

Satisfied with our validation accuracy, we are now ready to export our model, but just before we do so, let's perform a prediction on an individual image.

You can easily do this by calling the `prediction` method of your model instance (or `predictions` if you have multiple samples you want to perform inference on), as shown in this snippet:

```
let strawberryUrl = URL(
    fileURLWithPath: "/<PATH TO STRAWBERRY>")

print(try model.prediction(from: strawberryUrl))
```

If all goes well, then `Strawberry` should be output to your console. Now, feeling confident with our model, it's time to export it.

In keeping with the nature of Create ML, exporting is simply a single line of code:

```
try model.write(toFile: "<PATH TO FILE>")
```

From here, it's just a matter of importing the Core ML model into your project, as we have seen many times throughout this book.

We have almost concluded our brief introduction to Create ML; but before we move on, I want to quickly highlight a few things, starting with model parameters.

# Model parameters

In the previous section, I mentioned the usefulness of data augmentation for small datasets. So, how do you use this during your training? The options are exposed to you using the `MLImageClassifier.ModelParameters` structure, which you can pass an instance of when instantiating the classifier. One of the parameters is the `OptionSet` `CreateML.MLImageClassifier.ImageAugmentationOptions`, which allows you to toggle various augmentation techniques on and off.

`MLImageClassifier.ModelParameters` also allows you to specify the maximum number of iterations, version of the feature extraction, and validation data. You can learn more about these on the official web page at `https://developer.apple.com/documentation/create_ml/mlimageclassifier/modelparameters`.

# Model metadata

When working with the Core ML Tools package in Chapters 5, *Emotion Detection with CNNs*, and Chapter 6, *Creating Art with Style Transfer*, to convert a Keras model to Core ML, we saw how we could explicitly set the metadata, which is shown in Xcode. Create ML provides a way of explicitly setting this data by passing in an instance of MLModelMetadata when exporting the model. It provides you all the metadata we had seen when working with the Core ML Tools package, such as name, description and so on.

# Alternative workflow (graphical)

The last point before moving on to the next section! In this chapter, we have walked through programmatically creating, training, and validating a model. Create ML offers an alternative, where, instead of using code to build your model, you can use a graphical interface. This is accessible via the CreateMLUI library, where you simply create an instance of MLImageClassifierBuilder and call its showInLiveView method:

```
import CreateMLUI

let builder = MLImageClassifierBuilder()
builder.showInLiveView()
```

Once this runs, you will see a widget in the live view, which allows you to train the model simply by dragging and dropping in your training and validation examples. The following figure shows this widget after training and validation, and the panel for entering metadata:

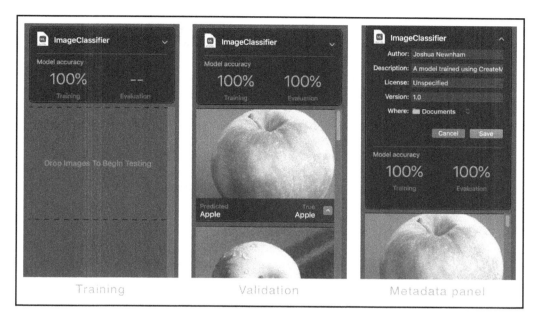

This concludes this section, the chapter, and the book. We will wrap up with some closing thoughts, including a list of some other tools to help you on your journey to creating more intelligent apps.

# Closing thoughts

This tool essentially democratizes machine learning by way of allowing anyone (who is able) to create custom models, but there is always a trade-off between simplicity and expressiveness. So, here is a short list of tools you may want to explore:

- **Turi create**: comes from a firm acquired by Apple in 2016; it provides tight integration with Core ML, allowing for easy deployment and custom models. It also provides a more comprehensive suite of machine learning models such as Style Transfer and segmentation. You can learn more about Turi create here: `https://github.com/apple/turicreate`.
- **IBM Watson Services for Core ML**: IBM Watson is IBM's AI platform, exposing an array of common machine learning models as a service. They have recently made available some of these services via Core ML models, allowing your application to leverage IBM Watson's services even when offline.

- **ML Kit**: Google announced an ML Kit in early 2018 as a platform for common machine learning tasks such as image labeling and optical character recognition. The platform also takes care of model distribution, including custom ones.
- **TensorFlowLite**: A lightweight version of the popular machine learning framework TensorFlow. Like Core ML, it enables on-device inference.

These are only a few of the options available to integrate machine learning into your application, and all this is likely to grow significantly over the coming years. But, as we have seen throughout this book, the machine learning algorithm is (literally) only one part of the equation; data is what drives the experience, so I encourage you to seek out and experiment with new datasets to see what unique experiences you can come up with using what you have learnt here.

Machine learning is evolving at an incredible pace. The website Arxiv is a popular repository for researchers to publish their papers; by just monitoring this site for over a week, you will be amazed and excited by the volume of papers being published and the advancements being made.

But, right now, there is a gap between the research community and industry practitioners, which in part motivated me to write this book. I hope that what you have read in the pages of this book has given you enough intuition behind deep neural networks and, more importantly, sparked enough curiosity and excitement for you to continue exploring and experimenting. As I mentioned at the start of this chapter, we have just scratched the surface of what is currently out and possible, never mind what will be around in 12 months.

So, consider this as an invite or challenge to join me in creating the next generation of applications. I look forward to seeing what you create!

# Summary

In this chapter, we introduced Create ML, a tool that makes it incredibly easy to train and deploy common machine learning models. We saw how easy it is to create an image classifier using a minimal amount of examples and minimal amount of code. We discussed how this was achieved through the use of transfer learning, and then covered some considerations to keep in mind with regard to your training data and the importance of splitting it for validation and testing.

# Other Books You May Enjoy

If you enjoyed this book, you may be interested in these other books by Packt:

**Mastering Machine Learning Algorithms**
Giuseppe Bonaccorso

ISBN: 978-1-78862-111-3

- Explore how a ML model can be trained, optimized, and evaluated
- Understand how to create and learn static and dynamic probabilistic models
- Successfully cluster high-dimensional data and evaluate model accuracy
- Discover how artificial neural networks work and how to train, optimize, and validate them
- Work with Autoencoders and Generative Adversarial Networks
- Apply label spreading and propagation to large datasets
- Explore the most important Reinforcement Learning techniques

## Machine Learning with Swift
Alexander Sosnovshchenko

ISBN: 978-1-78712-151-5

- Learn rapid model prototyping with Python and Swift
- Deploy pre-trained models to iOS using Core ML
- Find hidden patterns in the data using unsupervised learning
- Get a deeper understanding of the clustering techniques
- Learn modern compact architectures of neural networks for iOS devices
- Train neural networks for image processing and natural language processing

# Leave a review - let other readers know what you think

Please share your thoughts on this book with others by leaving a review on the site that you bought it from. If you purchased the book from Amazon, please leave us an honest review on this book's Amazon page. This is vital so that other potential readers can see and use your unbiased opinion to make purchasing decisions, we can understand what our customers think about our products, and our authors can see your feedback on the title that they have worked with Packt to create. It will only take a few minutes of your time, but is valuable to other potential customers, our authors, and Packt. Thank you!

# Index

# F

facial expressions  80, 81, 82, 83
FacialEmotionDetection  106, 108, 109, 111, 113
feature engineering  16, 54
frames per second (fps)  57

# G

GPU
  using  205, 206, 208
gram matrix  179

# H

Hey Siri  32
histogram of oriented gradients (HOG)  17
human-computer interaction (HCI)  15

# I

IBM Watson Services for Core ML  357
ImageNet Large-Scale Visual Recognition
    Challenge (ILSVRC)  20
images
  about  50, 51, 52, 53
  style, transferring  174, 175, 177, 178, 179
inference
  performing  76
  versus training  29, 31
International Conference on Machine Learning
    (ICML)  80
Internet of Things (IoT)  31
intersection over union (IoU)  126
Intersection over Union (IoU) coefficient  318
iOS keyboard prediction  23

# K

K-means  18
Keras model
  converting, to Core ML  183, 185, 186, 187,
    188, 189, 190, 191, 193
Keras Tiny YOLO
  converting, to Core ML  129, 131, 132, 134,
    135, 137
kernels
  padding  53

stride value  53

# L

Labeled Faces in the Wild (LFW)
  reference  317
layers
  accelerating  204, 205
learning algorithms
  about  37
  auto insurance in Sweden  37, 38, 40, 41
  supported learning algorithms  45
Long Short-Term Memory (LSTM)  280
loss function  30

# M

machine learning (ML)
  about  8, 9
  use cases  32
metal performance shaders (MPSes)  34
ML algorithms
  about  11
  Collaborative Filtering (CF)  11
  iOS keyboard prediction  23
  shadow draw  15
  Shutterstock  20
ML Kit  358
ML workflow  26, 27
model metadata  356
model parameters  355
model
  creating  351, 353
  training  352, 353, 354
  weight, reducing  209, 210, 212, 214
multi-class classification  347

# N

named entity recognition (NER)  34
natural language processing (NLP)  34
NDJSON
  reference  275
Netflix  11
non-max suppression  125

www.ingramcontent.com/pod-product-compliance
Lightning Source LLC
Chambersburg PA
CBHW080612060326
40690CB00021B/4669